NEURODIVERSITY-AFFIRMING PRACTICE FOR SPEECH AND LANGUAGE THERAPISTS

Are you a speech and language therapist (SLT) working independently, within a speech and language therapy team, or in training? Do you, or might you work with autistic or other neurodivergent people? This book will help you understand the changing narrative around how we support neurodivergent individuals, how to sit with complex thoughts and feelings you may have and how to grow your capacity to unlearn, adapt and shift your values and practice.

This essential guide considers what neurodiversity is and what it means to practice in a neurodiversity-affirming way, considering why we should be doing so and, importantly, how to do it. The book moves through the context of neurodiversity in recent times and considers key historical approaches within speech and language therapy. Chapters offer space for reflective practice based on what we know now, for both individual reflection and with colleagues as part of a wider team, before introducing practical strategies to challenge and change how we work with neurodivergent individuals. Throughout, the voices of autistic and ADHD speech and language therapists (SLTs) are included and amplified, sharing their lived experiences and perspectives to further support teams to develop neurodiversity-informed practice.

This book offers a safe and supportive space to explore a topic that can be uncomfortable and scary but must be delved into to provide neurodivergent people with access to therapists with knowledge, skills and advocacy approaches to best meet their needs. It will be crucial reading for all practising and training speech and language therapists.

Ruth Jones (she/her) is an independent speech and language therapist working across Wiltshire and Somerset. Her work involves direct work with individuals, families and education settings. Additionally, she delivers training to therapists and settings and offers clinical supervision to other speech and language therapists.

She works primarily with neurodivergent children and young people, and those who require additional support to access meaningful opportunities and their education. Ruth believes in child-led and neurodiversity-informed practice and her core values are around acceptance, curiosity and connection.

Ruth feels purposeful about using her role to challenge and encourage change in the field of speech and language therapy, and more widely within education settings and society to better improve outcomes for neurodivergent individuals.

NEURODIVERSITY-AFFIRMING PRACTICE FOR SPEECH AND LANGUAGE THERAPISTS

Supporting Curiosity, Compassion and Conversation

Ruth Jones

LONDON AND NEW YORK

Designed cover image: Getty Images

First published 2026
by Routledge
4 Park Square, Milton Park, Abingdon, Oxon OX14 4RN

and by Routledge
605 Third Avenue, New York, NY 10158

Routledge is an imprint of the Taylor & Francis Group, an informa business

© 2026 Ruth Jones

The right of Ruth Jones to be identified as author of this work has been asserted in accordance with sections 77 and 78 of the Copyright, Designs and Patents Act 1988.

All rights reserved. No part of this book may be reprinted or reproduced or utilised in any form or by any electronic, mechanical, or other means, now known or hereafter invented, including photocopying and recording, or in any information storage or retrieval system, without permission in writing from the publishers.

Trademark notice: Product or corporate names may be trademarks or registered trademarks, and are used only for identification and explanation without intent to infringe.

British Library Cataloguing-in-Publication Data
A catalogue record for this book is available from the British Library

ISBN: 9781032689401 (hbk)
ISBN: 9781032689326 (pbk)
ISBN: 9781032689463 (ebk)

DOI: 10.4324/9781032689463

Typeset in Interstate
by codeMantra

This book is dedicated to Neurodivergent people. Those who came before us and taught us so much; to those with us now, for whom we strive to do better; and to those yet to come, for whom we will do better.

CONTENTS

Acknowledgements and Thanks   *viii*
Contributors   *ix*
Positionality Statement   *xi*
Limitations of This Book   *xiii*
Glossary   *xiv*

One	The Context	1
Two	Integrating Intersectionality: A Neurodiversity-Affirming Approach to Speech and Language Therapy *Fatimah Bint-Hanif and Kate Boot*	22
Three	Neurodiversity Now	45
Four	Our Learning Process	58
Five	Putting it Into Practice	77
Six	Expressive Communication	96
Seven	Social Communication	122
Eight	Relationships and Sex Education – A Speech and Language Therapist's Role *Kate Boot*	139
Nine	Flipping the Narrative on Behaviour	165
Ten	Reflective Practice	181

Reading List   *199*
Index   *203*

ACKNOWLEDGEMENTS AND THANKS

I would like to acknowledge the written input, support and emotional labour from Harriet, Fatimah and Kate in writing their contributions to this book. For their time in reflecting and supporting me in my writing, and notably to Kate for accompanying me on a writing retreat!

I am privileged to have had the opportunity to both study and work as a therapist. I am so thankful to have learnt from the incredible young people, their families and my colleagues who have shaped my practice and perspective over the years.

CONTRIBUTORS

Kate Boot (she/her) is a white, queer, AuDHD Speech and Language Therapist, Sensory Integration Practitioner, and advocate for Neurodiversity-Affirming and Anti-Oppressive Practice. She specialises in supporting neurodivergent individuals, teams and therapists in developing language for their experiences and navigating systemic barriers.

Kate is known for her work at the intersection of neurodiversity, intersectionality and social justice, with a particular focus on challenging the whiteness and ableism embedded within the SLT profession. She provides consultation, supervision and training to shift clinical practice towards approaches that centre neurodivergent autonomy, lived experience and disability justice. Kate co-authored the *Royal College of Speech and Language Therapists' LGBTQ+ Affirming Zones of Practice* and actively works to dismantle oppressive structures in healthcare and education. Her contributions to this book include exploring the SLT's role in Sex and Relationships Education and along with Fatimah, the vital role of intersectionality in neurodiversity-affirming practice.

Fatimah Bint-Hanif (she/her) is a Speech and Language Therapist whose work is grounded in equity, belonging and inclusion. She is committed to person-centred, holistic care that honours the richness of individual identities and lived experiences.

Fatimah's work and research critically examines how structural systems – including racism, ableism, capitalism and colonialism – shape individual experiences, particularly those from historically underserved communities. In her contribution to this book (co-written with Kate Boot), she emphasises that true neuro-affirming practice is inseparable from intersectionality.

Alongside her clinical work, Fatimah has co-authored guidance with the Royal College of Speech and Language Therapists (RCSLT), delivered guest lectures and spoken at Clinical Excellence Networks. She is also committed to supporting the next generation of speech and language therapists and mentors students from underrepresented backgrounds within the field.

Drawing on both professional expertise and lived experience, Fatimah bridges the gap between theory and practice, advocating for neuro-affirming approaches that are accessible, culturally responsive and truly inclusive. She is dedicated to dismantling systemic inequalities, ensuring that neurodivergent and historically underserved voices are heard, centred and empowered to support meaningful change.

Harriet Richardson (she/her) is a Speech and Language Therapist and Neurodevelopmental Practitioner, who specialises in autism and ADHD assessments within a neuro-affirming framework. Hat completed a degree in Psychology & Speech Pathology in 2018 and now works in Melbourne, Australia and remotely completes neurodevelopmental assessments in the UK. In therapy, she supports adults with post-identification sessions after late-identification, as well as psychoeducation sessions for children and teenagers. She is a blogger, podcaster and public speaker and runs the social media account @hat.talks.uk which shares her experiences as an autistic, ADHDer.

Hat was identified as autistic in adult life and identifies as semi-speaking, using AAC part-time. She is passionate about autistic and ADHD wellbeing as a result of her experiences with mental health difficulties from early childhood. Hat is committed to the lifelong learning journey of neuro-affirming practice. In her spare time, you will find Hat constantly on the go, either running, golfing or spending time with her assistance dog at the beach. She always has her head in a book, watching Shrek on repeat or hyperfocusing on a new project.

POSITIONALITY STATEMENT

In embarking on this exploration of intersectional identities and neurodivergence, it is crucial to acknowledge my own position and the lenses through which I view this subject matter. I write this book as a white, middle-class, neurodivergent speech and language therapist. I recognise the strengths and limitations of my own perspective. My core contributors, Fatimah, Kate and Harriet, also bring their own unique viewpoints to this work. Together, we aim to build a more inclusive conversation, reflecting on our perspectives and experiences – both personally and professionally.

Throughout one's journey of learning, unlearning and growing awareness, Maya Angelou's words provide comfort and safety: 'I did then what I knew how to do. Now that I know better, I do better'. This theme weaves throughout the book, and is something that I recognise: this writing is my best, with the knowledge I have. I am always learning and developing and, as such, so will the viewpoints that I have shared.

Having navigated the complexities of neurodiversity-affirming practices, and the critical importance for an intersectional lens, I recognise that our lived experiences bring valuable insights and inevitable limitations. Drawing from personal experiences allows us to create an empathetic and nuanced approach, but it restricts our perspectives to the experiences we know. As the author of this book, I acknowledge that my core contributors and I do not, and cannot, fully represent the vast range of experiences within the neurodivergent community.

We are committed to amplifying marginalised voices and highlighting the diverse experiences of neurodivergent individuals, particularly those at the intersections of multiple identities. Throughout this book, we strive to maintain an inclusive and respectful dialogue.

As the author of this book, the commitment I made was to use my position of privilege to uplift the voices of marginalised individuals. While I strived to integrate a range of perspectives, financial constraints have limited my ability to compensate contributors fully, which reflects a broader, systemic issue of valuing marginalised voices. I am transparent about this challenge, as I do not want to perpetuate historical patterns of free labour for marginalised communities. To address this, I have bought and read books, followed and engaged with advocates and activists sharing their experiences, knowledge and learning and credited them within the text, hoping to respectfully include these voices even as we work within constraints.

By sharing this positionality statement, we aim to provide transparency about our perspective and encourage readers to critically engage with the material, actively questioning and reflecting on their own biases. As you read, we suggest you consider your own positionality. We encourage readers to reflect on their own identities and how these might influence their understanding of neurodivergence.

Throughout this book, we have included practical examples, reflective prompts and insights from a variety of voices, to provide readers with concrete ways to apply these concepts in everyday contexts. At the end of the book is a list of recommended places for you to seek more learning on the topics, from a range of different authors and creators. We hope this work empowers readers to actively challenge stigmas, incorporate inclusivity and advocate for neurodivergent rights, both within their personal lives and in broader social settings.

LIMITATIONS OF THIS BOOK

While this book strives to provide a range of insights and practical guidance on neurodiversity-affirming practices within the field of speech and language therapy, several limitations must be acknowledged:

1. **Scope of Diversity**: This book predominantly focuses on common neurodivergent profiles, such as autism and ADHD. It may not fully address the specific needs and experiences of individuals with less frequently discussed or emerging neurodivergent profiles.
2. **Contextual Variability**: The effectiveness of the strategies discussed can vary significantly depending on individual differences and contextual factors, such as cultural backgrounds, family dynamics and regional healthcare practices. For this reason, the book aims to offer space to reflect on your caseload and consider the implications of learning for your context in which you work and practice.
3. **Research Constraints**: Although this book is grounded in current research and best practices, the field of neurodiversity-affirming therapy is continually evolving. Some of the concepts and methods presented may be subject to change as new research emerges. Readers are encouraged to stay informed about the latest developments and consider this book as part of an ongoing learning process and seek out signposts provided.
4. **Practical Application**: This book aims to provide foundational knowledge and inspiration; however, it cannot replace the need for supervision and ongoing professional development. All therapists in line with professional guidance should ensure that they are meeting their recommendations and explore the implications for learning on providing safe and affirming care.
5. **Personal Experiences**: The perspectives and case studies included in this book are based on the experiences of specific individuals and practitioners. While these stories provide valuable insights, they are not universally representative. Readers should consider them as illustrative examples rather than exhaustive accounts.

GLOSSARY

There is key vocabulary to be aware of before we begin to delve into theory and ways of working. Language matters and before we go on, I implore you to read and understand these terms.

- **Ableism**: system of assigning value to people's bodies and minds based on societally constructed ideas of normalcy, productivity, desirability, intelligence, excellence, and fitness.
- **Allistic**: (adjective) a non-autistic person.
- **Anti-Oppressive Practice**: framework that aims to recognise and counteract the various forms of oppression that people face based on race, gender, class, sexuality, disability and other social identities. This practice involves critical self-reflection, understanding the power dynamics at play and actively working to dismantle systems of inequality and injustice.
- **Code Switching**: the practice of alternating between two or more languages, dialects, or styles of communication within a single conversation or context, depending on the social setting or conversational partner.
- **Colonialism**: practice or policy where one country establishes and maintains political, social and economic control over another country or territory.
- **Intersecting Identities**: the multiple, overlapping social identities that a person holds, such as race, gender, class, sexual orientation, disability and more.
- **Intersectionality**: the interconnected nature of social categorisations such as race, class, and gender, which can create overlapping and interdependent systems of discrimination or disadvantage.
- **Marginalised**: individuals or groups that are pushed to the edge of society or an organisation, meaning they have little social, economic or political power or influence.
- **Mysogynoir**: the specific form of prejudice and discrimination directed at Black women, where both race and gender intersect to create unique experiences of oppression.
- **Neurodivergent**: (adjective) the term used to describe an individual whose brain functions differently from a 'standard' or 'typical' brain.
- **Neurodiversity**: (noun) the term that encompasses all minds, a room full of people can be described as neurodiverse.
- **Neurodiversity movement**: the term used to encompass the ongoing social justice work seeking equity for neurodivergent individuals.
- **Neurodiversity paradigm**: the term used to describe the shift in thinking around Neurodivergent individuals to see them as valuable humans, rather than medical problems or disordered individuals.

- **Neuronormative**: (adjective) the term that describes an individual who lacks awareness of their ableism, and therefore places increased value and superiority on neurotypical ways of being.
- **Neurotypical:** (adjective) the term used to describe an individual whose brain functions in a 'standard' way.
- **Oppression**: Oppression is the systematic and pervasive mistreatment, control, or exploitation of a group of people by a more powerful group.
- **Reflective practice**: thinking critically about actions and experiences, to learn from them and improve future practice.
- **Reflexive practice**: emphasises the interconnectedness between the individual, social, cultural and institutional contexts in which they function, being aware of how these contexts shape and influence practice. This practice is a critical self-aware examination of how one's own background, beliefs, values and assumptions shape our actions and decisions.
- **Trauma Informed**: an approach that understands, recognises and responds to the effects of all types of trauma. Trauma-informed care involves acknowledging the widespread impact of trauma, recognising the signs and symptoms in clients, patients or communities, and integrating this knowledge into practices, policies, and procedures. It also emphasises creating a safe environment that avoids re-traumatisation and fosters healing and resilience.

1
The Context

A note from the author:

Before we begin, pause for thought on this quote from Heraclitus:

> The only constant in life is change.

For you to fully grow into a neurodiversity-affirming speech and language therapist, I am fairly sure there are things that you will have to change your mind on, or perhaps just awaken your mind to that are already in there. The whole process is not a specific set of skills, or therapeutic approaches but a mindset shift. This theme will weave throughout this book, with moments to pause and reflect to enable you to consider if you feel able to change your mind, or perhaps give you the conversation starters to help change the minds of others within the speech and language profession and beyond. It might give you validation of the thoughts and experiences you have already. What is important in this learning is noticing – what thoughts come into your brain as you read parts of this book – noticing them is a good first step. Are they excited thoughts? Are they dismissive? Are they uncomfortable? If we begin to notice what shows up in our thoughts and feelings on these topics, we can really start to begin our unlearning of all the systems that fight against affirming practice, and consider the ripples of change we can start.

I felt as though becoming neurodiversity-affirming was a journey when I first began my learning. But I have come to realise that the term implies there is an end destination. I am not sure one ever really becomes neurodiversity-affirming, but more that we become aware. Kate Boot suggested the term "neurodiversity affirming committed" to me, which, as I understand and explore more, feels a good fit. So this book, when I began, felt like it was about being part of a learning journey, but doesn't seem to be quite that after all. But I suggest you use this book as a journey, from your point of understanding and knowledge now at the start of the journey, to the final page being your end. I hope that by the time you finish your journey with the text, you will then find yourself becoming a neurodiversity-affirming committed therapist.

This book is written from my experiences, knowledge and learning. It draws on years of practice, listening to the neurodivergent community and training. There are some references, but mostly I have captured my sources of learning over time through a reading list at the back of the book, as place for you to go for onward learning on some of the topics and to become more informed by the community around you too.

The aim of this book is to offer space for reflection and exploration of these topics, and to signpost you to further places to learn more on topics.

Throughout the book I have been supported by Harriet Richardson, who has shared her lived experiences as a late diagnosed autistic, ADHD Speech and Language Therapist. I am forever grateful to all she has shared to better inform my practice, and indeed for her incredible contributions to enable you to develop your practice too through this book.

My Context

What is my context? I have had a lot of thoughts about this before writing the book and what makes me a good person to do this. Imposter syndrome has kicked in, and I've needed some reassurance. If I am totally honest, I am still not convinced. But what I have done is try to pull together some fabulous contributions, references and further reading lists to help me along the way and hopefully make this book a space to uplift the communities' voices and experiences and offer you a starting point to your learning with signposts to a range of further resources.

My interest in speech and language therapy began during school. I remember being sat at the computer in my dining room with a good friend browsing the UCAS website. My preferred studies during A Level were Biology, Psychology and English Language and I was interested in studying Psychology further, also considering a joint degree with French. I knew I wanted to study at university but it was tricky deciding what. My friend mentioned Speech and Language Therapy; I don't really recall how she knew about it, but my Dad was at the time sat within earshot of our conversation, and she mentioned that the NHS paid the course fees. Well, it is safe to say I didn't have much choice if it meant going to university was going to be cheaper, my Dad would have signed me up on the dotted line then and there! But, as we browsed it suggested that the course was an amalgamation of my preferred subjects and that, also, the grades required were within my reach.

During 6th Form I sought out work experience on Wednesday afternoon slots to go and work in an autism specialist school who had a speech and language therapist. I cannot recall whether she was employed there or part of the health care provision, but I spent time in the classroom observing her sessions, which cemented my interest. Off I went to study thinking that I was going to be a paediatric speech and language therapist.

At the end of my first year, I was now going to work as an adult acute therapist, working with stroke survivors and patients who were living with conditions such as motor neurone disease, and I had my first experience of alternative communication with a lady using a Light Writer and it was incredible.

By the end of my second year, I was going to work in the community hospital setting, mixing inpatient early intervention with community support for stroke survivors.

Then, I got my final year placement, which I will not lie was not without its stressors - tears on finding out, money troubles with the cost of having to fund the placement and stay away from university, as well as reduce my shifts in the pub I worked at to manage financially - and it was an adult learning disability placement. No way was that where I wanted to work, and to boot it was going to cause me immense pressure and stress, applying for hardship loans, and working all hours I could at the weekend to pay for it all.

Well, by the end of the first week, it was set, I was going to be a therapist in the learning disability sector! It is safe to say, the journey to getting into my chosen area of the field chopped and changed somewhat …

My first post was in a residential special school for autistic children with high support needs across all domains, where very shortly after I started, I found out my colleague was leaving for pastures new, and I was to be working solo while they recruited a second therapist. This was a real make or break moment for me in my career, and I am so pleased to be able to say, that post made me.

Shortly after my colleague left, they recruited to the post, and I can honestly say the pairing made for a real dream team, both full of enthusiasm for the role and passion. We still recall when we get together at the time. I cried delivering communication training because prior to being a therapist I had supported adults with learning disabilities in the transition from institutions to the community as a support worker. I had seen how a lifetime of presuming incompetence and lack of access to speech and language supports impacted on quality of life and how the staff team working in schools really needed to understand how precious this time was for the children there; in particular with the team of therapists available on site for the small number of children who resided there.

I worked in these settings up until the birth of my first child, and I worked with several incredible professionals who were part of the on-site multi-disciplinary teams, including psychiatrists, clinical psychologists and assistants, occupational therapists, music psychotherapists, mental health and learning disability nurses, behaviour support specialists. Honestly, I look back and think I didn't know how lucky I was to have all these amazing brains passing through my life, teaching me so much.

This, in turn, has led me to explore and wonder what it is like in other settings, and I have been astounded at the different levels of service available to neurodivergent individuals in different settings. To that end it is important I recognise that there are limitations to my knowledge about how different services will deliver support and the resources at their disposal. I now work as an independent therapist, with neurodivergent children within the home, mainstream and specialist provisions. I love what I do, bore anyone who knows me to tears with my passion and feel strongly about neurodiversity-affirming practice, and the whole narrative shift that goes along with it.

Being asked to write this book was a huge shock, and one that made me feel so excited I was like, heck yes! However … as I mentioned, imposter syndrome is very real. This is one of the scariest things I have ever done, and as I have read so much more to ensure I capture information accurately, in a balanced and reflective manner I have only realised how uneasy some of this work has made me. How challenged I have felt by my learning and how vulnerable it feels to think deeply about my practice, my values, my unconscious biases. I have sought safe spaces to explore these thoughts and questions and, importantly, learn to sit with some of the unease while I work it out. This is a journey of development of thinking, and I am not at the end, and I do not believe I ever will be, but I am purposeful and committed.

This questioning has only further developed as I have continued to explore intersectionality, as core to neurodivergent-informed practice, we cannot choose to affirm neurodivergent people's lived experiences to enhance our work and ignore other marginalised groups. As my supervisor and chapter contributor Kate Boot says, 'Neurodiversity affirming practice is intersectional affirming practice'.

I will try to weave through the themes of intersectionality within reflective points and questions. However, as a white cis-gender woman in the earlier stages of learning and exploring intersectionality and anti-racism work, I am not the person to speak on this topic, and so I would signpost you to this book: *A Vision from the Margin: Intersectional Insights on Navigating Diversity in Speech and Language Therapy* by Mariam Malik. Watch this space in Chapter 2 for a bit of a 'deeper dive' into the topic.

Intersectionality and anti-racism work was not something I had much awareness of even as recently as a year ago but one that has caused me a great deal of uncomfortable feeling. It has involved a significantly extended reading list than I first thought to write this book but also an incredible amount of connection, professional growth and personal development. While some of the vocabulary that we are going to explore can feel alienating, and the concepts very big, I can only implore you to continue and promise it will be worth it when I say that this work is meaningful, valuable and essential.

Neurodivergent-informed practice means listening to neurodivergent voices and this is where my collaborators come in. I bring to the table my own experiences of working with neurodivergent individuals but recognise that everyone's lived experience is different and that I cannot speak for all. What I can do is bring together, and signpost you to, valuable voices to inform the practice of speech and language therapists.

I feel like this really is my sales pitch. If I can get across the values and ethos of the neurodiversity movement and its application to speech, language, and life then the rest of this book will be a breeze for you to make changes to the way you work or feel validated in the way that you already do things.

I guess I anticipate that by picking up this book, you want to know more, to do better to support the neurodivergent individuals that you do or might work with in the future. So perhaps this isn't too much of a sales pitch, but more the beginning of creating purpose, excitement, and drive to know more.

Before moving into independent practice, I worked in a specialist school for autistic children with more medium support needs across all domains, and these children and young people were all using spoken language in the most part, accessing national curriculum and did not have the complex learning disabilities of the children I had worked with previously, and they taught me so much. I would listen in therapy sessions to their challenges and found myself often relating and understanding. As such, I sought more information to better understand myself and in March 2023 I was diagnosed with ADHD, which is something I think I am still processing. Since then, I have also been confirmed as perimenopausal which means I have been on a real journey about myself and how my brain and body works while writing this book so it has been one wild ride!

During the process of writing, I read a book called *Ego is the Enemy* (Holiday, 2016) and it talks about the difference between passion and purpose. I would have always called myself a passionate speech and language therapist, but what I have reflected on is that passion serves myself, what I really meant when I said that is that I am an SLT with purpose. My purpose is to improve the quality of life of neurodivergent individuals through informed practice, but also supervision, training and learning opportunities for other therapists and trainees. This book helps serve that purpose. It has been a total labour of love, so please, read on, look within and be gentle, my rejection sensitive dysphoria is raging. I have done my best.

Being neurodivergent-informed and neurodiversity-affirming committed is not a 'what to do' kind of conversation, this book will not give you a list of approaches or trainings that mean you are now a 'neurodiversity-informed' therapist. This book will aim to help guide the thinking and mindset that creates a neurodiversity-affirming committed practitioner. So, without further ado …

Harriet's Context

In 2022, I was clinically identified as autistic and shortly after, self-identified as ADHD. I had always been AuDHD but no one had ever realised, including myself. Every day I struggled in a world not suited to me, living behind a mask, and trying hard to do things that were expected of me but were inaccessible. I became a speech and language therapist in 2018, after a very traumatic university experience. During my time training, I experienced significant mental health difficulties and almost didn't complete my course and almost lost my life. I had always wanted to help people as a job and from high school had a keen interest in supporting Neurodivergent people. I was passionate about going into a career centred around supporting others and understanding how brains worked.

During my training, I lost all my passion for Speech & Language Therapy and felt that I would never be any good at the role. I entered newly qualified life with low self-confidence and uncertain of my place in the profession. Most of my peers went into a role in the NHS, where they learnt about the general role of an SLT and expanded their knowledge of a range of different settings and SLCN. In contrast, I wanted to immediately specialise in mental health and was told my way of thinking would 'never fit in the NHS'. I began my career working in specialist schools for Social Emotional Mental Health differences, with those who are Neurodivergent and/or had experienced developmental trauma. I connected and understood the children in a completely different way and was able to give a different perspective of things. I didn't realise at the time that this was due to my lived experience of being Neurodivergent. Fast forward six years, I am now an independent speech and language therapist and neurodevelopmental practitioner and primarily support neurodivergent people through ADHD and autism assessments and post-identification.

Being identified as AuDHD at 26 was the best thing that has ever happened to me and has completely changed my life and my view of myself and others. It felt like before 26, I was unable to be myself and was restricted to being what others wanted and needed me to be. I could never achieve the things everybody thought I should be able to achieve. Presently, my mental health has never been better, and I have never felt so much fulfilment in my career and relationships. I spent the first 25 years of my life being told I 'couldn't' do things and I would 'never be able' to do things and I believed each negative message I received. Having finally had my strengths and needs confirmed and recognised has allowed me to put supports in my life and be able to thrive with my areas of strength. Due to my AuDHD identification, I have finally met my people (neurokin) and I feel seen, appreciated and respected. Having connection with a community of like-minded people has been the most wonderful and truly life-changing experience. I would not change any aspect of my journey to this point, but I wish the younger version of me had known that her life would eventually make sense and she would finally be able to accept herself and have people around her who do.

I must note that in this book I will be discussing my experiences as an AuDHer. These are my experiences alone, it's important that people are aware that all Neurodivergent people are different. I cannot speak for others' experiences, but I will share my own, as well as information I have gained from interactions and conversations with my clients. My experiences of AuDHD are heavily influenced by my privileges, including being a low-support needs, cisgender, white woman. I would always encourage people to seek the experiences of people who do not look like me or communicate like me and have different life experiences to myself. We have included some information about other sources of information from people who are non-speaking, BIPOC, and queer at the end of the book. Neuro-affirming practice is much more than just a disability issue and to progress with neuro-affirming practice we also must work on being LGBTQIA+ affirming and anti-racist.

Another important thing to note is that as a neurodivergent SLT, I certainly do not know everything there is to know about neuro-affirming practice. As many others are, I am on the journey and continue to shift my practice in this direction but there is no end point, it is a process of continual learning. I will likely write of things in this book that I will change my perspective on in time as my knowledge develops. My intention is to share my current knowledge of neuro-affirming practice alongside my lived experience to support others' journeys through this process. As well as recognising and sharing my lived experience, I continue to listen to other voices in this community who have different experiences and learn from this. My views have evolved and shifted from listening to others in the community and continue to do so.

A note about language:

During my sections for this book, I will use specific terminology, which I would like to clarify. First, I appreciate the use of identity-first language when people refer to me with regard to autism (e.g. autistic person) however, I tend to use 'with ADHD' and 'ADHDer' interchangeably. As terminology around ADHD progresses, I may take a different stance. On that topic, it is important to note that a lot of the language used in this resource is likely to change as neuro-affirming work evolves and, therefore, the language that I use only reflects my knowledge and views at the time. Many in the autistic community opt for identity-first language, which I will use throughout this book. I will also use the term 'AuDHD', which is a combination of autism and ADHD. I will also use 'differences' and 'difficulties' at different points, as some of the differences I experience are in themselves differences, a neutral thing. However, I will also refer to some as difficulties, as this is my experience of them. For example, I would refer to my periods of mutism as communication 'difficulties' as it is something I find very challenging to navigate and can cause me some distress and negative experiences.

Your Context

Before delving into the concept of neurodiversity, I think it is important that we consider what it is to be a speech and language therapist, aspiring, studying or qualified. There is a set of values, or perhaps personality traits that underpin the profession.

The Royal College of Speech and Language Therapists (RCSLT, no date) define the job as follows:

> Speech and language therapy provides treatment, support and care for children and adults who have difficulties with communication, or with eating, drinking and swallowing.

To me here, there are a few key words to explore when we begin to think about what it is that underpins us, and predominantly they are support and care. We are supportive professionals who care about the individuals that we work with. Sometimes we care so deeply it is hard to switch off, sometimes we want to support so much that we go above and beyond in many ways to ensure that those individuals get what we feel they need.

We are a group of individuals who do what we do because we care. We sign up to our standards to continue to learn and develop, because we want to do the best that we can for the individuals we support. We read, listen and learn to ensure that we are at the forefront of practice. I'd hazard a guess that you have also on many occasions felt like you aren't doing enough, experienced imposter syndrome or got burnt out because of the pressure you placed on yourself to be all things to all people. Am I right?

The standards that we sign up to are those of the Health and Care Professions Council (HCPC) and when we qualify and register with them, we agree to uphold those standards. Part of that you are doing now: by reading this you are engaging in continuing professional development, a core principle of safe and effective practice within the guidelines (Health and Care Professions Council, no date).

> 1.3 – At the point of registration, a therapist must be able to keep their skills and knowledge up to date and understand the importance of continuing professional development throughout their career.

These standards also guide us that:

> 13.1 – At the point of registration, a therapist must be able to change their practice as needed to take account of new developments, technologies and changing contexts.

Both of these standards can only be upheld if, when working with neurodivergent individuals, therapists are keeping their skills and knowledge up to date, by engaging in continuing professional development that takes into account the changing contexts of the neurodiversity paradigm. In order to do this, we must embrace feeling uncomfortable, unlearning and digging into parts of you that perhaps you never knew existed. As we embrace neurodiversity, we must also work on other intersections and show up in conversations about anti-racism, power and privilege as well as anti-disability. Which is also part of the standards we agree to meet:

> 5.3 – At the point of registration, a therapist must be able to recognise the potential impact of their own values, beliefs and personal biases (which may be unconscious) on practice and take personal action to ensure all service users and carers are treated appropriately with respect and dignity.

Fatimah, one of the contributors to this book, introduced me to the concept of reflexive practice vs. reflective and when she shared more about it, I understood that the journey one takes delving into becoming more neurodiversity-affirming is one that is best expressed as reflexive, rather than reflective practice.

Reflective practice is simply thinking critically about an action or experience and learning from it to improve practice in the future. Reflexive practice takes this further; it begins to look not only at what was happening, but the people involved and encourages us to look at how our own backgrounds, beliefs, values and assumptions influence those actions we take, and decisions we make. It emphasises how these things are interconnected, that our practice is shaped by the social, cultural and institutional contexts within which we work.

So it seems to me, for us to meet that 5.3 point of our standards, we must seek to be more reflexive in our thinking, to become a more neurodivergent-informed practitioner, and bring our awareness to our unconscious bias about other intersections of marginalised populations that we support in our work.

REFLECTION

What do you really believe in?

To begin with unpicking our values, there are many tools to help you do this, and one of my favourites is from Brene Brown's website (Brown, 2023). To be a neurodivergent-informed practitioner, the first element is diving down into your own values.

I would advise here completing this activity for yourselves. It is a complex deep dive but worth doing, especially to then consider who you are surrounded by, and if they enable these values to be lived out in the work you do. Our colleagues are important when we are moving towards being a neurodiversity-affirming committed therapist and I know many therapists have left roles and taken up roles based on the work of the team and systems they are working within to feel satisfied that they can meet their HCPC standards, and their own set of values.

Brene helps us to work out what values are most important to us, she describes these as beliefs that 'help you find your way in the dark, that fill you with a feeling of purpose'. Her tool asks us to identify from a list two values that define who we are, and then work through how our behaviours support those values. My two core values are curiosity and learning, these play out in my parenting, my professional life and my being. Although, I won't lie that learning about things that don't interest me or are delivered in a manner that doesn't get me engaged is definitely a caveat to that value!

I live fully into these values every day within my work, being curious about the individuals I support and what drives them, and their families and support teams. What are the barriers to progress and improving quality of life? What does quality of life look like for these individuals?

What do you think are two core values that fill you with purpose? That are at the centre of your being and that radiate through how you learn, reflect and work.

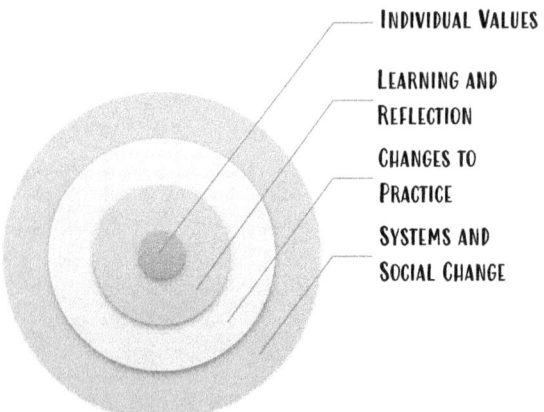

By beginning with ourselves and our values we can work out where we might need to shift our thoughts and consider our own flexibility and openness to new ways of thinking. Our values lead to our learning and reflection. In turn this can enable us to bring about change to our individual practice, influence others in their changes to practice through critical conversations, supportive reflections and nurturing supervision. If all therapists sign up to these standards and are doing this work, we can create a voice and be loud in order to effect change within our systems. Which in one moment in time can create somewhat of a large stumbling block, and at other times a giant brick wall. When challenging practice, we must be brave, curious and humble.

We know what we know, but we don't know what we don't.

So much of this work is about breaking down our own internal values and beliefs, some of which may be so unconscious you weren't aware of them and part of this isn't about just swapping a few approaches and introducing some new words to reports and goals. It is about developing an awareness of intersectionality, unlearning everything we thought we knew about ourselves, society and culture and building it back up once we are better informed. To that end, we will be exploring intersectionality within the book and how if we are to be truly neuro-affirming practitioners, we too must explore how our own social identities create subconscious discrimination and bring our awareness of privilege.

Society's Context

Intersectionality is defined as 'the network of connections between social categories such as race, class and gender, especially when this may result in additional disadvantage or discrimination' (Oxford Dictionary, no date). The term was coined by Kimberlé Crenshaw (1989). First and foremost, speech and language therapy is a predominantly white, middle-class, female profession; we are not the most diverse bunch.

> **REFLECTION**
>
> Thinking back, or looking around in your current lectures, what was the diversity in age, sexuality, gender, ethnicity, race?
>
> Are you aware of your privilege? If you have it, how can you use that to support the marginalised communities that we support as therapists?

I know from my experiences there was very little diversity, and this is a very similar picture and has been through my working life so far. There has been a lot of privilege in the groups of people I have trained with, and subsequently worked with. It is an essential task to explore and reflect on how these social categories show up for you, and the impact this might have on your unconscious bias about neurodivergent people and their families.

In order to identify your privilege, I would highly recommend you watch Naomi Ignatius, senior SLT, Neurosciences SLT Service video on YouTube. I have a link to this and other useful videos from the RCSLT on anti-racism in the reading list at the back of this book.

We are actively called upon by the HCPC within our professional standards to:

> 5.5 recognise the characteristics and consequences of barriers to inclusion, including for socially isolated groups.
>
> 5.6 actively challenge these barriers, supporting the implementation of change wherever possible.

Crenshaw (no date) states: 'Intersectionality is a lens through which you can see where power comes and collides, where it interlocks and intersects. It's not simply that there's a race problem here, a gender problem here, and a class or LBGTQ problem there'. The RCSLT is doing some critical work (Moore, 2022; RCSLT, 2024a, 2024b) in this area across our profession to seek to improve guidance for therapists and in turn expectations of how we work from the point of entry into the profession via degree or apprenticeship, through to supporting therapists in the workplace as well as considering the individuals we serve as therapists. We must as individuals and a profession be seen to challenge and advocate for those marginalised groups and amplify their voices, in a meaningful way.

We know that disabilities can create marginalised communities but as Talila Lewis (2019) states, ableism can be rooted across all marginalised groups and as a profession we must do better to identify this and increase access to services, and those that are judgement free and offer honouring and affirming professionals.

Pete Wharmby (2022) writes: 'interesting fact: we've absolutely no idea how many autistic people there are in the world'. What we know is that as we know more, there are probably similar numbers of autistic males and females, that there are also similar numbers of Black, Brown and white autistics. Pete summarises beautifully: 'wherever you find people, you'll find autistics'. It strikes me this is likely the case for a lot of neurodivergent profiles, where the research is mostly about white individuals, often boys, in terms of the diagnostic criteria and the narrative about other marginalised groups.

This to me feels the same for all varying neurotypes, and the discrimination that goes against them accessing services can start from the beginning, accessing information and health services, diagnosis, post-diagnostic support, access to specialist services and education. Most of my working career has been in independent specialist settings, and the children and young people I have worked with have mostly been white and male. However, I have no doubt there are as many female and neurodivergent people of the global majority out there, but they have not been able to access the services. Why is that?

In order to truly be neurodiversity-affirming committed, where we tackle ableism (which I will explore shortly) we must also tackle racism and be trauma informed. There are so many layers of complexity to these topics, and it can feel very overwhelming. At the time of writing this, I will be honest, I am in a place of confusion. I thought I was 'just' a speech and language therapist, who wanted to better serve the children and young people I work with.

Delving into these social issues was not necessarily something I ever thought about professionally or considered as a pivotal part to developing my practice. So often we believe continuing professional development (CPD) to be going on the latest training for the next great approach, attending a conference or a webinar. This kind of development is both personal and professional, and it is intense, and it does not give you a 'what will you do in a session tomorrow' kind of reflection, but more a sense of 'how do I shift my thinking?' and apply those thoughts in a conscious and meaningful way to make a change. But once you are aware and see these challenges, you cannot go back to the way you thought before and it gives us an opportunity to be part of the change for the better both in the diversity of therapists themselves, but also in the way that different individuals can access our services. Each individual will need to find a way to uplift the voices of others, to challenge the systems within which we work and advocate for best practice, that is truly best for the individuals that we support. It is about starting a ripple.

The language of neurodiversity and intersectionality is complex, it can be a little alienating, confusing and perhaps actually not be conducive to welcoming and promoting inclusivity. There are many glossaries out there and the vocabulary can be explained, but the best thing to do is to listen to people talk about this. Social media (despite so many flaws) has brought about a change in the way we can access learning and explore complex topics, and I really advocate the use of if when becoming more neurodiversity-affirming. By accessing information via social media, we can investigate these topics from experts in the truest sense, sharing their lived experience, and in small and manageable chunks. I will collate a list of great places to seek more information about these topics, as well as references at the end of the book. This is caveated with two points:

1. All information must be used as part of our critical thinking skills as therapists and weighed up based on the individuals that we serve.
2. One neurodivergent person, cannot speak for the whole population, but only for their experiences.

I talked earlier about passion vs. purpose, and I think there is such clarity in these differences when we are delving into these topics, listening to people who we might say are passionate, but it is their purpose that drives that perception. We are listening to people who are making it their purpose to better inform those who deliver services like speech and language therapy. We, in turn, can make it our purpose to learn, and then our purpose to inform those around us.

So where can you go from here, to better inform yourself and bring awareness? Listen and learn from other's views, seek out those who do not share the same social categories as you, both neurodivergent and speech and language therapists. We can learn so much from listening to those with lived experiences. Make space to do this, set aside time, record it as continuing professional development and see it as part of the on-going learning and growth that we as therapists are required to do.

The History of Neurodiversity

The term neurodiversity has been around since the late 1990s. Recently an article published by Botha et al. (2024) highlighted that despite the term being often attributed to the work of Judy Singer, a social scientist, in her 1998 thesis, it had been used collectively before that date. More recently it has gained traction with the neurodiversity movement and advocacy communities, who are driving change for neurodivergent individuals and promoting equity. In time the terms neurodivergent and neurodivergence were coined by Kassiane Asaumasu, a neurodiversity activist.

Being neurodivergent is not a diagnosis or medical term, it is a term that we might consider an 'umbrella' for lots of different traits and diagnostic labels. Many individuals will identify with a neurotype and consider themselves neurodivergent, some with and some without a diagnosis. This should be considered valid, and it is an important shift, taking away the significance of requiring a diagnosis from a health care professional or team. This is particularly important when we consider three groups of people:

1. Those who we might be working alongside as adults who are recognising their neurotype as divergent and identifying that way but due to lack of services might not receive a diagnosis, or not feel one is required. Here we must be able to accept and support reasonable adjustments for them within the workplace or say for example if we are in the role of practice educator on placement.

> **REFLECTION**
>
> If a colleague or SLT student shared, they identify as ADHD, how would you respond? Might you ask if they have a diagnosis? If they don't, how would that sit with you?

2. Those service users who have similar challenges accessing services for diagnosis, but who themselves, or their parents and team around them recognise and identify them as neurodivergent. There are many individuals in this situation, and the number is increasing with waiting lists and better understanding and recognition of neurodivergent profiles, in particular autism, ADHD and specific learning difficulties, but within an under-resourced diagnostic service.

> **REFLECTION**
>
> What are your thoughts: Does a diagnosis matter in terms of the support you will give? How crucial is a diagnosis for access to support services? Perhaps again another part of the broken system that neurodivergent people are required to navigate in order to live if the answer to that is 'very crucial'.

3. The parents of children we might be working with. We know that a lot of neurodivergent profiles are genetic, and therefore there is a likelihood that if we are supporting neurodivergent children, their parents may too be neurodivergent.

> **REFLECTION**
>
> How do you adapt your communication style when handing over information to neurodivergent parents? What reasonable adjustments do you make for them in terms of their access to the service and their capacity to engage in supporting their child? Remembering appointments, taking away information and understanding and applying it?

We can consider a range of both acquired and developmental differences under the umbrella of neurodivergent: some individuals experience changes to their neurology that are lifelong following periods of illness or accident, while others experience these differences as part of their neurology from the point of conception. What is important is that neurodivergence is an identity and so if someone identifies as neurodivergent, we must honour and respect that.

The Context 15

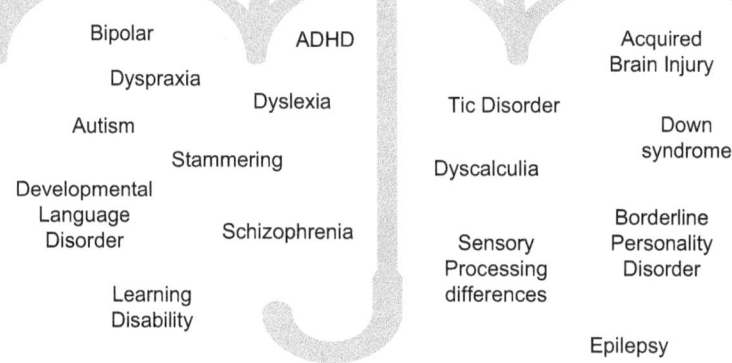

Adapted from Wise (2023)

The Umbrella has been developed and used by many individuals; this image has been adapted from Sonny-Jane Wise, who released an updated 'Smorgasbord of Neurodivergence' which I recommend you have a look at. As the practice of being neurodiversity-affirming is linked to seeing individuals through the right humanist lens we can take the concept and apply it to all differing Neurotypes. For the purpose of this book, I will be focussing towards Neurodevelopmental differences.

Neurodivergent individuals throughout history would have been viewed as different, eccentrics, and perhaps put into institutions. Outcomes were mostly poor, society's judgement causing trauma, mental health problems and loss of life, or being admitted and having a poor quality of life within large hospitals with practices that sought to fix the individual and rid them of their neurodivergence through unethical, abusive and traumatic practices.

Dignity and autonomy for neurodivergent individuals were not necessarily a consideration, these people were perceived as less than, as incapable of thoughts and therefore needing to be 'done to' within medical practice. Practices such as electro-convulsive therapy, punishment and aversion therapies were all recommended for treating neurodivergence, in particular autism and those neurotypes that present with distress behaviour.

Herein lies part of the problem, individuals presenting with meltdowns, significantly distressed behaviour that puts themselves and others at risk. This was seen through a medical lens, where the problem was the person, that the person needed treating in order to stop these behaviours.

Society's judgement of those obvious behaviours meant they needed medical care to cure them. Alternatively, those individuals who might not have presented with this and masked behaviours were deemed odd, left-out and judged for their social communication style and personalities, and also bullied and traumatised.

In time, more behavioural approaches began to be introduced for individuals. While on the surface they seemed less intrusive and more reward focussed, ultimately the aim was to make neurodivergent people more neurotypical in their presentation. Cue another generation of individuals made to feel that they were less, that they needed to change to fit in and that neurodivergence was their problem.

This viewpoint stems from the medical model, a lens that suggests neurodivergence is a disordered way of being, that it needs treatment and intervention and strict diagnostic criteria based on evidence-based assessment tools. We see this on a very visible level in the diagnostic labels of many neurodivergent profiles:

> Obsessive compulsive DISORDER
> Attention DEFECIT hyperactive DISORDER
> Autism spectrum DISORDER
> Bipolar DISORDER
> Borderline Personality DISORDER

The terms themselves identify neurology as disordered, as medically less than a typical brain and body. These profiles can be totally disabling for individuals who experience them, but are they a disorder? Or are they part of the rich tapestry of life, as we see within the natural world and call it biodiversity?

Over the years there have been shifts with new ways of enabling individuals, systems such as positive behaviour support, special education provisions, specific teams within the health care sector for these profiles and the introduction of concepts around neurodivergence awareness days, weeks and months.

As part of the process of becoming neurodivergent informed, I advise that you consider your preconceptions about neurodivergent individuals and their families.

REFLECTION

When you are assessing, supporting, writing about neurodivergent individuals, what is the narrative you create?

We all have history behind us that has shaped our learning when we trained, our on-going continuing professional development, the courses we take, the books we read. The world is developing and growing but there is still an awful lot of practice that takes place through a medical model lens.

Ableism

It seems fitting here to introduce the concept of ableism. This concept is core to understanding why neurodiversity-informed practice is so important, but also one that brings about some significantly uncomfortable thoughts and feelings about previous practice. Ableism is defined as: 'discrimination in favour of non-disabled people, by Scope, the Disability charity' (Scope UK, no date).

As Talila Lewis (2019) states in a working definition of ableism: 'you do not have to be disabled to experience ableism'. The definition speaks to ableism being based on society's 'constructed ideas of normalcy, intelligence and excellence. Thise constructed ideas of normalcy, intelligence and excellence are deeply rooted in anti-Blackness, eugenics and capitalism'.

When we explore our values, we begin to look inwards and here is where we can uncover ableism. This is often not a conscious thought process, just something that we have grown up with, that society, our training and placement and practice experience develops in our thinking. Lewis states: 'this form of systemic oppression leads to people and society determining who is valuable and worthy based on people's appearance and/or their ability to satisfactorily produce, excel and behave'.

Internalised ableism, albeit unconscious, is the next stage on the journey. Looking within to how our own thoughts shape the way we perceive neurodivergent individuals, unknowingly creating a narrative about their being and, in turn, a way of assessing, goal setting and working with them.

Ableism within neurodiversity goes deep! When we think about physical or visible disabilities, ableism might look like limited access to a shop for a wheelchair user, or no toilet facilities for someone who needs physical support such as bars to be able to independently access them. This is where society discriminates against disabled people. The UK is constantly moving forward with this: better access to facilities, increased numbers of changing places with more equipment to enable better access, but there is still a long way to go.

For the neurodivergent population, the surface has barely been scratched. Some cinemas now offer special showings, supermarkets have relaxed low arousal times and airports are introducing sensory rooms. Within speech and language therapy, the times, they are a changing ... but at a slow pace.

Ableism within our field tends to lend itself towards us assessing neurodivergent individuals as though they are neurotypical, comparing their skills developmentally and plotting their 'age equivalent'; using standardised assessments that are not written to the perceptions or norm referenced for neurodivergent individuals. It means we are settings goals to develop their communication skills to match our neurotypical expectations; seeking to engage neurodivergent children through carrot dangling sensory rewards when these strategies are regulating and access should be unrestricted; keeping a child's preferred activities until they've done our adult-led 'boring' ones; and teaching what we might deem 'appropriate' social skills, but actually what we are doing is teaching neurotypical social skills, encouraging neurodivergent individuals to see themselves as different, and less, and that they need to mask who they truly are in order to succeed.

It is a way of thinking that means we are not accepting the individual as they are, we are not working with their neurotype and strengths, and instead we are trying to change the way they do things to fit in with the world around them. We often think about the concept of trying to fit a round peg in a square hole. The more you hit that peg, the more damaged it becomes. It is wedged, unable to move, either forwards or backwards, and this is the case for a lot of older neurodivergent individuals, who have accessed therapy that is teaching them to stop the way they think, act and are. Then, wedged, they are needing support to be gentle with themselves, to bring their awareness to their differences and in time embrace and champion them as their own authentic selves. We must stop trying to be the hammers that are damaging pegs.

Generally, this is where the shift begins, considering what it is we are trying to change, and, importantly, why?

The Deficit Basis

When we think of neurodivergence, we are moving towards thinking of positive things:

- Empowerment
- Autonomy
- Authenticity

However, historically, a neurodivergent profile was viewed through a medical lens. This lens saw individuals as broken, pathologising their profiles and encouraging early intervention to fix and change how a person presents to fit into the neurotypical way of being.

The language itself of 'disorders' creates a narrative that is heard and perceived by society as negative, and in turn has created a negative narrative of self for any neurodivergent individuals, that they have to work hard to challenge and develop an authentic understanding of self, and in turn the advocacy skills to be who they are and seek the support they require.

We still hear the term intervention a lot; I would challenge the term intervention in itself. When we begin to think about our language, we can think about the different narratives that we create. Intervention kind of suggests fixing. Look at the Cambridge dictionary definition of intervention: 'the action of becoming intentionally involved in a difficult situation, in order to improve it or prevent it from getting worse' (Cambridge Dictionary, no date).

> **REFLECTION**
>
> Take a moment to pause and think about those words: we say that we are working with 'difficult situations' to 'improve' or prevent worsening. Imagine for a moment that is in relation to someone you care about?

We must consider the implications when we talk about 'intervention'. While we may be seeking an improvement in an individual's skills and quality of life, there is a question about who thinks the situation is difficult. So what instead? Personally, I suggest we consider the use of 'support' instead of 'intervention'. We offer speech and language therapy to support skill development, to support quality of life. We offer services that support neurodivergent individuals to understand themselves and develop their advocacy skills. We are not viewing neurodivergent people as difficult situations, we do not view their situations as hopeless, in need of hours and hours of specialist support. We view them as humans, with differences, where we can be involved as required to support them in their development of self in order to ensure their well-being.

Conclusion

Challenging our ableism, for me, is about asking the question 'so what?' This can be where we start to challenge what we do as therapists, and when and why. Let's challenge ourselves, to really begin to question our referrals, and the work that we have previously done to support neurodivergent individuals. When a problem is brought to you, someone wants support with an issue, ask it of yourself and them.

> 'My child doesn't look at me when I talk to them' – so what?
> 'They never sit still in my lessons' – so what?
> 'I just talk about what I love and it's hard to listen to other people' – so what?

These examples give an idea of some of the challenges that a neurodivergent individual might face, in light of a society that places more value on neurotypical communication and regulation strategies. So, while the answer to some of these questions might mean there is an impact on well-being, we start to consider how we then support this.

My thoughts, based on what we now know listening to the neurodivergent community, are:

- 'My child doesn't look at me when I talk to them' – Let's talk about how that makes you, the adult, feel? You feel as though they aren't listening, but are they not? Maybe their listening looks different to how you expect them to.
- 'They never sit still in my lessons' – Ok, let's explore the challenges here. Are they distracting you or others? What is their movement looking like? How do you offer them access to movement proactively? What equipment is provided within their desk space to enable some movement. It sounds like this individual needs movement to regulate. What is dysregulating about that classroom environment for them? Have you asked them?

- 'I just talk about what I love and it's hard to listen to other people' – It sounds like that is important to you. What do your friends and family think about your interests? How do you feel this is impacting your relationships and quality of life? How do you let people know about your neurodivergence and the differences they might experience communicating with you?

Changing the way we think about these challenges, shifting the perception we hold ourselves, enabling the individual and the people around them to shift too, is how we challenge some of this internalised ableism.

Chapter Summary

- Your values matter: check yourself, reflect on how your social categories show up and impact on your unconscious bias, and engagement with individuals and families.
- Your language matters: know the vocabulary and use it in the right way.
- Your voice matters: as professionals supporting individuals and families the way we talk about neurodivergence, the reports we write, the goals we set all matter.
- Your mindset matters: ask those critical questions when you are working with neurodivergent individuals, check in with your biases, think about the potential outcomes and long-term impact of support you are offering.

References and Resources

Botha, M., R. Chapman, M.G. Onaiwu et al. (2024) 'The neurodiversity concept was developed collectively: An overdue correction on the origins of neurodiversity theory', *Autism*, 28(6), 1591–1594.

Brown, B. (2023) 'Living into our values'. https://brenebrown.com/resources/living-into-our-values/ (accessed on 15/08/2023).

Cambridge Dictionary. (no date) intervention – definition. https://dictionary.cambridge.org/dictionary/english/intervention (accessed on 07/10/2023).

Crenshaw, K. (1998) 'Demarginalizing the intersection of race and sex: A Black Feminist critique of antidiscrimination doctrine, feminist theory, and antiracist politics'. *Oxford University Press eBooks*, pp. 314–343. https://doi.org/10.1093/oso/9780198782063.003.0016 (accessed 15/09/2024).

Disablism and ableism. Disability charity Scope UK. (no date). www.scope.org.uk/about-us/disablism (accessed 15/08/2023).

Health and Care Professions Council. (no date) Speech and language therapists. www.hcpc-uk.org/standards/standards-of-proficiency/speech-and-language-therapists/ (accessed on 13/07/2024).

Holiday, R. (2016) *Ego is the Enemy*. London: Profile Books.

Lewis, T. (2019) *Ableism*. [Instagram] 10/03/2019 (accessed on 24/08/2024).

Moore, M. (2022) 'Progressing our work on equality diversity and inclusion'. www.rcslt.org/news/progressing-our-work-on-equality-diversity-and-inclusion/ (accessed 16/07/2024).

Oxford Dictionary. (no date) intersectionality noun – Definition, pictures, pronunciation and usage notes. *Oxford Advanced Learner's Dictionary*. www.oxfordlearnersdictionaries.com/definition/english/intersectionality?q=intersectionality (accessed 15/09/2024).

Royal College of Speech and Language Therapists. (no date) 'Speech and language therapy'. RCSLT. www.rcslt.org/speech-and-language-therapy/ (accessed 15/08/2024).

Royal College of Speech and Language Therapists. (2024a) 'Supporting LGBT-QIA+ colleagues in the workplace: A guide for all'. RCSLT. www.rcslt.org/learning/diversity-inclusion-and-anti-racism/supporting-lgbtqia-colleagues-in-the-workplace-a-guide-for-all/ (accessed 16/07/2024).

Royal College of Speech and Language Therapists. (2024b) 'Supporting diversity, equality and inclusion – Resources'. *RCSLT.* www.rcslt.org/learning/diversity-inclusion-and-anti-racism/external-resources/ (accessed 16/07/2024).

Wharmby, P. (2024) *Untypical: How the World Isn't Built for Autistic People and What We Should All Do About it.* London: Mudlark, Harper Collins Publishers.

Image Adaptation Reference

Wise, S,J. (2023) The Neurodivergent Umbrella. [Instagram] 19/02/2023. www.instagram.com/p/Co29RLrhgWT/?utm_source=ig_web_copy_link&igsh=MzRIODBiNWFlZA== (accessed 25/08/2024).

2

Integrating Intersectionality

A Neurodiversity-Affirming Approach to Speech and Language Therapy

Fatimah Bint-Hanif and Kate Boot

We would like to thank Wing Yee Lam and Amy Cats for their time in reviewing this chapter's draft and providing us with valuable insights that have greatly enhanced this final version and extended our personal growth in this area. We also extend our gratitude to other reviewers, including those who preferred to remain unnamed, for their thoughtful feedback and contributions.

Welcome and Grounding: Embracing Positionality, Compassion, and Collective Learning

We're Fatimah and Kate, and we're here to explore the concept of intersectionality so that our practice can be neurodiversity-affirming committed, rather than 'neuroaffirming-lite'. Before we share our perspectives, it's important to acknowledge that the author reached out to invite other voices with intersecting identities to contribute to this book; however, responses were limited. We recognise that the process of connecting with others who can contribute is complex. The networks we can access are often selective and limited, and it is important to acknowledge that those with privileged access to resources or platforms are typically the ones asked to contribute. There are many other valuable voices in this field that deserve to be heard.

We come to this chapter from distinct yet complementary positions. Fatimah writes as a British, Muslim cis-gender woman with a heritage from South Asia and Southern Africa. Kate brings her perspective as a white British, late-discovered AuDHD, queer, cis-gender woman from a working-class background, who also has access to middle-class social and cultural capital. Our different experiences have enriched this work, offering varied insights into neurodiversity-affirming practice.

We joined this project as a late addition, working within focused timelines to create meaningful and thoughtful content. We write with awareness that our perspectives, while informed by both personal and professional experience, cannot and should not speak for all. Our positions offer unique viewpoints while leaving space for other individuals.

The language used in this chapter aims to be accessible, inclusive, and respectful, reflecting diverse perspectives and experiences. It is not, however, apologetic. This book contributes to the ongoing conversations about neurodiversity-affirming speech and language therapy practice. In order to maintain the status quo, deficit-based narratives are often reinforced-framing individuals and communities by what they are perceived to lack rather than what they bring. These narratives are historically white-led and influenced by colonialism which has minoritised, de-humanised and pathologised individuals. In our commitment to decolonise the profession, we will use culturally sensitive and affirming language, recognising that many communities experience multiple marginalisations, including neurodivergent individuals.

While helpful for understanding, we acknowledge that language labels cannot capture individual complexity. Terms such as 'global majority', 'marginalised' and 'underserved' are used for clarity while recognising they cannot fully describe everyone's identities and experiences. These preferences often reflect personal, political, and cultural contexts – what feels empowering to one person may feel restrictive to another. Language continues to evolve, as does our understanding of inclusive communication. We invite readers to engage critically with the text, recognising that our collective understanding of respectful and affirming language is constantly developing.

The breadth of experiences within marginalised communities deserves expansive exploration beyond what a single chapter can offer. We feel it was fundamental to highlight how intersectionality significantly shapes neurodiversity-affirming practice while recognising this is a single contribution to more extensive insight.

We recommend engaging with diverse voices and perspectives beyond this chapter, particularly those from historically underserved communities. This topic deserves deeper exploration through engagement with community voices, academic research, and lived experiences beyond what we could include here.

Compassion and Collective Learning

The discussions in this chapter may challenge your existing biases, beliefs and assumptions. We encourage you to approach these ideas with a critical mindset, recognising that this engagement is fundamental to understanding and supporting the lives of real people impacted by these topics. Our discussions are not just theoretical; they actively shape the daily lives of individuals and communities around us.

As you think about these ideas, know that everyone starts from their own place of understanding. Learning is a cyclical process of growth. What matters is taking that next step in understanding because the way we recognise inequalities, power, and privilege helps us build a more equitable world. While this understanding is essential, it shows only part of the picture. Real change happens when we translate these insights into everyday actions and practices. As Maya Angelou reminds us:

> *Do the best you can until you know better.*
> *Then when you know better, do better.*

We understand that learning about intersectionality might make you uncomfortable – particularly when confronting how systems of power and privilege have shaped our world. Any momentary discomfort of learning exists in stark contrast to the realities of historically underserved communities, for whom these topics are not reflective exercises but daily experiences shaped by generations of systemic oppression and ongoing harm from colonial structures that persist in our education, organisations, practices, and ways of thinking. Yet discomfort can become a catalyst for change when we choose to examine it deeply and honestly. As Robin DiAngelo reflects:

> The key to moving forward is what we do with our discomfort. We can use it as a door out – blame the messenger, disregard the message, and continue on unchanged. Or we can use it as a door in by asking, 'Why does this unsettle me? What would it mean for me if this were true?'

For some, you may reflect individually, while others may partake in group discussions with their colleagues, peers, friends, family, community groups or within supervisory relationships in university, workplaces or on placement. As you engage in these conversations, it's essential to acknowledge that we all bring different levels of privilege to the table, which can shape our perspectives and experiences. We encourage you to consider using a framework for facilitating group conversations, particularly where groups include people with intersectional identities for whom these discussions may resurface trauma, cause harm, or trigger distressing experiences.

Supportive Reading Guidelines

Throughout this chapter, you may encounter ideas that bring up discomfort or require a pause for deeper reflection. Using regulation tools can help you process these moments with care, creating a more balanced reading experience. Here are some suggested regulation tools to support your journey:

- **Pause and Reflect**: Take intentional breaks to process key concepts while creating a space for deeper understanding and reflection.
- **Movement Breaks**: Regulate your emotions by, for example, stretching or taking a walk.
- **Regulation Tools**: Reading while moving can help with regulation, for example, using fidget aids or other sensory tools.
- **Journaling**: Use a journal to engage in reflexive practice, considering your thoughts, feelings, and opinions.

- **Mindfulness Techniques**: Ground yourself with breathing techniques to help you refocus.
- **Self-Compassion**: Approach your learning with kindness and patience.

Intersectionality: What Is It?

What Are Intersecting Identities?

Intersecting identities are how all of your identities come together. We all have intersecting identities. Think about yourself for a moment; what do you consider to be your identity? This relates to aspects including, but not limited to, age, gender identity, race, ethnicity, nationality, sexuality, class, religion, languages spoken, education level, and disability status. The different parts of your identity don't exist on their own; they overlap – this is what we mean by intersecting identities.

What Is Intersectionality?

Intersectionality describes how identities interact with systems of power and oppression in complex and overlapping ways. The term 'intersectionality' was formally coined by Black legal scholar Kimberlé Crenshaw in 1989, emerging from her work on how race and gender discrimination create distinct experiences of oppression in Black women's lives (Crenshaw, 1989, 1991). This theoretical framework articulated decades of Black feminist scholarship and activism, mainly through the work of the Combahee River Collective (1982), bell hooks (1981) and Patricia Hill Collins (1990). These understandings were simultaneously shaped by and intertwined with disability justice scholarship (Bailey, 2019) alongside contributions from Black LGBTQIA+ scholars like Audre Lorde (1984) and Barbara Smith (1983). Their collective activism demonstrated how different forms of oppression operate together. At its core, intersectionality recognises identities are inherently interconnected and shape how individuals experience the world. Audre Lourde stated:

> There is no thing as a single-issue struggle because
> we do not live single-issue lives.

This understanding of interconnected oppression is what scholar Patricia Hill Collins terms the 'matrix of domination' – how different systems of oppression work together to create distinct experiences of marginalisation (Collins, 1990). These systems should not be viewed separately or in isolation; it is crucial to understand how they interact and reinforce one another rather than simply adding race, gender, class and disability together (Collins, 2000). This framework fundamentally challenges the single-axis thinking that has historically dominated academic and professional discourse.

To help you understand intersectionality, imagine standing at a busy junction where different roads merge. Just as multiple streets intersect, various aspects of our identities intersect in our lives. These intersections aren't just points where identities meet; they create unique experiences that cannot be understood by looking at any single identity in isolation.

For example, a religious woman from an ethnic majority group may face discrimination that intertwines sexism, racism and religious intolerance. For instance, they might be stereotyped as submissive or oppressed due to sexist assumptions tied to their faith while also encountering hostility or exclusion because of racialised religious prejudice. This is a distinct form of marginalisation which emerges from how oppressive systems can work together. Kimberlé Crenshaw makes it clear:

> If you're standing in the path of multiple forms of exclusion,
> you're likely to get hit by both.

We have observed this limitation in some spaces that claim to be 'neurodiversity-affirming'. For example, discourse around 'unmasking' often presents universal strategies, failing to consider how this experience differs across communities. The risks and consequences of unmasking vary significantly depending on a person's intersecting identities – including racial trauma, cultural stigma plus economic and social barriers (Pearson and Rose, 2021). It is important we don't blindly adopt approaches which have the potential to exclude and 'other' people with multiple marginalised identities but perpetuate the same systems of oppression that have historically pathologised and stigmatised these communities through deficit-based models.

Crucially, intersectionality emerged from resistance and survival strategies, not just theoretical analysis. As bell hooks (1981) emphasises, marginalised people have long understood that their experiences couldn't be separated into neat categories – their lived realities have always reflected the interplay of multiple identities and oppressions. While we all possess multiple identities, those with intersecting marginalised identities often encounter compounded oppression and inequality, while those holding multiple privileged identities may benefit from overlapping advantages. These power dynamics are not accidental – they are maintained through systemic inequity, institutional policies, cultural norms and social practices that privilege certain identities while marginalising others. Only by understanding and challenging these interconnected systems and acknowledging our own positions of privilege within them, can we work towards meaningful change.

The Critical Distinction

Understanding **the difference between intersecting identities and intersectionality is crucial**. While intersecting identities describe the multiple aspects of identity someone holds, intersectionality provides the analytical framework for understanding how these identities interact within systems of power and oppression. As Davis (2008) warns, without this distinction, intersectionality risks becoming a buzzword rather than a tool for systemic change. It is important to get the terminology correct otherwise you erase the perspectives and experiences of the very people it was designed to represent.

Reflection Time

For some, these ideas may feel new, prompting curiosity. For others, they may feel like a familiar echo of lived experiences - a recognition of struggles faced daily. You might find yourself connecting with a range of emotions: validation, discomfort, recognition, or even hope for change.

Intersectionality invites us to consider identity and power from different perspectives, helping us understand our roles as practitioners and as individuals. Now that we've journeyed through these concepts, let's take a moment for personal reflection. Think of this as a conversation with yourself - a space to explore how these ideas connect with your own lived experiences or perhaps to see things from a perspective you haven't encountered before. What matters most here is your openness and willingness to engage deeply with these questions in a way that's meaningful for you.

Reflective Questions:

- How might viewing someone through a single aspect of their identity limit our understanding of their experience?
- How do our assumptions about a person shift when we consider their intersecting identities rather than a single aspect?
- How does our professional privilege influence our understanding and practice?
- How do you feel institutions (like schools, universities, workplaces, or healthcare systems) often overlook the unique needs of those with intersecting identities?
- Where do you see resistance to discussing privilege and oppression in professional spaces?

Moving from Theory to Action:

- Where do we see systemic inequalities in our practice?
- What concrete steps could you take to challenge systemic inequities in your organisation?
- How can you advocate for changes within your organisation to better serve communities with intersecting identities?
- What resources or support networks could you connect with to help dismantle systemic barriers affecting your clients? How do we acknowledge being facilitators of the masters' tools, while actively working towards harm reduction?
- What training could you access to ensure you are equipped?

Creating Systemic Change:

- What changes could address systemic barriers and inequalities within our organisation?
- How might your position of privilege be used to advocate for systemic change?
- Where do we see systemic inequalities in our practice, and how can we address them?

Intersectionality and the Relationship with the Neurodiversity Paradigm

Intersectionality in Speech and Language Therapy

Similar to many other professions, speech and language therapy has historically been shaped by a Global North, predominantly white, paradigm that systematically excludes and erases the experiences of neurodivergent individuals with intersecting marginalised identities (Abrahams et al., 2023; Mallipeddi and VanDaalen, 2022; Nair, Farah and Boveda, 2024). This oversight is not just incidental; it represents a structural failure that perpetuates harm through assessment frameworks, therapy approaches and advocacy efforts.

The systemic exclusion of these experiences reflects the broader societal structures of power and privilege, which are embedded in professional practices. As a profession that centralises the social construct of language and communication, the impact of this exclusion ripples through every aspect of our work, shaping how we conceptualise, assess and support neurodivergent individuals. This has significant implications for the quality and equity of care provided, particularly for those whose experiences fall outside the dominant cultural and socioeconomic frameworks.

By recognising this historical and structural failure, we can begin to challenge and dismantle the biases that shape our profession, striving to create more inclusive, intersectional and equitable practices for all individuals.

The Importance of Intersectional Practice

You might wonder, 'What does intersectionality have to do with my work?' or 'How is intersectionality valuable within neurodiversity-affirming speech and language therapy practice?' These questions reflect a professional lens, but let's take a step back: 'What does intersectionality have to do with how I see and engage with the world around me?' This question invites reflection not just as a practitioner but as a human being navigating a diverse and interconnected society. It also reveals a fundamental misunderstanding of what it means to truly affirm neurodivergent individuals. To be genuinely neurodiversity-affirming committed, we must understand and embrace intersectionality – because the two are inseparable.

Neurodivergent individuals do not exist in a vacuum; their experiences are profoundly shaped by the intersections of their identities, each bearing its own weight of privilege or systemic oppression. For instance, the experience of a Black neurodivergent child is not simply a sum of their neurodivergence and racial identity – it is shaped by the way racism, anti-Blackness and ableism interact to create unique barriers. These barriers manifest in healthcare, education and daily life: their masking may be intensified by racial stereotypes, their communication style judged through the dual lenses of racism and ableism and their access to support further restricted by systemic issues tied to capitalism, colonialism and imperialism.

As practitioners – and as people – it's vital to recognise that we're not working with speech, language, communication or swallowing needs in isolation. We are engaging with whole individuals whose lived experiences are deeply influenced by the intersections of their identities. Recognising and addressing these intersections doesn't make our jobs more complicated; it makes our practice more ethical, more effective and more aligned with the realities of those we support. Moreover, it pushes us to think critically about how we contribute to systems of equity or inequity in every sphere of life. Intersectionality isn't just about professional competence – it's about how we move through the world with respect, understanding and the commitment to create spaces where everyone can thrive. It's about how we challenge ourselves professionally, considering how SLT upholds and constructs tools of oppression, for example, through professional protectionism related to deficit-based forms of practice.

Understanding Systemic Oppression in Practice

To fully grasp the urgency of intersectional practice, we must understand how systems of oppression operate and intersect. As Talila Lewis powerfully articulates:

> able·ism /ˈābəˌlizəm/ noun
>
> A system of assigning value to people's bodies and minds based on societally constructed ideas of normalcy, productivity, desirability, intelligence, excellence, and fitness. These constructed ideas are deeply rooted in eugenics, anti-Blackness, misogyny, colonialism, imperialism, and capitalism. This systemic oppression that leads to people and society determining people's value based on their culture, age, language, appearance, religion, birth or living place, 'health/wellness', and/or their ability to satisfactorily re/produce, 'excel' and 'behave.' You do not have to be disabled to experience ableism.

This definition illuminates how ableism intertwines with other forms of oppression, creating compound barriers for multiply-marginalised individuals. It demands that we examine how our profession has historically upheld these systems of oppression through our practices, assessments, therapy approaches and service delivery models.

Intersectionality is fundamental to neurodiversity-affirming speech and language therapy practice. Our profession must move beyond the restrictive medical model that has historically dominated our field – a model that has systematically excluded and marginalised many of the people we serve (Chapman and Botha, 2022; DeThorne and Gerlach-Houck, 2023; Donaldson et al., 2023; Humphries et al., 2016). This necessary transformation isn't merely about changing terminology or updating policies. Instead, it demands that we confront an uncomfortable truth: our traditional approaches have often failed to capture, understand and support the full range of human experiences and identities, therefore actively harming these groups.

Further, when we understand the concept of intersectionality and consider it within frameworks offered by people like Talila Lewis, we can critique how we show up in the profession. Let's give an example.

For instance, if we present ourselves as 'neurodiversity-affirming speech and language therapists' but fail to address intersectionality or engage in ongoing learning about intersectional identities, we risk perpetuating harm. By not actively engaging with the complexities of how race, class, gender, disability and other identities intersect with neurodivergence, we inadvertently uphold the very systems of white supremacy and capitalism that have long influenced our field.

These practices must be integrated into all aspects of our work: university curricula, institutional policies, health models, professional development and everyday practice. Without this awareness and action, we perpetuate the marginalisation of individuals whose identities don't fit within narrow, traditional frameworks and uphold normalcy. Whether we are teaching, practising, researching or collaborating, it is our responsibility to actively dismantle these harmful structures. Only by doing so can we create truly inclusive spaces that recognise and affirm the full diversity of human identities.

Learning from Disability Studies

For years, Disability Studies have been quietly influencing our profession, pushing us to question our assumptions and practices (Wickenden, 2023; Wolbring and Nasir, 2024). While not every scholar in this field explicitly names intersectionality in their work, their insights align deeply with intersectional principles (Walker, 2014). This influence has helped us recognise how overlapping identities create unique experiences of privilege and oppression – experiences that profoundly impact how individuals engage with therapy and navigate healthcare systems.

Power and marginalisation operate in complex ways throughout society, shaping lives at individual, community and systemic levels (Benson et al, 2024). When we understand this, we begin to see how some experiences become hyper-visible in our profession while others are systematically erased or ignored. This understanding is crucial – it helps us recognise how our own professional practices might inadvertently contribute to this erasure, even as we strive to help.

The Neurodiversity Paradigm: A Path Forward

The Neurodiversity Paradigm is a perspective that views neurocognitive differences as natural variations of the human brain rather than deficits or disorders which are pathologising. The Neurodiversity Paradigm builds naturally on these insights, calling us to embrace human diversity in all its forms (Chapman and Botha, 2021; Long, 2022; Neurodivergent Consultant, 2023). This isn't about simple acceptance – it's about recognising that neurodivergent experiences are valid. When we truly embrace this paradigm alongside intersectional understanding, we create space for more authentic, effective therapeutic relationships that honour each person's unique combination of identities and experiences.

By bringing together intersectionality and the Neurodiversity Paradigm, we strengthen both approaches and create more meaningful therapeutic practices. However, this isn't just about theoretical frameworks – it's about real people, real lives and our professional responsibility to provide care that genuinely serves diverse communities. As we move forward, we must remain both hopeful about the potential for change and critical of our current practices, constantly asking ourselves how we can better serve those who trust us with their care.

The Neurodiversity Paradigm, when properly understood and implemented, serves as a framework for liberation. It demands we move beyond surface-level acceptance to actively challenge societal structures that privilege specific ways of being while marginalising others. This paradigm calls for:

- Radical acceptance of diverse ways of thinking, being, and communicating.
- Active resistance against normative pressures and expectations.
- Recognition of how different forms of oppression intersect with neurodivergence.
- Celebration of neurodivergent experiences within their cultural and social contexts.

Confronting Professional Realities

The stark reality of speech and language therapy demographics in the United Kingdom (HCPC, 2023) reveals how systemic barriers continue to shape our profession. Our workforce remains overwhelmingly white (87%), cis-gender (98%), non-disabled (90%) and heterosexual (86%) – statistics that reflect deeply embedded structural barriers to entry and progression. The future of speech and language therapy must reflect the diverse communities we serve, and this transformation begins with acknowledging our current reality while actively working towards a more representative profession.

Cost of Inaction

Avoiding intersectionality in our practice isn't a neutral stance – it actively perpetuates harm through every assessment we conduct, every therapy session we deliver and every interaction we have with neurodivergent individuals and colleagues belonging to marginalised groups. When we maintain a one-size-fits-all approach, we fail to recognise how different systems of oppression intersect to create unique barriers and challenges for our clients (Nario-Redmond, 2020). This means that we're complicit in upholding systemic inequalities that harm and marginalise people further.

This failure ripples through their lived experiences: accessing services becomes increasingly difficult for neurodivergent individuals from marginalised communities, and therapeutic goals may be misaligned with clients' actual needs and experiences. The cost isn't theoretical – it manifests in trauma, damaged trust between practitioners and communities, missed therapeutic support and inappropriate interventions.

Every time we **choose** not to engage with intersectional practice, we contribute to widening healthcare disparities and maintaining systems that privilege certain voices while silencing others. This is about recognising that our current approaches actively exclude and harm the very people we aim to support. We cannot continue claiming we provide neurodiversity-affirming practice and effective, ethical care while ignoring how intersecting identities fundamentally shape neurodivergent experiences.

Trauma-Informed, Intersectional and Anti-Oppressive Approaches to Neurodiversity-Affirming Practice

Trauma-informed practice in the context of neurodiversity-affirming approaches recognises that the experiences of neurodivergent individuals are deeply intertwined with past and ongoing trauma. This trauma can be personal, stemming from life experiences, or systemic, resulting from societal marginalisation and oppression. A key component of trauma-informed care is understanding that trauma impacts the brain and body, affecting an individual's ability to trust, engage and participate in therapeutic processes. For neurodivergent individuals, this might manifest as communication, sensory and/or social interaction differences, all of which can be exacerbated by ableism, racism, sexism and classism. Trauma-informed approaches seek to create safe, supportive spaces where individuals feel seen, respected and empowered to share their experiences without fear of judgement or re-traumatisation (Harris and Fallot, 2001).

Incorporating an intersectional lens into trauma-informed practice is essential to fully address the complexities of neurodivergent people's lives. Trauma-informed practice that is intersectional recognises these compounded forms of oppression and works to deconstruct the systems that perpetuate them, ensuring that therapeutic approaches are not only safe but also culturally relevant and sensitive.

Decolonialism is another critical aspect in the development of trauma-informed, intersectional, neurodiversity-affirming practices. Many traditional models of diagnosing and treating neurodivergence are rooted in the Global North, colonial frameworks that pathologise behaviours without considering the cultural contexts in which they arise. By adopting a decolonial approach, practitioners acknowledge the historical and cultural biases embedded within diagnostic categories and treatment protocols, creating more inclusive, culturally responsive practices. Decolonising neurodivergent support means not only challenging the cultural assumptions that shape diagnosis and intervention but also reimagining care practices that honour diverse ways of being (Tuck and Yang, 2012).

Finally, anti-oppressive practice is integral to trauma-informed care for neurodivergent individuals. This approach explicitly critiques the power dynamics and social hierarchies that uphold oppressive structures. Anti-oppressive practice emphasises that the goal of therapy is not to 'fix' or 'intervene' neurodivergent individuals but to affirm their identity, validate their experiences and empower them to navigate systems that were not designed with their needs in mind. In practice, this means challenging the harmful societal norms that equate productivity with worth and instead embracing a more holistic view of an individual. It also means recognising the role of institutional and systemic barriers – such as the underrepresentation of neurodivergent people in healthcare or education – while advocating for more significant equity and inclusivity in service provision.

Together, these frameworks – trauma-informed, intersectional, decolonial and anti-oppressive – work to create a more compassionate and effective approach to supporting neurodivergent individuals. By understanding the complex ways in which trauma, identity and systemic oppression intersect, practitioners can better serve those who have been historically marginalised and create environments that genuinely affirm neurodivergent experiences.

Moving Forward: Intersectionality, Positionality, and Professional Growth

Neurodiversity-affirming practices cannot thrive in isolation; they must be deeply rooted in a nuanced understanding of intersectionality. Current approaches that claim to be neurodiversity-affirming risk being superficial if they do not engage with the complex systems of oppression that individuals navigate daily. At the same time, it is essential to recognise the limitations of working within these systems, which often constrain the potential for truly transformative practice.

By reflecting on these constraints, we can better understand the ways in which systemic frameworks influence our professional responsibilities and impact the individuals we support. This awareness compels us to think critically about how to navigate these elements, while maintaining our commitment to equity and inclusion. To move towards genuinely neurodiversity-affirming practice, we must balance working within unjust systems while advocating for structural change, ensuring our approaches remain grounded in compassion and a deep understanding of intersectional experiences.

Neurodiversity-affirming practice is not a checklist; it is a heartfelt commitment to supporting individuals in all their identities. As practitioners, it is our duty to build meaningful therapeutic relationships using person-centred approaches to ensure the individual is central, and this relationship should be grounded in core therapeutic values (for example, respect, empathy and honesty). Individuals should be considered experts in their own experiences, and this means tailoring any therapeutic support to the needs of the individual.

Neglecting intersectionality not only perpetuates harm but also reinforces existing power structures, ultimately further excluding marginalised communities. This oversight can lead to practices that exacerbate inequities, even when our intentions are well-meaning. While neurodiversity-affirming, intersectional and trauma-informed approaches are critical, we must also recognise the limitations imposed by working within systems steeped in oppression, as highlighted by Audre Lorde's 'master's tools' analogy: 'The master's tools will never dismantle the master's house' (2018). This means that we cannot achieve actual change or dismantle systems of oppression using the same methods, structures or mindsets that created and sustained those systems. These systems – shaped by racism, ableism, classism and other forms of discrimination – position us in roles of unique power and privilege while capping the potential for truly transformative practice.

Acknowledging these constraints is vital because they demand we navigate complex ethical dilemmas, such as fulfilling professional responsibilities that may unintentionally reinforce systemic harm. To honour neurodiversity-affirming practice within these limitations, we must critically evaluate the tools and frameworks we inherit, often designed to uphold the very systems we seek to dismantle. This reflection challenges us to be creative and intentional in balancing our obligations with the need to protect and empower others. By embracing intersectional experiences and working towards equitable systemic change, we can begin to create genuinely inclusive spaces that hold the potential for profound and meaningful progress.

Recognising Our Own Positionality

As we start unfolding this topic, we must consider our own identities and how these hold significance. Each of us has characteristics that shape our identities, including (but not limited to) our age, gender, race, sexuality, ethnicity, religion, socioeconomic status and disability. Some aspects of our identities may come with power and privilege, while others may lead to inequality and marginalisation. It is essential to mention that power and privilege are not static; they can shift depending on the context. Whether we're fully conscious of it or not, through our identities, we each carry a unique combination of privilege and marginalisation. Our identities can shape our perceptions, impact our day-to-day lives, and influence the way we approach our work.

To understand these influences more deeply, we invite you to pause for a moment of guided self-reflection. We will do this by using the *Wheel of Privilege and Power*. There are many examples of these wheels available, and in practice, we have used several to engage in critical discussions with others, considering intersectionality, intersectional experiences, and the positions of power or privilege some of us get to speak from in specific contexts. For this chapter, we're choosing to reference the *Wheel of Privilege and Power* as we feel it is one of the least problematic diagrams in terms of language use and harm to marginalised groups.

This exercise requires openness and willingness to explore your position in society, not as an act of self-critique but as a necessary foundation for understanding intersectionality and neurodivergence. Allow yourself to sit with any thoughts, feelings or reactions that arise in the process. Remember, this reflection isn't about judging yourself; it's about taking the first step toward equitable practices and genuinely committing to understanding the influence of intersecting identities. Please be mindful about completing this activity in group settings. We would encourage those doing so to hold in mind a few key points: (1) people from within marginalised groups are not homogenous in their opinions and experiences, (2) in sharing our opinions, we'd encourage you to consider what Blair Imani (2021) advises: 'speak to share, not to change minds'.

Language preferences vary from person to person, and individuals may use different labels to describe their identities. These preferences can evolve over time and may be influenced by various factors, including personal experiences and the broader views of a group. It's important to recognise and respect that not everyone within a group shares the same language choices, and we should approach these differences with understanding and openness. Creating space for diverse perspectives helps promote inclusivity and mutual respect.

To begin, let's take a closer look at the *Wheel of Privilege and Power* together. Sadly, we did not get approval to share the image in this manuscript. You can search for the wheel using an internet search engine. The wheel includes various categories that make up our identities, with each category representing areas where privilege or marginalisation can exist.

REFLECTION

1. Exploring Your Identity Categories. For each category in the *Wheel of Privilege and Power*, identify where you sit:

    - Does this aspect of your identity bring you unearned advantages or create barriers?
    - How might this aspect impact your access to resources or your sense of safety?
    - Are there situations where this aspect of your identity feels more or less 'visible'?

2. Understanding Context and Privilege
   - When does your experience of privilege or marginalisation shift depending on the situation?
   - How do different settings affect your experience of privilege?
   - In what ways do your various identities interact with each other?
   - How do your privileges manifest in different professional contexts?

3. Personal Journey in the Profession
   - How have your identities influenced your journey into speech and language therapy?
   - What barriers or advantages have you experienced in your career?
   - How do your identities shape your clinical perspective?
   - What aspects of your identity influence your therapeutic relationships?
   - What blind spots might you have due to your position?

4. Power and Influence
   - How does your position affect your ability to make changes?
   - Where do you hold power in your professional role?
   - What responsibilities come with your privileges?
   - How do your identities influence your professional voice?
   - What aspects of your identity give you credibility or create barriers?

Understanding the Impact of Intersecting Identities in Neurodivergent Clients

To provide truly effective speech and language therapy, it is essential to recognise that intersecting identities fundamentally shape our experiences, access to support and therapeutic outcomes. These intersections are not just additional factors to consider – they are central to how neurodivergent individuals navigate the world and engage with therapy services.

To help you reflect on these critical intersections, we have included some illustrative examples intended for educational purposes. These examples are not exhaustive; the ways in which identities intersect and influence lived experiences are varied. While these examples are useful starting points, they are no substitute for the ongoing work required to deepen your understanding.

It is important to actively seek out knowledge, challenge your own assumptions and engage in meaningful learning about the diverse experiences of the individuals you support. This work includes being open to feedback, reflecting on your own position and biases and remaining committed to growth.

Cultural and Race-Related Factors

Research demonstrates that cultural perspectives and racial identity profoundly shape experiences of neurodivergence and engagement with therapy services. Different communities bring rich and diverse understandings of neurodivergence, communication, and support needs (Hirota, Cheon and Lai, 2024).

However, systemic and structural inequities create significant barriers for these communities. Research highlights how these individuals often navigate additional barriers within health and social care settings (Ajayi Sobuto, 2021). Unequal access to resources, biased service delivery and healthcare disparities continue to disadvantage many communities, further exacerbating health inequalities (The King's Fund, 2023).

Key Considerations:

- Develop cultural humility through continuous learning and self-reflection.
- Create assessment processes that recognise diverse cultural communication patterns.
- Design therapeutic approaches that align with families' cultural values and practices.
- Build partnerships with community organisations and leaders.
- Ensure service delivery reflects and responds to local community needs.
- Use tools, such as a White Privilege checklist, to explore power, privilege and positionality in practice.
- Apply anti-racism frameworks (e.g. Andrew Ibrahaim's Anti-Racism model) to inform equitable, systemic change.
- Refer to RCSLT guidance on equity, diversity, inclusion and anti-racism to inform practice.
- Use therapy materials and resources that reflect the cultural and racial identities of the individuals and communities you support.
- Join or create networks and reflective spaces for professional to discuss equity, culture and anti-oppressive practice.
- Create networks that specifically support culturally and racially diverse colleagues.

Socioeconomic Status and Class

Socioeconomic status significantly influences the experiences of neurodivergent individuals and their ability to access appropriate support. Structural barriers, such as inequitable access to healthcare, educational resources and specialised therapies, often create challenges for those from lower socioeconomic backgrounds, highlighting systemic issues rather than individual limitations.

Research highlights how economic circumstances influence access to therapeutic services (Sharland et al., 2023). Families from low-income areas often balance work commitments, family responsibilities and service engagement, offering invaluable insights into practical solutions and community resources. Understanding the realities of access to technology, financial pressures, transport considerations and time constraints helps shape more effective and inclusive service delivery.

Class-related perceptions and biases can further influence access and engagement. For example, assumptions about productivity and capability linked to working-class communities may create barriers to accessing speech and language therapy. Personal experiences of navigating class-based preconceptions, such as regional accents being associated with specific socioeconomic backgrounds, highlight how cultural perceptions can shape interactions and access to care. Moreover, the middle-class nature of speech and language therapy as a profession underscores the importance of addressing disparities in education and stability tied to class.

Key Considerations
- Create therapy plans that maximise impact within available sessions.
- Develop accessible programmes that consider financial and time constraints.
- Provide therapy in community spaces that are both accessible and familiar.
- Implement flexible systems that accommodate varied work patterns and transport options.
- Advocate within services for equitable access to therapeutic resources and support.
- Reflect on and challenge personal and systemic biases related to class to foster equitable practices.
- Collaborate with organisations that can support these communities in addressing broader needs.

Gender and Neurodivergence

Research demonstrates that gender significantly influences how neurodivergent traits are expressed and understood (Mo et al., 2024; Davidson, 2016). Considering this within the context of intersectionality and anti-oppressive practice, shouldn't we explore the expectations and social constructs that certain individuals navigate in our patriarchal society? For example, autistic individuals may display varying degrees of overt autistic traits, which can shape how others perceive them. Their gender expression and ability to meet societal conventions of productivity and thresholds of respectability – criteria often influenced by ableist norms – may significantly impact their experiences with masking. When we consider additional intersectional layers and how they influence individual lived experience, such as misogynoir, highlights the complex interplay between visible traits, societal expectations, and the pressures to conform.

Key Considerations:

- Actively recognise and validate diverse presentations of neurodivergent traits across women, non-binary individuals and gender-diverse populations.

- Update assessment practices to account for gender-based differences in trait presentation and masking behaviours.
- Create gender-inclusive environments through appropriate pronouns, language and documentation systems.
- Build knowledge of how gender expectations influence communication patterns and neurodivergent expression.
- Implement regular training on gender diversity in neurodivergent populations and its impact on assessment and therapeutic support.

LGBTQIA+ Identities and Neurodivergence

Research indicates that neurodivergent traits, especially autism, are more prevalent within LGBTQIA+ communities (Warrier et al., 2020). LGBTQIA+ neurodivergent individuals bring unique perspectives to social communication and gender expression. While celebrating these intersecting identities, it's essential to acknowledge that some individuals navigate complex social dynamics. This can include:

- Managing varied expectations around gender expression and communication styles.
- Building trust in therapeutic settings, particularly following past healthcare experiences.
- Seeking providers who understand and affirm both neurodivergent and LGBTQIA+ experiences.

Creating affirming therapeutic environments supports clients in bringing their whole authentic selves to sessions. Research emphasises the value of inclusive practices and culturally responsive care (Rimes et al., 2018; Durso and Meyer, 2013).

Key Considerations:

- Use the LGBTQIA+-affirming Zones of Practice (RCSLT and UK SLT Pride Network, 2023).
- Create visibly welcoming environments through inclusive signage, resources, and forms that reflect diverse gender identities and relationships.
- Implement comprehensive staff training on LGBTQIA+ cultural competency, including proper use of pronouns, chosen names and understanding of gender diversity.
- Establish clear anti-discrimination policies and procedures that explicitly protect LGBTQIA+ service users and staff.
- Build referral networks with LGBTQIA+ affirming healthcare providers and community organisations.
- Regular self-audit of service delivery.
- Demonstrate commitment through active engagement with LGBTQIA+ communities and regular updates to policies based on service user feedback.
- Use the RCSLT guidance about supporting LGBTQIA+ colleagues (2024).

Keep Going: An Invitation to Continue Growing

Learning about intersectionality and neurodivergence is an ongoing journey, one that requires continual growth. As our understanding evolves, so too should our approaches to these topics. We invite you to actively engage with the importance of intersectionality, whether through self-reflection, discussions with friends or collaborative dialogues with colleagues.

To support your ongoing, self-directed learning, we encourage you to take the insights from this chapter and apply them practically. We thought the following suggestions could help you to support your own learning:

Practical Strategies for Neurodiversity-Affirming, Intersectional Practice

1. **Decolonise assessments and therapeutic approaches**
   Speech and language therapists must use inclusive and responsive assessments, as standardised tools often fail to account for the diverse communication styles, values and social norms of marginalised communities, leading to misdiagnosis or underdiagnosis. Additionally, therapeutic approaches should be supportive of the specific individual, considering their background. To address this issue, speech and language therapists should:

   - **Integrate dynamic assessments and therapeutic approaches** that allow for flexibility and better reflect an individual's skills, needs, and abilities in the context of their background.
   - **Adopt a person-centred approach** that values the lived experiences of clients and their communities, especially those from intersecting marginalised identities.

2. **Ongoing learning and professional growth**
   Engaging in ongoing learning about intersectionality and neurodivergence is essential to providing inclusive and equitable care. As our understanding of these topics evolves, so too must our clinical practices. This journey of growth requires:

   - **Self-reflection**: Regularly assessing one's own biases and examining how these influence clinical decision-making.
   - **Engagement with neurodivergent voices**: Listening to and learning from individuals with intersecting identities, particularly those who are often marginalised, to better understand their needs and experiences.

3. **Practical strategies for ongoing professional development**

   - **Initiate dialogues on intersectionality** within your workplace or academic setting, if it feels safe to do so.
   - **Join Clinical Excellence Networks** to connect with others in the field and learn from a diverse range of practitioners.
   - **Follow advocates and thought leaders** who focus on neurodiversity, intersectionality, and inclusion to stay informed on the latest issues and research.

- **Attend workshops and webinars** focused on neurodivergent-affirming practices to deepen your knowledge of neurodiversity and intersectionality in clinical practice.
- **Read journal articles and books** on equity, inclusion, and neurodivergence and apply these insights to your practice.
- **Reflect on your own biases** and be open to confronting them to ensure that your practice is inclusive and affirming.

4. **Confronting societal inequities**

   Speech and language therapists must recognise that the societal structures and systemic inequalities that marginalise certain groups are also embedded within the systems we work within. These biases do not simply affect individuals; they permeate the frameworks and practices that inform our work. To fully appreciate and support neurodivergent experiences, we must be willing to confront these external influences. Our awareness and critique of these factors are non-negotiable. Without actively affirming and recognising the intersecting identities that shape each person's experience, we risk replicating the same exclusionary practices that have marginalised people for generations.

   In practice, this means that:

   - SLTs must **actively engage in deconstructing biases** within both themselves and the systems they work within to ensure that their practice is truly inclusive.

5. **Affirming intersecting identities** is crucial, as failing to do so risks perpetuating the very exclusionary practices that neurodivergent individuals have long experienced. Recognising the full humanity of clients means appreciating and addressing the complexity of their experiences.

Each of these steps can help you grow as a practitioner to build a more inclusive perspective. By incorporating them, you support an evidence-informed, neurodivergent-affirming practice.

Remember that your own identities, experiences and privileges profoundly shape your insights and perspectives on intersectionality. It's precisely because of this diversity in perspective that keeping these conversations alive is essential; intersectionality is not just an add-on but a critical foundation for truly neurodivergent-affirming practice.

We also cannot ignore the impact of societal attitudes, structural inequalities and institutional biases, which do not just impact individuals in isolation; they can also permeate the systems within which we all operate. The societal factors that perpetuate inequity do not exist outside of our practices; they are often interwoven with the very frameworks we rely on to support people. To fully appreciate and support neurodivergent experiences, we must be willing to confront these external influences. Our awareness and critique of these factors are non-negotiable. Without actively affirming and recognising the intersecting identities that shape each person's experience, we risk replicating the same exclusionary practices that have marginalised people for generations.

Conclusion

As authors, Fatimah and Kate, we have delved into the undeniable truth: individuals are whole, multifaceted beings, and their identities are woven together in ways that demand recognition. Ignoring these intersections does not just perpetuate harm—it erases lives, voices, and histories that have fought relentlessly to be seen.

For speech and language therapists, affirming neurodivergent experiences demands an unflinching commitment to intersectionality. This is not an accessory to our work – it *is* the work. It calls for radical self-reflection, relentless dismantling of exclusionary systems, and unapologetic advocacy for structural change. Anything less sustains a status quo steeped in inequity and injustice.

The truths shared in this chapter are not revelations – they are the echoes of wisdom long voiced by marginalised communities, especially Black women, who have carried this labour for centuries. To continue delaying action is to be complicit. It is time to stop waiting, to stop tiptoeing and to centre these voices with the urgency they deserve. Progress is not passive – it is loud, it is disruptive and it is overdue. The responsibility lies with all of us to create a profession that embodies equity and affirms the full humanity of every individual we serve.

Chapter Summary

- Your awareness matters: being aware of intersectionality and its implications for practice across your work is key to affirming identities and supporting positive outcomes for the individuals we support.
- Your active engagement matters: this work is not just about listening and learning, it is a call to action, to ongoing learning, to reflecting with others and sharing your learning.
- Your next step matters: the chapter offers ideas of what that could be, pick a few key goals to weave into your professional development plans.

References and Resources

Abrahams, K., R. Mallick, A.S.J. Hohlfeld et al. (2023) 'Emerging professional practices focusing on reducing inequity in speech-language therapy and audiology: A scoping review', *International Journal for Equity in Health*. [Online]. https://pubmed.ncbi.nlm.nih.gov/35449088/ (accessed on 01/04/2025).

Ajayi Sobtubo, O. (2021) 'A perspective on health inequalities in BAME communities and how to improve access to primary care', *Future Healthcare Journal*. [Online], 8(1), 36-39. https://doi.org/10.7861/fhj.2020-0217 (accessed on 25/10/2024).

Bailey, M. (2019) *Misogynoir Transformed: Black Women's Digital Resistance*. New York: NYU Press.

Benson, R., B. Duffy, R. Hesketh and K. Hewlett (2024) 'Attitudes to inequalities', *Oxford Open Economics*. [Online], 3(1), i39-i63. https://doi.org/10.1093/ooec/odad069 (accessed on 16/10/2024).

Chapman, R. and M. Botha (2023) 'Neurodivergence-informed therapy', *Developmental Medicine and Child Neurology*. [Online], 65(3), 310-317. https://doi.org/10.1111/dmcn.15384 (accessed on 1/11/2024).

Collins, P.H. (1990) *Black Feminist Thought: Knowledge, Consciousness, and the Politics of Empowerment.* New York: Routledge.

Collins, P.H. (2000) *Black Feminist Thought: Knowledge, Consciousness, and the Politics of Empowerment.* 2nd ed. New York: Routledge.

Combahee River Collective ([1977] 1982) 'A Black feminist statement', in G.T. Hull, P.B. Scott and B. Smith (eds) *All the Women Are White, All the Blacks Are Men, But Some of Us Are Brave.* New York: Feminist Press, pp.13–22.

Crenshaw, K. (1989) 'Demarginalizing the intersection of race and sex: A Black feminist critique of antidiscrimination doctrine, feminist theory and antiracist politics', *University of Chicago Legal Forum.* [Online], 139–167. http://chicagounbound.uchicago.edu/uclf/vol1989/iss1/8 (accessed on 1/11/2024).

Crenshaw, K. (1991) 'Mapping the margins: Intersectionality, identity politics, and violence against women of color', *Stanford Law Review.* [Online], 43(6), 1241–1299. https://doi.org/10.2307/1229039 (accessed on 5/10/2024).

Davidson, J. (2016) 'The invisible women: Autism and the gender gap', *Autism.* [Online], 20(6), 740–747. https://doi.org/10.1177/1362361316656596 (accessed on 19/10/2024).

Davis, K. (2008) 'Intersectionality as buzzword: A sociology of science perspective on what makes a feminist theory successful', *Feminist Theory.* [Online], 9(1), 67–85. https://doi.org/10.1177/1464700108086364 (accessed on 28/10/2024).

DeThorne, L.S. and H. Gerlach-Houck (2023) 'Resisting ableism in school-based speech-language therapy: An invitation to change', *Language, Speech, and Hearing Services in Schools.* [Online], 54(1), 1–7. https://doi.org/10.1044/2022_LSHSS-22-00139 (accessed on 22/10/2024).

Donaldson, A.L., E. Corbin, A.H. Zisk and B. Eddy (2023) 'Promotion of communication access, choice, and agency for autistic students', *Language, Speech, and Hearing Services in Schools.* [Online], 54(1), 140–155. https://doi/full/10.1086/689543 (accessed on 22/10/2024).

Durso, L.E. and I.H. Meyer (2013) 'Patterns and predictors of disclosure of sexual orientation to healthcare providers among lesbians, gay men, and bisexuals', *Sexuality Research & Social Policy.* [Online], 10(1), 35–42. https://doi.org/10.1007/s13178-012-0105-2 (accessed on 11/11/2024).

Harris, M. and R. Fallot (2001) *Using Trauma Theory to Create Trauma-Informed Care.* San Francisco: Jossey-Bass.

Health and Care Professions Council (HCPC). (2023) Diversity data: Speech and Language Therapists 2023. [Online]. www.hcpc-uk.org/resources/data/2023/diversity-data-speech-and-language-therapists-2023/ (accessed on 30/10/2024).

Hirota, T., K.A. Cheon and M.-C. Lai (2024) 'Neurodiversity paradigms and their development across cultures: Some reflections in East Asian contexts', *Autism.* [Online], 28(11). https://doi.org/10.1177/136236132412856 (accessed on 23/11/2024).

hooks, b. (1981) *Ain't I a Woman: Black Women and Feminism.* Boston: South End Press.

Humphries, T., P. Kushalnagar, G. Mathur et al. (2016) 'Avoiding linguistic neglect of deaf children', *Social Service Review.* [Online], 90(4), 589–619. https://doi.org/10.1086/689543 (accessed on 22/10/2024).

Imani, B. (2021) *Read This to Get Smarter: About Race, Class, Gender, Disability & More.* London: Ten Speed Press.

Long, É. (2022) '"Difference which makes a difference" (Bateson, 1972): how the neurodiversity paradigm and systemic approaches can support individuals and organisations to facilitate more helpful conversations about autism', *Journal of Social Work Practice* [Online], 37(1), 109–118. https://doi.org/10.1080/02650533.2022.2142768 (accessed on 12/10/2024).

Lorde, A. (1984) *Sister Outsider: Essays and Speeches.* Trumansburg: Crossing Press.

Lorde, A. (2018) *The Master's Tools Will Never Dismantle the Master's House: Audre Lorde.* London: Penguin Classic.

Mallipeddi, N.V. and R.A. VanDaalen (2022) 'Intersectionality within critical autism studies: A narrative review', *Autism in Adulthood: Challenges and Management.* [Online], 4(4), 281–289. https://doi.org/10.1089/aut.2021.0014 (accessed on 1/12/2024).

Mo, K., E. Anagnostou, J.P. Lerch et al. (2024). Gender diversity is correlated with dimensional neurodivergent traits but not categorical neurodevelopmental diagnoses in children. *Journal of Child Psychology and Psychiatry*. [Online]. https://acamh.onlinelibrary.wiley.com/doi/pdf/10.1111/jcpp.13965 (accessed on 3/12/2024).

Nair, V.K., W. Farah and M. Boveda (2024) 'Is neurodiversity a Global Northern White paradigm?', *Autism: The International Journal of Research and Practice*. [Online]. https://doi.org/10.1177/13623613241280835 (accessed on 1/11/2024).

Nario-Redmond, M.R. (2020). *Ableism: The Causes and Consequences of Disability Prejudice*. New Jersey: John Wiley & Sons.

Neurodivergent Consultant. (2023) Embracing the Neurodiversity Paradigm: Celebrating Differences. www.neurodivergentconsultant.org/blog/embracing-the-neurodiversity-paradigm-celebrating-differences (accessed on 16/11/2024).

Pearson, A. and K. Rose (2021) 'A conceptual analysis of autistic masking: Understanding the narrative of stigma and the illusion of choice', *Autism in Adulthood: Challenges and Management*. [Online], 3(1), 52–60. https://doi.org/10.1089/aut.2020.0043 (accessed on 25/10/2024).

Rimes, K.A., M. Broadbent, R. Holden et al. (2018) 'Comparison of treatment outcomes between lesbian, gay, bisexual and heterosexual individuals receiving a primary care psychological intervention', *Behavioural and Cognitive Psychotherapy*. [Online], 46(3), 332-349. https://doi.org/10.1017/S1352465817000583 (accessed on 17/11/2024).

Royal College of Speech and Language Therapists (RCSLT) (2023) [Online]. 'LGBTQIA+ Zones of Practice: A guide to affirming speech and language therapy practice' [pdf]. www.rcslt.org/wp-content/uploads/2024/02/LGBTQIA-Zones-of-Practice-FINAL-with-intro.pdf (accessed on 17/11/2024).

Royal College of Speech and Language Therapists (RCSLT) (2024) [Online]. 'Supporting LGBTQIA+ colleagues in the workplace: A guide for all'. www.rcslt.org/learning/diversity-inclusion-and-anti-racism/supporting-lgbtqia-colleagues-in-the-workplace-a-guide-for-all/#section-7 (accessed on 17/11/2024).

Royal College of Speech and Language Therapists. (no date) 'Addressing health inequalities: A guide for speech and language therapists'.www.rcslt.org (accessed on 16/11/2024).

Sharland, E., K. Rzepnicka, D. Schneider et al. (2023) 'Socio-demographic differences in access to psychological treatment services: evidence from a national cohort study', *Psychological Medicine*, 53(15), 7395-7406. doi:10.1017/S0033291723001010.

Smith, B. (1983) *Home Girls: A Black Feminist Anthology*. New York: Kitchen Table: Women of Color Press.

The King's Fund. (2023) 'The health of people from ethnic minority groups in England'. www.kingsfund.org.uk/insight-and-analysis/long-reads/health-people-ethnic-minority-groups-england (accessed on 30/10/2024).

Tuck, E. and K.W. Yang (2012) 'Decolonization is not a metaphor'. [Online] *Amandla! Magazine*. (accessed on 4/12/2024).

Walker, N. (2014) 'Neurodiversity: Some basic terms & definitions'. [Online]. http://neurocosmopolitanism.com/neurodiversity-some-basic-terms-definitions/ (accessed on 13/10/2024).

Warrier, V., D.M. Greenberg, E. Weir et al. (2020). 'Elevated rates of autism, other neurodevelopmental and psychiatric diagnoses, and autistic traits in transgender and gender-diverse individuals', *Nature Communications*, 11, 3959.

Wickenden, M. (2023) 'Disability and other identities? How do they intersect?' *Disability, Rehabilitation, and Inclusion*. [Online], 4. https://doi.org/10.3389/fresc.2023.1200386 (accessed on 25/10/2024).

Wolbring, G. and L. Nasir (2024) 'Intersectionality of disabled people through a disability studies, ability-based studies, and intersectional pedagogy lens: A survey and a scoping review', *Societies*. [Online], 14(9), 176. https://doi.org/10.3390/soc14090176 (accessed on 25/10/2024).

3
Neurodiversity Now

Neurodiversity in the Current Context

With the growth of the internet and social media, neurodivergent voices are now louder and more accessible that ever, no longer do folks need to be published, part of research or trainers and speakers to be heard. Following the right hashtags can open a whole world of information that can really help you to explore and delve into the lived experience of a range of support needs.

The first thing we need to really think about is that one neurodivergent person cannot speak for the majority, so the more exploring you do, the better. Once you have heard from one neurodivergent person, you have heard from one neurodivergent person. While many people have similar lived experiences, the range of different support needs mean that there can be subtle differences, or massive great chasms.

We have explored what intersectionality means in Chapter 2. Here, we can consider how intersectionality shows up in this work you are doing, are all the voices you are exploring the same race, gender and class as examples. It is important to ensure that you seek to do better in terms of growing the range of experiences you are hearing about and understanding, as we know the population of children, adults and families that we support can be diverse, we do not want to lean into just one area of learning about experience.

In Chapter 1, I used the term high support and medium support needs. There is a shift to move away from functioning labels, particularly when thinking about autistic individuals and towards support needs; we must ensure we are hearing from individuals across the range, whether this is through parent advocacy or individuals sharing their own experiences.

Functioning Labels:

- high functioning
- Asperger's syndrome

- low functioning
- severe autism

What is wrong with those descriptions? Well, they create a certain narrative, and that in itself can be disabling. An individual labelled as high functioning yet who experiences disabling differences in their sensory processing and executive functioning skills, who is therefore struggling with accessing group learning, is then expected to get on with it, because they're high functioning, or worse, and then they are labelled as unable to thrive and written off.

Likewise, a low functioning individual who is non-speaking is written off because they cannot communicate, they are given little expectation for success. But with the right communication support they can prove their potential, and are able to achieve success in learning and meaningful occupations.

So, moving to describing support needs gives a better understanding and narrative of an individual. While there is no way to specifically do this, a lot of neurodivergent individuals would deem themselves as:

- low support needs (LSN)
- medium support needs (MSN)
- high support needs (HSN)

If we think about assessments and reports, it can be helpful to break this down as a speech and language therapist. I tend to explore support needs through the Education, Health and Care Plan (EHCP) domains of communication and interaction, social, emotional and mental health, physical and sensory and cognition. Here, we can then break down the differing needs across domains, which gives a descriptive and hopefully more meaningful and individual narrative of the person. It can also capture the varying profiles, often to referred to as spikey. This is something to explore, and discuss with colleagues across professions too, as for example in the case of children, Educational Psychologists (EP) and Occupational Therapists (OT) might be involved in the assessment and support, and ensure that as teams we are all using the same terminology. While we may describe support needs in terms of cognition, communication and interaction and social, emotional and mental health, our EP and OT colleagues will create consistency if they do the same for their input across their domains too.

For example, a person might have low support needs for physical and sensory and cognition but require medium support for communication and interaction and high support needs for social, emotional and mental health. This creates a much more personalised and meaningful narrative of the individual, that a simple 'high functioning' or 'low functioning' label may not. The individuals we are supporting deserve better narratives, that are fair and accurate of their presentation, both in their strengths and challenges. This seems like a clear way to capture that for them.

We can go further as therapists if required and perhaps explore the varying aspects of communication and interaction in terms of the level of support needs, breaking down into attention/listening, play and interaction, understanding and expression as required. Sticking with consistent ways of describing support needs will develop an understanding across individuals, their support networks and other professionals as to their requirements for adjustments; this feels particularly pertinent within the EHCP process and when working with local authorities and teams who assess the needs of the child or young person based on professional reports.

Practice Example

Report Language:

X has high communication support needs for their expressive skills. They need access to robust alternative communication tools. With access to the right tools, they present with low play and interaction support needs, and if their high sensory support needs are met and they are well regulated they can sustain attention for around 20 minutes.

The things we are learning now about being neurodivergent is that the historical practices that they have been 'supported' with have caused generations of mental ill-health and poor social and emotional outcomes. These adults we can now learn so much from are helping us to understand that the way they have been treated, the narratives created around them, the misdiagnosis leading to ineffective treatment and supports have all had a devastating impact on their well-being. For many, their late diagnosis has been their awakening and an opportunity to work through the harm that their former years left them with. As professionals, with a duty to continue our learning, we must seek to be better informed, to better understand in order to support a more positive narrative for them.

The Impact of Diagnosis and the Positive Narrative: Harriet's Perspective

Being late-identified as an autistic, ADHD person, for me, has been multi-layered. There comes a relief that is indescribable, an answer to so many questions asked throughout my life:

- Why does no one understand me?
- Why am I like this?
- What is wrong with me?
- Why can't I just fit in?
- Why does everything feel so much harder for me?

It gave me so much forgiveness and compassion for myself and allowed me to start to embrace who I am at my centre, not the masks I'd been hiding behind all throughout life. It made me challenge the identity I had formed and through that I figured out I really was very different from everyone else's perception of me. It really was a life-changing revelation and something that completely shifted my world. However, the process of being identified late in life has also shattered my entire world. Though many days I feel positive about having the knowledge of my more authentic identity, there are also times where I really wish I hadn't known about being neurodivergent. My perspective of what my future can and should look like was flipped upside down overnight, I had to realign my sense of self and reconfigure the world around me. The big wedding I had dreamt of was never going to happen, the hope of finally having a reciprocal and 'typical' best friendship was out of the question. I had to rethink my plans of having children, marrying my partner and continuing in the speech therapy profession. The late identification led to the reopening of old wounds and having to process trauma I wasn't consciously aware of. I had to have difficult conversations, end relationships and put firm boundaries into the ones I was desperate to keep hold of. I questioned everything, and I mean everything. Who I was, what I had done in my past, what had been done to me, who was a good influence in my life, what choices I had made authentically and those I had made to please others, my wardrobe, my career choice, the decoration of my home, my relationships. Everything.

When I do adult autism assessments, during the feedback session, I tend to explain what the late diagnosis process has looked like for me. I often liken it to the grieving process, where there are many different emotions and experiences to go through before finding acceptance and being able to move on. That being said, this has not been a linear process for me, and although I spend more time in the zone of self-acceptance, I also navigate between anger that people didn't support me earlier and I still feel shame for my disability. Being identified as autistic seems to be a complex and individual process for the people and their close ones, who I have interacted with online and those I spend time with in my professional experiences.

At the two-year mark, post-identification I learnt that I had been living in my diagnosis journey to an unhealthy extent. Everything in my life had become about AuDHD, the special interest I had in understanding my neurology became all-consuming. Every waking thought was about neurodivergence, all my conversations, work projects, the books that I read and my friendships. I was constantly analysing my mind and trying to lean into the autistic traits I thought I must have. I pushed myself to stim when I felt emotions. I avoided things I thought that would overwhelm me. I became very far from the person I was pre-identification, and it was my parents who noted that. They told me that I had seemed to become a very serious person and didn't have the same quick sense of humour or adventure that I had before. They felt that I was consumed by this need to figure out my brain and it left no room for the parts of me that were just me and not necessarily related to autism. It also meant that I become more distant from my present and shut myself off from people. In the February two years after my autism identification, I had a sudden realisation that my prominent neurotype was ADHD and many of the things I had been doing was pushing my autistic neurotype into prominence and I was masking my ADHD as a result. It felt like I had to do a full 180 on my mission over the past two years.

Having an AuDHD neurotype is complex and very difficult to manage. Although 30–70% of people who are autistic also have ADHD* there is not too much understanding about how the two neurotypes interact. For many people, they can experience a predominant neurotype within this overlap and the prominence of each neurotype can differ day to day. There are certainly days where I experience autism more prominently and I'm not able to take public transport by myself or go to sensory loud environments. On these days socialising can be very difficult and feel uncomfortable. Throughout most of my life, my ADHD has featured more strongly and is more closely aligned with my personality and experiences. Growing up, it was very difficult for me to understand my identity, due to these conflicts, for example I could never decide if I was an introvert or extrovert because it would differ day to day and in different situations. When doing combined autism and ADHD assessments, I find that clients can present very differently on different days, some assessment sessions having more clear traits for ADHD on one day and the next no noticeable ADHD traits but obvious autistic traits. This makes AuDHD assessments very difficult with both ADHD and autism masking each other and differing day to day.

It's very important to also listen to those who were identified earlier in life, as their experiences, both positive and negative, give a different view. Sonny Jane Wise discusses this online.

The social vs medical model

When I was first identified as autistic I heavily favoured the Social Model of disability. I never used the mentality of it being a 'superpower' but I said things like 'the world disables me not autism'. I thought that now that I understood my brain, things would get easier and I wouldn't have so much difficulty. I felt that the way the world was made things difficult for me, not necessarily autism. I strongly rejected everything about the Medical Model of disability with its pathologising language. I didn't see a middle ground between the two models until I discovered the neurodiversity paradigm. I now seen my autism as a disability, which would continue to be disabling even if neurotypical society became ND-friendly. I would still struggle with periods of mutism and need alternative and augmentative communication (AAC). I would still have difficulty with self-care. I would still experience sensory overloads and shutdowns and meltdowns and migraines. I would still need support. Due to my monotropic thinking style and all or nothing approach I initially viewed autism mostly from my experience, as well as the other white, low support needs autistics I interacted with and followed online. I talked for the community and sometimes over other voices. I thought I was doing the right thing for all of us and that all our experiences of autism were similar in a lot of ways. But I was very wrong in that assumption. The more I started to expand my social media circle and listen to BIPOC and medium and high support needs autistics and their parents, I began to see more technicolour in this journey. There were grey areas, that honestly were hard for me to wrap my monotropic brain around. So I sat back for a while and I listened and I unlearned many of the things I thought I had learned about autism and what it means to be autistic. I started to question parts of the neuro-affirming practice I had entered into. That is when I realised that neuro-affirming practice has no end goal, no polished look, it's a journey that is lifelong. I will make mistakes throughout this journey but I reflect on them and keep moving, keep listening and keep learning. Because being AuDHD does not automatically mean I am neuro-affirming.

Strengths-based Practice: Harriet Richardson

A key to changing the way we are working is shifting from seeing Neurodivergent individuals as their deficits, fixing their problems, often telling them what their problems are as opposed to engaging them in communicating what the challenges are and working with their strengths.

What we know is that for a lot of Neurodivergent people their neurotypes can give some incredible strengths. There is a lot of conversation about how we describe these, and some people like to think of it as a 'superpower', others however find this devalues the challenges that they can face. Personally, I like to ask the individuals I am working with but tend to take the view that these are not superpowers, but strengths as any individual we are working with would have. By labelling superpowers, we can invalidate the challenges that individuals can face, and this feeds into shifting how we describe Neurotype challenges using specific support needs labels, rather than functioning ones. But more about that later!

When we focus on these strengths to engage individuals with assessment and therapy, not only do we see improved engagement but also better outcomes. The changes start here.

Double Empathy Theory

Alongside ableism, a core theory we need to know about in particular in relation to autism is the Double Empathy theory. I feel though that this applies for all neurodivergent profiles and can be thought about more broadly. This work by Dr Damian Milton (2012) suggests that when persons of differing neurotypes come together they will find it hard to empathise with one another, because each individual experiences the world very differently. Add to this the differences in communication style from differing neurotypes and social expectations that compound the challenges of empathising with each other.

| Autistic/ND Individual communicates in a way that fits with:

- Their experiences
- Their way of seeing the world
- Their neurology

Leading to masking, feelings of isolation and challenge communicating with neurotypical people | 

Both parties may struggle to understand the other's thoughts, and therefore differences in the way they behave. | Neurotypical Individual has expectations of the way others 'should be' based on:

- Their experiences
- Their way of seeing the world
- Their neurology

Judgements are then made when others do not 'conform' to these expectations |

These differences can cause a breakdown in communication and understanding, which is pivotal for speech and language therapists to be aware of and make reasonable adjustments to how we work in order to try to compensate. We can often find that people of similar neurotypes make meaningful connections more easily because of their shared experiences and ways of processing the world and communicating. We will explore this further throughout the book, and its implications for practice, and importantly changes we can make to ensure access to meaningful and effective speech and language therapy services.

We have to consider as therapists that if we are not neurodivergent, we cannot fully understand the experiences of the people that we serve who are. Even if we are, we still only have our lived experience. Being aware of this, exploring it with people and their families and support networks is important, this will also cross over to working with colleagues and families who are also neurodivergent, navigating complex systems. This also is exacerbated for those neurodivergent individuals who sit across multiple intersections, and it is our role as therapists to bring our awareness to this and be humble in our knowing, and not knowing about the experiences.

> **REFLECTION**
>
> Do you consider how truly deep your understanding and empathy can be if you aren't living that life? How do you mindfully discuss this with individuals, their families and support networks to better enable them to understand this too?

It brings me back to an experience of working with a family, whose child was autistic and ADHD, and found eye contact incredibly difficult. This child's language and communication skills were functional for them, and they were happy with their skills and at that point in life they felt their skills met their requirements for study and social interactions at school and beyond. This child's parents found it very difficult that they didn't give eye contact, both with them, but also with interactions they supported their child with such as with other professionals, family members and so on. They wanted to work on eye contact. It was a difficult conversation to have, but we explored with the child what they felt their listening looked like, what giving eye contact felt like and how it took over their brain, meaning their communication skills decreased because so much cognitive energy was taken up with managing the eye contact, which at times felt physically painful for them. We were then able to use the double empathy problem to explain these differences in processing with the family to enable them to understand why this wasn't a meaningful goal and would encourage masking, and potentially disable their child's communication skills. This shift in thinking and understanding is so important, to avoid that judgement of communication skills that do not sit within a neurotypical individual's expectations.

I have introduced the concept of 'so what', another key question is 'says who?'. In this example, we think about eye contact being required for listening, and successful interaction, but ask 'says who?'.

In order to do better, we also need to consider how our role in both professional and personal life can offer opportunities for advocacy of the neurodivergent community. When listening to conversations, are you hearing people describing experiences of meeting, or working with someone and their frustrations at how this person 'doesn't get it', 'is too slow', 'just a bit weird'. Consider how in these moments we can show up for the neurodivergent community and offer a different narrative, we can't say that all these people our friends, family and colleagues describe are neurodivergent, but we can offer space for pausing and reflecting. Reflecting the Double Empathy theory within conversations can enable the wider community to flip the narrative too. We all have judgements, I think it is human nature, but perhaps we can try to not quite so much and to be curious and kind, and support our friends, family and colleagues to do the same.

Personally, I know that this has happened for me when speaking with my husband. Things that he might have found tricky with colleagues, through his knowledge through listening to me go on (and on, and on!), meant he was given an internal award for supporting a neurodivergent colleague with reasonable adjustments. Which, of course, I am super proud of him for. There will be people in your life that can do this work with you too, to make neurodivergent folks included and enabled to reach their best.

Neurodivergent Communication

What we can better understand now is how neurodivergent individuals communicate, because we can listen to the neurodivergent community who are willing to share their experiences to better inform us and develop our practice.

Historically, there has been a focus on speech, or prerequisite skills for access to AAC; we might have also known what an individual wanted but did not honour that communication, and instead required them to use their AAC to tell us (or cringe) they've shown us what they might like, and we reply 'use your words'. I have done many observations where a child is shown two items to choose from, they point to the one they want and are redirected to a communication aid. Why? That's a good point to reflect on.

We have seen info-dumping (where a neurodivergent person might share lots of information all at once about their enthusiasm) being viewed as a negative way of communicating, that blocks out the listener, doesn't allow for turn taking in conversations and isn't being aware of the other person's thoughts and feelings. How about if we see it being their way to build a connection? Someone is showing their trust, enjoyment and safety in your company to share with you this information about something that is so important to them.

A feature of some neurodivergent profiles is also how they join in a conversation and show empathy and understanding. This is often by referring back to themselves, for example you share a situation that is difficult, the individual then says, 'Oh yeah, it's just like this time that X happened to me' and proceed to tell you about it. For a neurotypical person, this might create a feeling of discomfort, of not being listened too, that the neurodivergent individual is just 'always talking about themselves'. Flip that, to an individual who is listening, processing and relating, and sharing their experiences as a way to say they've understood. How do we support this as a speech and language therapist? This is the double empathy problem playing out in life.

It is also a common feature of autistic communication particularly, where it is direct, small talk isn't seen as meaningful and so they get to the point. Society's expectations may find neurotypical people affronted by this type of communication. Why? Because majority rules? Because that's how we were brought up? Again, a point for reflection.

> **REFLECTION**
>
> I'd argue no way of communicating is better, it's just different and we need to consider if neurotypical feelings matter in this instance more than encouraging a Neurodivergent person to change who they are?

Promoting neurotypical social skills as optimal encourages neurodivergent individuals to mask their authentic selves and put themselves at risk of well-being decrease and mental ill-health and burnout to save a neurotypical person feeling a bit uncomfortable, have a think about it next time you're in this situation.

As part of developing our neurodivergent informed practice, we must begin to honour all forms of communication, and importantly advocate this to colleagues, families and individuals that we support. A lot of our work in this is as much about how we talk to others about neurodivergent individuals, as much as changing the way we think and practice. We have the capacity to make changes to those around us.

If you consider the learning you are going to be taking in from reading this book, and changes you might make, you might feel like 'I'm only one speech therapist' but if you speak to two teachers, who engage with two parents and two teaching assistants, who share it with their neighbours and partners at home, suddenly this shift in thinking is getting out there. It is a case of planting the seed, as we know from little acorns grow the mighty oak trees and while it takes time and nurturing, we can see a shift, both within our profession but also within wider society.

You speak to your colleague, a teacher and a parent.

They speak to their partner, TWO Teaching assistants, a sibling and a colleague

They speak to their partner, TWO Teaching assistants, a sibling and a colleague, their parent and a close friend.

Monotropism

Introducing here another theory that is important: Monotropism. This was developed initially by Dinah Murray, Mike Lesser and Wendy Lawson (2005). This theory can help us make sense of the way that neurodivergent people experience the world, in terms of their interests and engagement and specifically for autistic individuals. A monotropic thinker would have their attention strongly grounded in a small number of interests at a time, focussing deeply and intently, and finding it challenging to move that focus if they are not ready too. This theory has been similarly applied to other neurodivergent profiles, such as ADHD, and termed hyper-focus; what we know for other profiles that are not autistic is that this can likely look like deep attention for a topic, but these topics will more likely shift and change over time.

This is as opposed to a polytopic mind which might focus a little bit on everything. This might apply to our day to day lives, where we can think about what we are doing, what needs to happen next and also what to put on a shopping list for next week. It might be when we are communicating with people we can focus on their words, as well as their bodies and what is happening behind them and still process, to understand and respond in the interaction.

Neurodivergent Individual	Neurotypical Individual
- I have this exciting new project today, to write a new training resource about social communication. - Doesn't notice the phone ringing, the need for a snack, or the toilet or a drink. - Doesn't hear someone asking if they want a coffee.	- What is for tea? - I've got three emails I must send today. - I'll just answer that phone call then get to those emails. - Dealing with the problem from the call that arose, and I'll now write those emails.

As with most experiences of neurodivergence, this is different for different people. It can be a rich strength for some people, and for others disabling when it means that focus does not shift to meet basic needs, like eating, sleeping and going to the toilet. For some we might see it in the way they like to play, and the routines around this they create, for others this might be in a specific enthusiasm they want to read about, research and talk about. For some it might be a deep passion about a topic that is fleeting for a few days, weeks or months before the next thing comes around.

> **REFLECTION**
>
> How do you view this theory? Can you think about some of the individuals you have supported who likely have monotropic thinking? How can you honour that within the work you do?

The Systems

What we know for a lot of the wider community is that diversity, equity and inclusion (DE&I) is a hot topic, rightly so. Companies are recognising the strengths of neurodivergent profiles, they are paying neurodivergent people to come and speak to their teams about lived experiences and reasonable adjustments in the workplace, books are being written to support neurodivergent individuals access learning and the workplace. While far from perfect, and often a bit 'lite', the promotion of DE&I work, introduction of new roles, teams and policies is pushing the conversation to the front of the workforce in some sectors, and as discussed before, these are the ripples beginning, that hopefully make waves, led from the front with some of the biggest companies seeking this information.

Companies such as Google, LinkedIn, Jessica Kingsley Publishers and Warner Bros have been working with autistic individuals to gain their views and experiences. The BBC have given space for autistic voices through documentaries by Christine McGuinness which highlighted the specific challenges that autistic women can face, and also Chris Packham's programmes 'Inside Our Autistic Minds'. The more that information about neurodivergent experiences are shared, the better understanding is across all of society, and this is the wonderful thing about the internet and social media enhancing our access to this information.

It is important here though that I speak about the challenges. A lot of social media content is developed for free, by disabled individuals sharing their experiences, some of whom cross over several marginalised intersections. Consider not just reading their free posts, but supporting these individuals in other ways, by sharing their information, clicking on their donation pages, buying their books. Or speaking to your service about getting individuals to speak on the topics to enhance understanding, both in terms of the workplace and supporting neurodivergent colleagues, but also for us as professionals to seek understanding. Some of the most powerful experiences I have had through CPD opportunities has been to listen to the lived experiences of autistic individuals, while they can only speak to their experiences and not the whole community it offers an important insight that is key as a professional.

While there is movement in the adult workplace due to the progress with DE&I work, it does seem that the strides here are perhaps within children's services, learning and education, baby steps at the moment.

Education settings (from early years, through to higher education) are bound by so many structures, policies and processes that it can often seem impossible to shift how we work, not to mention the perceptions and abilities of individuals and the systems to make a change.

Settings that one feels should have a basic awareness of even the term 'neurodiversity' do not, policies for inclusion and behaviour are based on archaic behavioural practices that do not fit the learning styles or profiles of neurodivergent learners (and it could be argued neurotypical ones at times). The concept of what is a reasonable adjustment may seem like an inconvenience. In order to move forward, again, we can think of ourselves as advocates for these individuals within the systems we work in. We may be met with challenge, but, ultimately, we must do the best we can by the individuals we are supporting. So, develop our skills to manage and overcome this challenge we must!

> **REFLECTION**
>
> How do you feel approaching potentially difficult conversations? What skills do you have? What skills do you need to develop to do this effectively?

Imagine for a moment you observe a child in a classroom as part of an assessment. They are diagnosed with ADHD and Dyslexia. The task is delivered by the teacher at the front of the classroom to the group and they are left to complete it. The child you are observing is repeatedly told to stop fidgeting. They leave their seat multiple times and are made to return. They are shamed when they have not remembered a piece of equipment: 'Well everyone else in the class heard me say it, and managed to get their ruler, as well as their pencil, rubber and paper'.

If we revisit the Double Empathy theory, if that teacher is not neurodivergent, they perhaps do not understand what it is like in this child's brain and body.

> **REFLECTION**
>
> What would your thoughts be after this observation? How would you go about sharing those with the Teacher? What feedback and recommendations might you make?

It is also important to consider the narratives around neurodivergent profiles, which Ellie Middleton (2023) raises as an interesting point within her book, that even within positive conversations there are still subtle differences in how people discuss supporting neurodivergent individuals. For example, autism is all about embracing your differences, yet a narrative exists for ADHD that is more about 'hacking your brain'. Here the difference is subtle but moving more towards an ADHD brain being a challenge to overcome, as opposed to an autistic one being something to embrace and nurture, which seemed like a really interesting observation. I wonder what narrative applies to other neurodivergent profiles, such as specific learning difficulties, borderline personality disorder or tic disorders?

It is helpful to develop your own recommendations, books for people to read, websites and blogs that are helpful or people to follow on social media, as you progress these conversations and having bitesize places to send people for information is great. In order to promote and importantly grow the neurodiversity movement, we need to ensure we have accessible information for people. I'd consider here when working with parents and carers places they might seek more information, as well as for other professionals or personal connections you are speaking with on the topic.

Conclusion

Finally, within the context of neurodiversity as it is now, as we want it to grow and develop, find your own community. In order to feel safe to explore the challenges this might bring to your own views, values and practices you must lean into a group of people who are comfortable with the topic and able to support and reflect with you, peer learning groups, social media networks and like-minded colleagues can all form part of this space.

> **REFLECTION**
>
> I would encourage you as we come to the end of this chapter to think quite deeply about your values, and your communication skills. To improve the quality of life of individuals, we need to ensure that we are uplifting their voices and advocating for change and reasonable adjustments. How can you do this? Do you feel confident too? What is stopping you?

Chapter Summary:

- Your curiosity matters: how you shift your perspectives and lens through which you view neurodivergent individuals you support.
- Your language matters: when describing individuals and speaking about their support needs, to shape narratives around them.
- Your knowledge matters: knowing some of these key theories enable us to talk in a concrete way about thinking and communication styles in an affirming way to open conversations with others.
- Your voice matters: while at times we work in difficult systems, our voice can make a change and we have to use these positions for the good of the communities we support.

References and Resources

Middleton, E. (2023) *Unmasked*. London: Penguin Life.
Milton, D.E.M. (2012) 'On the ontological status of autism: The "double empathy problem"', *Disability & Society*, 27(6), 883-887.
Murray, D., Lesser, M. and Lawson, W. (2005) 'Attention, monotropism and the diagnostic criteria for autism', *Autism*, 9(2), 139-156.

4
Our Learning Process

My Experience

When I qualified in 2010 autism was covered within the curriculum. I do not recall anything about ADHD, dyslexia, dyspraxia or other neurodivergent profiles. I still have the handouts from the autism lectures, it was three hours presented by a guest therapist from the local NHS services. The handouts explained the use of visual schedules, structure within the environment and principles from the TEACCH approach (Treatment and Education of Autistic and Related Communication Handicapped Children). Then, that was it. We had whole modules on learning disabilities, and within this we explored things like AAC, Makaton and Total Communication Strategies. We had placements during training and some of the students will have met autistic children in a paediatric placement, in mainstream and special schools. Some had learning disability placements as they were known, but this was usually only if you had already had a paediatric and adult placement.

We used to do weekly problem-based learning, and this was a brilliant way to explore and apply learning. On a Monday we received a case study and had groups in which we worked. Throughout the week we had lectures on the topic and so by Friday we came back together to explore applying the learning to the case study.

The model within which we learned was the ICF (International Classification of Functioning, no date) which was I suppose the beginning of thinking about individuals holistically. This is still used within courses today as a way of supporting future therapists to consider individuals.

Within the case study we would work through the information and classify it within the ICF categories, see below. It is described by the World Health Organisation (WHO) as 'a classification of health and health-related domains. ICF is the WHO framework for measuring health and disability at both individual and population levels'.

These domains can be seen below, and within these domains the ICF explores 'impairments', 'limitations' and 'restrictions'. It is a medical model tool, that while recognising the impact of the environment and that disabilities exist within contexts, focuses on the individuals' challenges. While we must recognise that neurodivergent profiles are disabling, what this tool fails to do is explore with future therapists a social model of disability, and a strengths-based approach.

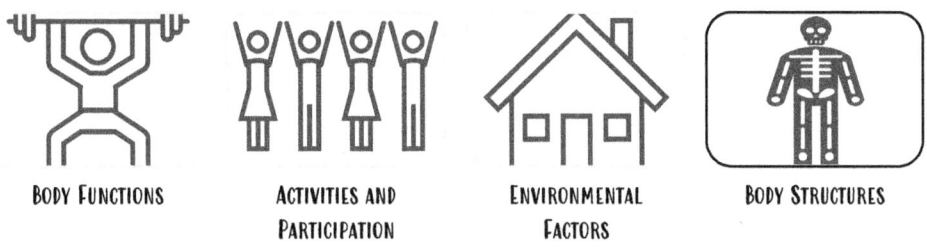

| Body Functions | Activities and Participation | Environmental Factors | Body Structures |

What we know is that speech and language therapy is such a broad occupation, and the scope of work is huge, therefore curriculum pressures are high to cover all the required learning to qualify. However, what we also know is that considering the broad nature of neurodivergence it is likely that in any field a qualified therapist goes to work in that they are going to support neurodivergent individuals. Therefore, it is important that the curriculum grows and shifts and is flexible to the evolving nature of the neurodiversity paradigm.

Our Learning After School

Before we explore some student's experiences, I think it is helpful for us to consider what we learnt, and how we have sought out more information as we have gone through our careers if you are already a registered therapist.

The process of continuing professional development, as discussed in Chapter 1, is a key component of our registration to practice and something we all sign up to do. We can be flexible about what and how we do that but must ensure we are evidencing the things we do. On the most part experiences seem to be that learning about neurodivergent profiles during study is limited, and therefore it is the role of the practice educators to support student therapists, and the role of the qualified therapists to seek out and access the right learning after qualifying.

As neurodiversity as a way of thinking becomes more well known, this has led to a bit of a minefield of courses, resources and new business opportunities. It can feel a bit overwhelming as to what to study, read and use precious training budgets on! While courses can be helpful, they offer a wonderfully luxurious experience of dedicated head space to think and reflect about a topic, I would argue that where we start is with what we are learning and doing now. So, as we learn and grow, space for safe discussions with colleagues and student therapists is a good way to start.

If you are a placement educator, find out what your student therapists are learning. Perhaps give them a task to seek out more information and report back to your team? Offer them space to facilitate discussions within the service about neurodiversity-affirming practice. How do you bring the conversation around language change to team meetings?

At the top of the service through to the bottom are you supporting each other with making some of the simple language shifts we have discussed in Chapter 1, 2 and 3? Learning and development is on-going and so while what we learn 'in school' is important, what to some extent is more important is on-going learning. In particular within the field of neurodiversity where the knowledge and experiences we have access to, that we can learn from only continue to gain traction, breadth and platforms for sharing.

As part of on-going learning, myself and the contributors have been collating a list of resources, book recommendations, podcasts and webinars that can support you on this journey and these can all be found at the back of this book. I would encourage you to investigate any potential CPD opportunities you are exploring in terms of their input or delivery by neurodivergent individuals as well as those individuals' knowledge and experience of the field of speech and language therapy, if that is what the course is about. So much learning can be done by focusing our efforts on understanding the ways neurodivergent individuals see the world, and this can inform us and enable us to then think and ask that 'so what' question when we come to working with and supporting them. Who better to learn about dyslexia from than a dyslexic person?

Current Students

At the time of writing a search on the UCAS website highlighted 20 universities providing a range of speech and language therapy courses, including options for placement years, learning abroad, master's and bachelor's degrees. Some bachelor's level degrees were three years, where others were four (UCAS, no date).

During research for this chapter, I completed simple questionnaires with students who offered their time in January–March 2024. A summary of this information is below.

Do you have lectures within your course that include within the title/description the term Neurodiversity/divergent?	56% Yes 44% No
Within lectures on neurodivergent profiles (autism, ADHD, specific learning differences etc) is the term ableism discussed?	50% Yes 50% No
Have you learned (or will you learn) about the difference between viewing neurodivergent individuals through the social and medical models?	56% Yes 44% No
Has your placement experience given you chance to work directly with neurodivergent individuals?	80% Yes 20% No
What would you say you about your learning so far about the Neurodiversity movement and its implication in speech and language therapy practice?	Exceeded Expectations: 4% Met Expectations: 52% Below Expectations: 44%

As can be seen in the figures there will be around 50% of graduates with formal learning on the topic of neurodivergence that is delivered in an affirming way and discusses the complexities of ableism. It is clear that placements are incredibly valuable in their impact on this learning and that the role of the placement educator is going to be huge in terms of shaping and supporting the reflections of future therapists during their development about how they view, support and advocate for neurodivergent individuals within their practice.

From the responses collected, participants noted that there were opportunities to learn about neurodiversity within optional talks and modules, and that if this was therefore an area of interest students can choose their learning.

Some respondents praised the depth to which lectures explored the neurodiversity paradigm, ableism and prejudice that neurodivergent individuals may experience. Others stated that terms like ableism were discussed 'rarely' and that neurodivergence has only been 'viewed through a medical model and deficits-based profile'.

From those who responded to the survey, 80% said they had experience of working with neurodivergent individuals during their placement, but added 'yes, but I saw them for speech sound therapy'; 'I worked with one child who had queried ASD'.

So, do our population of future therapists feel confident to support neurodivergent individuals?

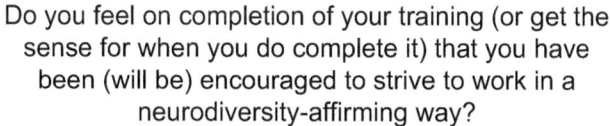

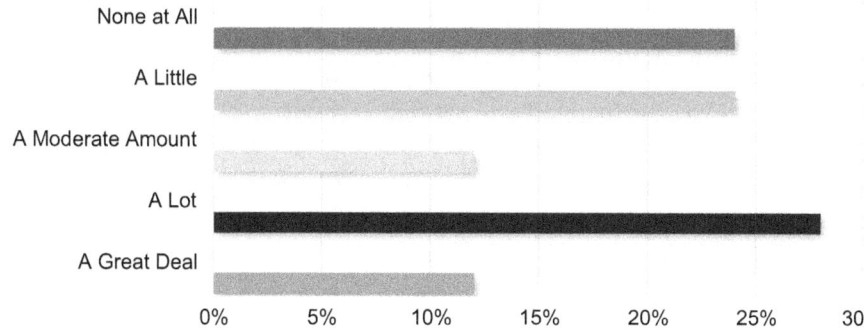

In short, not really. What was encouraging was that participants responded with:

> 'As a cohort we weren't happy with what we were taught on autism so we asked for extra lectures which we were then given'
>
> 'Majority of understanding has been conducted through self-directed study'
>
> 'This came up on my current placement, I emailed my lecturers to ask if this was on the syllabus they said it's not and couldn't recommend any books'
>
> 'A couple of lecturers spoke very passionately about neuro-affirming care and rethinking the way neurodiversity may have been perceived and treated – both generally and specifically in SLT. While the message did not come from all lecturers, I feel those that spoke on it were very impactful'

What I can summarise from this small piece of research is that there are, as ever, a few passionate and loud therapists, using their positions as lecturers and placement educators to enable improved access to learning for future therapists, which in turn will enable better outcomes for the individuals that we serve.

We see a passionate and proactive group of future therapists seeking out their own learning, advocating for their learning requirements within their training and who will no doubt go on to champion the neurodiversity paradigm as it shows up within their work.

But we also see a lot of quiet on this topic, within the one place that would be most expected and appropriate to be loud.

REFLECTION

Are you involved as a practice educator or an employer of newly qualified therapists (NQP)? How can you incorporate neurodiversity informed practice into the learning your students and NQPs will have? Are you involved and working with universities? How can you enhance the offering and open conversations with these institutions? If you offer work experience for aspiring therapists, can this topic be explored with them?

Again, any conversations you are having are planting that seed, and with the right purpose and curiosity, this may spark those individuals to have more conversations, not just with their education colleagues, but also with their family and friends, and we move another step closer to a more curious, kind and inclusive society for neurodivergent individuals.

Neurodivergent Students: Harriet's Experience

University was not a safe place for me, in any respect. Being an undiagnosed AuDHDer I was unable to sit through and listen to lectures, due to my attention style and language processing difficulties. I relied on my peers to hand work in on time and be motivated to get started on a project. I was chronically late to lectures without being allowed into the room when I got there. I remember sitting in the lectures and looking around at everyone else, listening intently to the lecturers whilst nothing stuck in my brain. I remember feeling so alone in a room full of people. No one else seemed to be unable to process the words or make sense of what they were reading on the PowerPoint. Each and every lecture I tried my hardest just to 'sit and listen' but I felt like there was something obviously 'wrong with me' when each time I failed. Quickly, I would give up because I'd lost track of the lecture, and I would write journal entries on my computer or craft things out of the handout. At other times, I would self-injure under the desk, so frustrated that I couldn't listen, or move or get out the restlessness inside me. I would return home after a full day of lectures having learnt nothing and having to read the textbooks and research things online instead. In fact, I believe I taught myself almost the entire syllabus outside of my lecture hours. Each day I sat in the same room for hours, doing nothing, learning nothing and going home exhausted.

Living away from home meant a significant demand on my mental health because I was unable to live independently whilst studying. I barely left my room by year three and experienced worsening anxiety, depression and suicidal ideation. My parents would come to visit me at the weekend and would leave unable to comprehend the state I was living in, my hair hadn't been washed in weeks, I could barely cope with showers, brushing my teeth sporadically, my living space never cleaned and living off a diet of chocolate, pasta, and cheap sauces. Because I was diagnosed with clinical depression and anxiety, I was given some accommodation on placements, but they were provided begrudgingly. I knew I was perceived as the student who didn't put enough work in and didn't deserve the results I obtained; I could always read a room. I was barely surviving and no matter how many times I went to the disability service for support, or my parents contacted my tutor airing their concerns, nothing changed. I believe the only reason I was able to stay on the course was the support of my course peers and friends, who I lived with, and they encouraged/forced me to go into university on mornings, got me to placements on time and fed me nutritious food. In fact, they are probably the reason I'm still alive.

I could have benefitted so much from a proper referral to the disability services, all the information was there had I just been given a compassionate ear. I could have told them that I was struggling to stick to deadlines, process auditory information, sit still, collaborate on group projects, understand instructions for coursework, organise my learning, time keep, process research papers, and organise myself for placements. With that information, it was quite clear there was something other than mental health difficulties going on. Having some noise cancelling headphones, extended deadlines, regular tutor check-ins, recorded lectures, closed captions, and additional processing time would have really helped my university experience, among other aids.

Placements were certainly the most challenging part of university for me, as a person who constantly analyses everything they do. I was so scared of getting things wrong because I knew I was constantly being watched and assessed, not just in my clinical practice but on the car journeys to clients, my ability to be on time and understand what was being asked of me. I was masking to such a high degree, and it was exhausting. I recall a placement I had alongside my friend on the course. I was in such a deep state of burnout that I could barely function. She would wake me up on a morning, make sure I had everything I needed for the day, get us to the train on time and let me sleep all the way there and on the way back, waking me when it was our stop. At one point, I started to fall asleep during a morning meeting because they were talking about things we couldn't input in, and my friend would nudge me to keep me awake. I cannot explain how exhausted and ill I was. Now I understand that I have chronic health issues, I can finally tell people that I'm not being rude or unprofessional, I literally cannot control my levels of exhaustion. Although I learnt most of what I learnt from placements, I was constantly in a state of fight or flight and found that barely any of my clinical educators were compassionate or understanding of my differences. I would constantly receive the same feedback that I didn't ask enough questions, both socially and in relation to my learning, but they didn't understand my learning style. After each day, I would go home and research what I wanted to learn because I thought that by asking it would come across as me not knowing what I should do. When I experienced migraines (which are often), my clinical educators wouldn't accept me texting in rather than calling, as I explained I could not speak when I was experiencing a migraine. Many of my clinical educators just didn't get me and struggled to find topics of conversation outside of the work we were doing. I realise that now it was because I find small talk extremely difficult and tend to avoid it, instead focusing conversations on the structure of the workplace. I constantly felt so misunderstood.

As part of my final year of university, I had a placement, which I thought would be my last before I qualified. As a result of increasing concerns for my mental health, I was given a placement near to my accommodation so that there was no public transport required and a later start time. Unfortunately, without knowledge of my sensory needs I was given a hospital-based placement, which meant loud lights, medical smells, and busyness. I got frequent migraines, and my anxiety was through the roof, with daily sensory overload. On top of this, my clinical educator had no understanding of my mental health difficulties and made no effort to provide support or make accommodations. I constantly went home in tears and was unable to sleep the two nights of my placement days. I was told that I wasn't trying hard enough on the placement and emails weren't responded to by my educator because they had 'annoyed' her. I was barely interacted with by the team and couldn't sit in their office and had to eat my lunch by myself. It got to a point where my anxiety levels meant I couldn't leave the house to go to placement or for anything else. I was in bed almost 90% of the time and could barely speak to people, needing constant care from others. I raised workplace bullying with the university, but they would not do anything about it because they didn't want to damage the relationship they had with the placement. I was failed by one mark in my last week and told that I should consider a change of career and that I would never be able to work full time. This meant that I couldn't graduate with my peers and needed to repeat the placement later. I carry a lot of trauma related to this and it was followed by a suicide attempt. It could have been prevented had my mental health difficulties been taken seriously, had reasonable adjustments been put in place, had there been compassion from the professionals involved and if my university had listened to my concerns. No one should ever be made to feel like that in the workplace. Instead of questioning 'what's wrong with the person' it should be 'what can I do/we change to help this person succeed?' By making no accommodations and expecting the other person to develop on a placement, we are setting up students to fail. It is the role of the clinical educator to support and guide the student to thrive, not be shamed and bullied.

Universities and clinical educators who have disabled students have to do better to support them. Although I wasn't identified as autistic and ADHD at the time, there was an awareness of the extent of my mental health difficulties, and these were not adequately supported. It is the role of a workplace to provide reasonable accommodations to help employees thrive, which is the same responsibility of educators and tutors. I'm aware that I am not the only neurodivergent SLT who has experienced workplace bullying, traumatic university and placement experiences and ableism in the profession. It is not the responsibility of neurodivergent SLTs to educate professionals on how to support neurodivergent employees and students. It is their responsibility to practice compassion and acceptance of difference. Our profession should be centred around curiosity rather than judgement. In my own experience, just by having clinical educators who were supportive, it may have prevented a suicide attempt. The impact of kindness and acceptance is something that shouldn't be underestimated.

Things that would have helped me through university:

- Curiosity rather than judgement of professionals and honest conversations.
- Flexible deadlines and check-in for the need for support.
- Flexible learning opportunities, including practical learning and video resources to watch to support repetition after lectures.
- Handouts printed for note making.
- Captions and access to recorded lectures to pause for note writing.
- Seating considerations for supporting distraction and background noises.
- Sensory aids available and environmental considerations.
- Check-ins with lecturers to ask additional questions or provide clarification.
- Clear and direct language with specific instructions and information, especially with regard to assignments and placements.
- Understanding of things taking longer to learn and needing additional processing time on placements.
- Support travelling to and from placements, such as buddy systems, arranging placements without use of public transport or help with planning the route.
- A culture of acceptance of difference and different learning and communication needs.
- Ensuring group projects have a close connection to prevent anxiety around social situations with less familiar people.
- Welfare checks and serious consideration of mental health difficulties.
- Transcription and audio recording equipment.

Evidence-based Practice

When we are learning, we are taught wholeheartedly to follow the evidence base. Using approaches that have been tried and tested with a range of research methods, and 'gold standard' of research means it is likely a 'gold standard' of support strategy. But, from whose perspective?

Let us begin here by revisiting the HCPC standards from Chapter 1 (no date). When qualified, a therapist must be registered in order to practice, and as such we sign up the following standards relevant to evidence-based practice:

> 1.3 keep their skills and knowledge up to date and understand the importance of continuing professional development throughout their career
>
> 4.2 use their skills, knowledge and experience, and the information available to them, to make informed decisions and/or take action where necessary
>
> 4.7 use research, reasoning and problem-solving skills when determining appropriate actions
>
> 4.8 understand the need for active participation in training, supervision and mentoring in supporting high standards of practice, and personal and professional conduct, and the importance of demonstrating this in practice
>
> 4.8 understand the need for active participation in training, supervision and mentoring in supporting high standards of practice, and personal and professional conduct, and the importance of demonstrating this in practice
>
> 11.1 engage in evidence-based practice
>
> 13.10 critically evaluate research and other evidence to inform their own practice

So, we all agree that in order to practice within our professional guidelines evidence-based practice is important. But what is it?

According to the Royal College of Speech and Language Therapists (RCSLT):

> Evidence-based practice (EBP) is the integration of best available evidence, clinical expertise and service user preferences and values.
>
> (RCSLT, no date)

What I think we must highlight here with a view to working in a neurodiversity-affirming committed way, is the term 'service user preferences and values'. We can read the research articles, attend training sessions and webinars, but we have to also consider the opinions and experiences of service users.

Our Learning Process 67

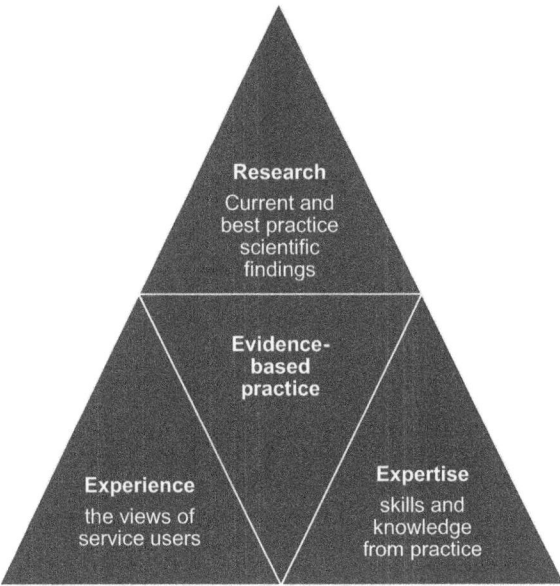

As therapists, part of our evidence base must come from listening to neurodivergent individuals.

- How did therapy make an autistic individual feel?
- What experiences did a person with bipolar have accessing therapy?
- How did the approach used within therapy sessions support an ADHDer?

We must consider the research, take into account things like the NICE guidelines for working, but seek to include more consistently the voice of the users of speech and language services and the neurodivergent community beyond. This includes listening to those who didn't have access to services, but what they might have liked should they have been able to.

When taking into account evidence and service user voices, we then add in our clinical expertise, often referred to as practice-based evidence. This is particularly relevant when we think about working with neurodivergent individuals.

Growing Up in a Medical Model World: Harriet Richardson

There was always something 'wrong with me'. I was always 'the problem'. At school, if I was always the one being picked on, it automatically became 'my fault' because I was the common denominator. In fact, bullying happened so often that people didn't believe me or became exasperated at my 'inability' to stand up for myself and avoid bullying. Children picked up on the language adults used to describe me: 'Hat is sensitive', 'Hat is difficult'. The labels I acquired throughout life have been awful. For that reason, it makes me frustrated when people say 'I don't want them to have a label' because the label 'autism' or 'ADHD' is, in my opinion, much better than 'lazy', 'defiant' or 'challenging'. When there's something different about people, others are very quick to make judgements and identify 'problems'. Anything that deviates from the norm immediately becomes something to fix or change just because it is different. In my case, so many things were changed about me, not because they were wrong, but because they made me stand out.

- I was pushed to spend time with girls because it wasn't age appropriate for me to continue playing with boys at the end of junior school.
- My ways of sitting weren't socially acceptable for girls, so I was taught to sit on my hands to stop myself wriggling. I was forced to have two feet on the floor while I ate my food.
- I was forced into eating 'appropriate foods' for breakfast like every other child, to the extent that I was sick, hid food from people in tissues and cried whilst I ate.
- My emotions were 'too big' so I was conditioned into stopping myself from crying and holding in frustrations. Instead, I created tension in my body, leading to chronic pain.
- My maturity and play were not in line with my age, so I was prevented from playing games deemed 'too young' for me. I was shamed if I acted immaturely for my age.
- I was forced into speech when it exhausted me because other people found it rude when I didn't verbally respond. Pointing, writing and gesturing were not accepted.
- My stims were supressed and I was told they were socially inappropriate and disgusting, due to licking my fingers after experiencing wet to dry textures.
- I was continuously forced into environments, which gave me meltdowns and migraines, including swimming galas, hospitals and parties. If I complained about the noise of a vacuum or the texture of food, I was invalidated.
- I was always made aware that my loudness, impulsivity and child-like excitement were 'annoying', and I needed to tone it down to make sure other people liked me. My personality and energy were completely dimmed.

These things happened because people presumed that they knew better and that my experiences were 'wrong'. I experienced trauma because people didn't listen to what I was experiencing. People thought because I was different that I should conform to what everyone else was doing, rather than encouraging me to embrace those differences and supporting others to understand me. I had to mask every day in a classroom because my need for movement and dynamic attention was not suited to learning. Teachers believed that if I wasn't looking at them while they were speaking, I wasn't listening. It was thought that I was being rude because I didn't want to complete a jigsaw with someone, and just wanted to do my own. I was perceived as difficult because I didn't want to share what I had won at a fayre with the friend I had taken with me, because I'd won it, not them. I was seen as having tantrums and in need of strict punishment when I melted down on a tennis court and smashed up a racket. All these incorrect assumptions are based around societal norms, which are ableist and only apply to a certain group of people. We are not accepting of people existing outside of these norms, not just with neurodivergent communication styles and behaviour, but cultural differences too.

I see so many services and intervention approaches discussing a 'reduction in autism/and or ADHD symptoms' and it is so triggering as a neurodivergent person, because I experienced trauma through a society which, on the surface, looked to reduce my neurodivergent traits. However, they never lessened, they were always just internalised. I developed compensatory strategies to best hide my neurodivergent traits, including:

- I sat on my hands and self-injured to stop more noticeable stimming.
- I spent time alone to avoid social misunderstandings and conflict.
- I never took my toys or belongings outside of the house to prevent myself losing them or having to share them with others.
- I stopped eating in school so that I didn't have to cope with the sensory environment of the canteen.
- I spent time with louder, confident children so that I could hide behind them and not have to do as much work socially.
- I participated in sport constantly to manage my need to move and distract people in the classroom.
- I held my body at tension, especially my jaw and fists to prevent myself from stimming and talking too much.

Throughout my life, many people have been confused by me because of inconsistencies in my skills. As a disabled person, I have significant fluctuations in my strengths and needs. As a child, I had advanced language skills, spoke very early, communicated like an adult at times and could understand advanced concepts. My written language skills were GCSE level in junior school, and I was always in the older age groups for sport. But there were also significant contradictions. During tennis coaching, I had incredible hand-eye coordination and could use technique many adults could not, however I could never master footwork and needed people to move my limbs physically for me to be able to copy them. I could pick up any sport on the first try but couldn't walk upstairs without watching my feet. I could have detailed conversations about my interests but couldn't relay a simple narrative of my school day. I could recall detailed, complex knowledge about dinosaurs but couldn't remember what my parents asked of me as soon as I left the room. All these inconsistencies led to adults telling me I just wasn't trying hard enough, because these things didn't make sense. Instead of being supported and having adjustments, I was reprimanded for being disabled.

The Research Is Just Beginning

In terms of having an evidence base, we have all the historical research that has gone into diagnosing and supporting neurodivergent individuals. Most of which has been focussed on white males, through a medical lens that individuals need to be more like neurotypicals because there is a right and wrong way to be. So, we must look to the evidence and be critical about its application to the individuals that we are supporting and working with now, in the current contexts of society and the ever-changing shifts in thinking.

First, neurodivergent profiles are broad, both in the fact that so many people identify as neurodivergent, but equally in that for each individual profile, for example autism, there is a whole spectrum of experiences, of strengths and of challenges. Research does not cover this breadth, particularly for multiply neurodivergent individuals.

So, we must hold at the forefront of our minds that we need to think flexibly about application of research and lean into quality supervision and mentoring to enable us to learn from each other's clinical expertise.

Research is constantly shifting in the field of neurodiversity, to be more honouring and supportive, as opposed to othering and dictating. What I mean by this is historically evidence has been for therapeutic approaches that seek to 'neurotypicalise' neurodivergent people; teach them how to be more neurotypical to fit in, teach their brains to think like neurotypical people's and treat their neurodivergent profiles as different to a wild degree from the norm.

As the neurodiversity paradigm shift is happening, so is critical appraisal of thinking and approaches, and in turn the research. But we know that research takes time and at the moment the practice-based evidence is ahead of the evidence-based research.

So what can we do in order to bridge the gap, while research is on-going?

1. Seek out and listen to neurodivergent voices, depending on the profiles you work with, ask your own service users, or social media accounts (ensure you consider how you explore varying intersections, for example don't just follow lots of white males with Tourette's).
2. Critically analyse your current toolbox of evidence-based practice, is it affirming? Does it honour the individuals or is trying to change their ways of thinking to be neurotypical?
3. Lean into good supervision, clinical excellence networks and mentoring. We can all be learning from each other on this journey to better practice.
4. Seek out information on general neurodiversity/intersectional topics to explore and broaden your understanding; there are some great books I have included in a reading list at the end of this book.

There are complex conversations going on within our profession around this topic, and some of the shifts in practice that we are seeing, and a nuance and level of critical thinking that is having to be explored. It seems there are a lot of egos in this space, and differing opinions and what and how neurodiversity-affirming practice can show up. Personally, as I explored in Chapter 1, there is no place for ego, we should when meeting our registration requirements be open and think critically, explore and seek supervision to guide our thinking, and ultimately be here for the good of our service users, not our own ego. We can disagree, of course, but at times there feels a lack of kindness and flexibility in these on-going conversations. It has to be about respectful and kind conversations, even if in the end we still disagree.

In addition to the core standards for evidence-based practice, a qualified therapist has also agreed to:

8.7 recognise that leadership is a skill all professionals can demonstrate

8.10 act as a role model for others

8.11 promote and engage in the learning of others

Here we can turn to our roles as advocates within the neurodiversity movement, how we can empower our service users, challenge practice in others and shift the systems that often disable neurodivergent individuals.

Speech and language therapists are in a unique position, the HCPC even states in its guidelines that we must recognise the position of power that we hold, and in turn, see how we can use this to our advantage while recognising the privilege.

Therapists can often be seen as superior, which is totally ridiculous. We are humans, with a set of skills, based on knowledge and supported by experience. But, so is everyone. A parent has a set of skills, based on knowledge and supported by their experiences of their child; consider a teacher, a doctor, a social worker, we are all the same and those outer layers of knowledge and skill should not dictate how we perceive ourselves, or others perceive us.

When working with individuals and families we must be humble in our knowledge and skills, listen and acknowledge their lived experiences. It is important we check ourselves, our values and any bias that shows up when listening to individual's stories and experiences at the point of contact and during their support from our services.

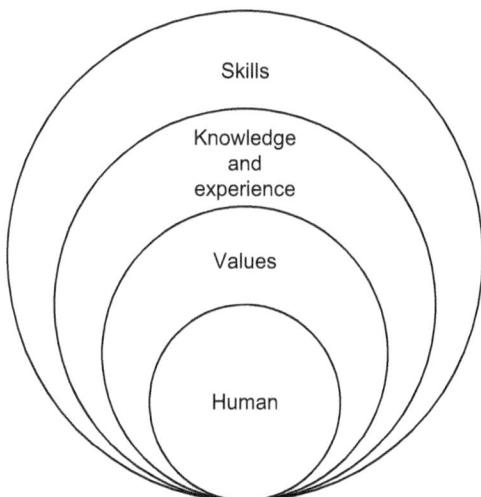

Now, consider the neurodivergent individual who equally is a human, with a set of skills, based on their knowledge and experiences, and more often than not due to the other people in their lives and those experiences have a negative sense of self, feel unsafe and have learned to minimise and mask, or become distressed and unsafe with those feelings.

We can use our position of privilege to uplift the voices of our service users, to champion them and their views about their support and goals. Often attributed to Mahatma Gandhi is the quote: 'be the change you want to see in the world'. I feel we should all hold on to that, when we start to feel fragile and uncomfortable in our advocacy roles as therapists. This must be done in a way that feels safe, but I would also ask you to consider why you feel unsafe challenging practice, or processes that negatively impact neurodivergent service users. Think back to the concept of reflexive practice.

> **REFLECTION**
>
> Ask yourself, what are my values? How does the way other people think about me, affect me? How does my silence (or voice) impact the service users?

Consider, how you explain to a teacher the impact their narrative about a neurodivergent pupil has? How would you explore with a doctor who is citing lack of eye contact as an obstacle to granting hospital leave? Could you have a conversation with a parent who is desperate for their child to stop flapping? Thinking about these too, how does intersectionality play a part when we are thinking reflexively about these conversations. Our experiences of these situations will all be different as we work in different geographical areas, as well as within different systems within health, social and educational settings.

Autism from a Narrow Lens: Harriet Richardson

One of the first questions I get asked when I disclose my autistic identity is 'how did you not know sooner?' It's a very valid question! As an SLT I have worked with autistic children all through my career, even in a diagnostic service as one of my university placements, yet I did not identify my own differences. Neither did clinical educators, lecturers or colleagues. Part of this, I believe, is due to what we learn about autism on our university journey. I recall learning about outdated theories, such as Theory of Mind and all autistic people having low empathy. We learnt about the 5:1 ratio of autistic boys to girls, but not because it was easier to identify boys but because it was a 'disorder of the male brain' primarily. We didn't learn about masking or less stereotypical autistic traits, so when I started in the autism diagnostic service it felt really easy to identify whether a child was autistic or not just by one observation at school. I am so thankful I didn't venture into autism assessment as an NQT because I'm not sure I could cope with the guilt of how many autistic children I would have misidentified.

Going into my first role, I felt very confident in my knowledge of autism, what it was and what it wasn't. Like many professionals, we are taught that what we learnt at university is the gold standard, the research is undeniable, and we should always listen to those who have been working for longer, as they have far more experience. Just like so many others, I believed I knew what was right for the young people I worked for, not them. I believed that I was superior in my awareness of autism. I was so unbelievably wrong! I spent the following three years questioning so many clients' autistic identities because they were 'too much like me', I believed they just had anxiety 'just like me'. I'm so ashamed of that. It wasn't until I actually started to listen to autistic people and their experiences that I really learnt what autism was. And then, when I listened, I related, and I quickly unlearned everything I thought I knew about what it was to be autistic. I learnt that I was autistic just by listening to one account of a late-identified autistic woman, not five years of study or four years of clinical practice.

Through the rise of late-identified ADHD and autistic adults, more information is being shared on social media. The understanding of autism and ADHD has widened in some respects, but it has also narrowed in others. Many people who do not fit the profile of 'late-identified', 'high-masking', speaking and white are not often being heard and that's problematic. Those who are non-speaking and BIPOC do not tend to be heard in these spaces, which impacts how we work as professionals. If we only hear one viewpoint, we aren't going to be able to provide support for the wide range of people that we come across in our roles. With this in mind, university curriculum has a real place in ensuring that the wide variety of voices and experiences are heard, and we are not just digesting information from the voices who shout the loudest. As professionals, we also have a duty to ensure that the information we receive is inclusive of a range of perspectives and considers intersectionality.

As professionals, we have a habit of seeing ourselves as the only people with knowledge. We can so easily discount the experiences and viewpoints of our clients and their parents/carers because we feel that we 'know better'. I still have to catch myself in assessments where I make assumptions based on patterns I've seen or how I've interpreted things. Our profession is about care and support, as part of that, we must be curious and rather than making judgements. We must listen as much as we observe and talk.

Evidence-based Practice vs Lived Experience: Harriet Richardson

Throughout my career, I have used my own experiences of autism and ADHD to guide my clinical practice. Through that lived experience, I have also challenged evidence-based practice, social skills training being one example. It was very obvious to me that Social Skills Training didn't 'improve social skills' for autistic people but instead taught masking, which was really what was being measured. It was obvious because it was something that I had experienced myself, not matter how much coaching I had around social interactions, it still wasn't natural for me, and it never will be. Now I work in assessment services, my lived experience is an important part of the work that I do because I continue to challenge aspects of clinical practice. For example, when I see people coming for an autism and ADHD assessment, I ensure that I ask them questions about their internal experience, which I can identify with and pick up on. When other clinicians question one of the neurotypes because it hasn't been observed, I am able to provide a lot of evidence that they meet both criteria, simply because of my lived experience of both neurotypes. Without having that understanding of my own neurology, I would have dismissed many children's neurodivergent identities due to lack of understanding and insight. For that reason, I will forever be glad that I didn't go into diagnostic work until after I was identified.

Pulling it All Together

In order to work in a neurodiversity-affirming way, and to explore the impact of our practice and the evidence base, we have to seek to better understand the experiences of the individual. Psychologists and other professionals use a tool known as formulation often to identify a presenting problem for an individual and explore things that cause the problem and cause the problem to continue. I believe that an adapted version of this tool can be an incredibly helpful way to consider the experiences of neurodivergent individuals visually and structurally in a holistic way.

This can help us flip the narrative (Elly Chapple, no date), an important concept in how we show up, speak about and write about neurodivergent individuals. Our advocacy, championing of neurodiversity-affirming committed work, can enable a shift in an individual's narrative about themselves, if they see a change in the narrative about them in the world around them. With better understanding and the right lens, we can help promote a positive sense of identity for neurodivergent individuals, which in turn will improve their quality of life and well-being, and as speech and language therapists that is our goal.

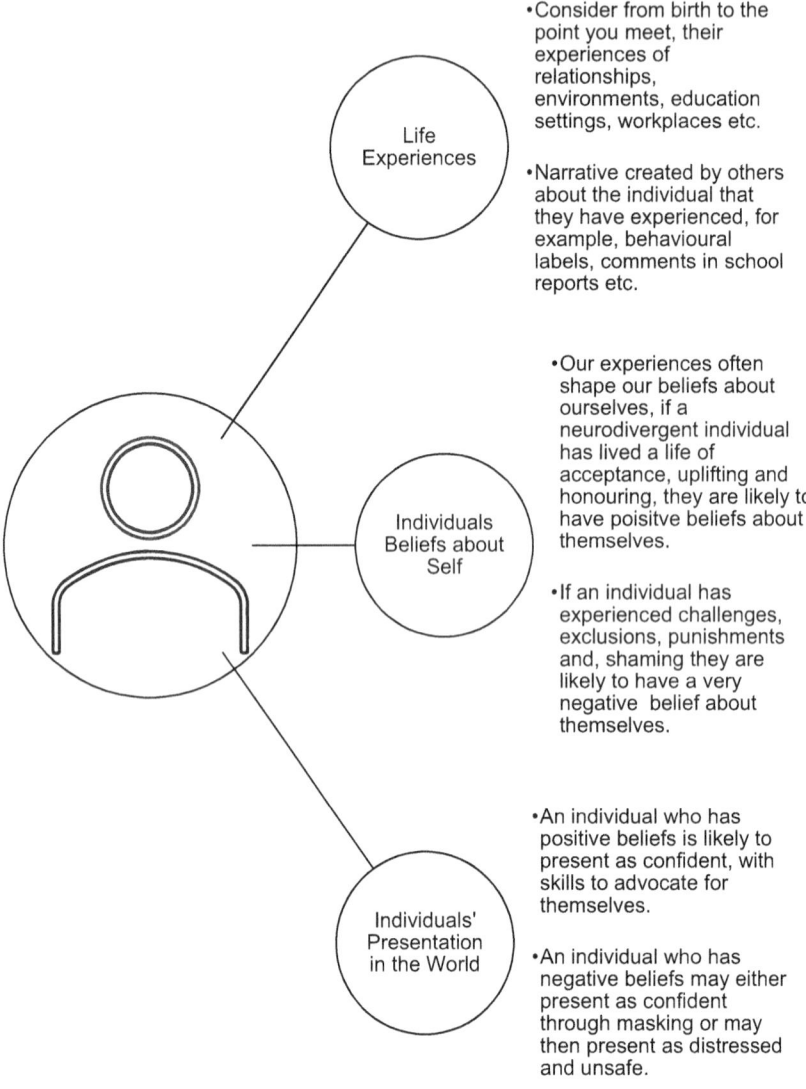

We must take these differing experiences into account as we grow and develop our practice in supporting neurodivergent individuals; if we better seek to understand their experiences this knowledge can shape our practice and develop better experiences for them, while also adding to our practice-based evidence.

We as therapists can help promote a sense of safety and security for these individuals, by taking our guidance, as above, and being leaders. No matter your years of experience or your level within a team, you can still take a leading role, in providing challenge, supporting reflection and initiating a change in how historical practices are reviewed and updated to be neurodiversity-affirming.

Within our systems, we can lead and act as role models for other colleagues across health, education and social care to discuss language we use, how we work and set goals and amplify the voices of our service users.

To that end, we have an opportunity to engage others in learning with us, ideas could include:

- Easy access short webinars for staff teams.
- Learning clubs, where you bring information you have sought and reflect as a team.
- Book clubs, see the reading list at the back for some great titles to start with.
- Information leaflets for parents.
- Team case explorations; discussing a particular individual and challenging the process of assessment, support and goal setting.
- INSET and twilight training for education teams.
- Language leaflets for colleagues across sectors regarding goal setting, narratives and affirming strengths-based profiles within documentation and reports.

Conclusion

Some therapists and other colleagues are going to feel uncomfortable. They may be challenged by people they believe to not be as experienced, or 'below' their rank, in a world where we are trying to better the services and experiences of the people we support, their feelings don't matter.

We all must access supervision, where we can explore uncomfortable feelings, we can speak to our support networks and access self-care to ensure we can keep ourselves well as we do challenge and learn. But this is not about us.

Chapter Summary

- Your actions matter: when supporting neurodivergent students of therapy. University can be a difficult place for neurodivergent learners; if you are a student, or work within the university system think about what you can do to enable your colleagues or learners to enable them.

- Your voice matters: if you are involved, let's enhance learning for students. At university, learners are not covering neurodiversity consistently, and it is not a fixed part of the curriculum.
- Your way of working matters: if you are a practice educator you can play a huge part in the opportunities for future speech and language therapists to enable their learning about neurodiversity-affirming committed practice.
- Your practice matters: delivering quality therapy is a triad of practice-based evidence, evidence-based practice and lived experiences to become neurodiversity-affirming committed.
- Your perspective matters: the way we view others and ourselves matters, no one person's experiences and knowledge can trump another's.
- Your learning matters: it is about so much more than just support strategies and we must explore beyond.

References and Resources

Elly Chapple (no date) #flipthenarrative – Can Do Elly (pdf) (accessed on 20/05/2024).
Evidence-based practice. (no date) RCSLT (members only page) (accessed on 11/04/2024).
HCPC Speech and language therapists. (no date) hcpc-uk.org (accessed on 11/02/2024).
International Classification of Functioning, Disability and Health (ICF). (no date). www.who.int/standardss/classifications/international-classification-of-functioning-disability-and-health (accessed on 11/04/2024).
UCAS. (no date) 'Choose your future'. https://ucas.com/ (accessed on 16/07/2024).

5

Putting it Into Practice

Where it Begins

This chapter will not explore a comprehensive list of dos and don'ts but will cover some of the core support strategies and how we can shape and develop their use in order to be more neurodiversity-affirming.

Raelene Dundon in her recent book, *A Therapist's Guide to Neurodiversity-Affirming Practice* (Dundon, 2023), offers seven principles of neurodiversity-affirming practice that we can take and wrap around our more specific speech and language therapy tools.

Principles of Neurodiversity-Affirming Practice, Dundon, 2024	Presume competence
	Promote autonomy
	Respect all communication styles
	Be informed by neurodivergent voices
	Take a strengths based approach
	Honour neurodivergent culture
	Tailor supports to individual needs

It is helpful here to consider our practice not only within these principles, but equally to several key principles and theories so that we can as a profession offer space that is safe and secure that will enable and uplift individuals within their assessment.

Warda Farah suggests that we 'provide spaces of reprieve, where others can be free to language in ways they want to'. This can 'enable others to feel good about who they are and remove the expectation and mask of standardised language' (Chapman and Mears, 2024).

When an individual comes to their speech and language therapy appointment, or if we are assessing an individual in their environments, we must think about this. We cannot see speech, language and communication in a silo when we are thinking about neurodivergent individuals, and as such we must consider:

- Sensory processing and the sensory environment (Ayres, 1972)
- The Nervous System and Polyvagal Theory (Porges, 2021)
- Attachment Theory (Maslow, 1943)
- Maslow's Hierarchy of Needs (Bowlby, 1988)
- Executive Functioning Skills (Sumpter, 2021)

These theories enable us to consider the holistic view of how a neurodivergent individual shows up in the world and consider how these things can both enhance and disable their speech, language and communication. We as speech and language therapists can speak on these topics within our assessments and reports within our knowledge and experience and we can seek out referrals to other trained professionals as required. There is a balance between seeking to affirm and assess the whole individual and sticking to our experience and training.

Sensory Processing and the Sensory Environment

The theory of sensory integration was first discussed and explored by Dr Jean Ayres in the 1970s. For a lot of neurodivergent individuals, in particular autistic individuals, their sensory systems differ in the way they receive and process sensory information.

In order to process language, one must be regulated and what we now know is that with the sensory processing differences neurodivergent individual may experience there may be a constant underlying dysregulation their brains are dealing with.

There are eight sensory systems to be aware of:

- Visual
- Tactile
- Auditory
- Olfactory
- Gustatory
- Vestibular
- Proprioceptive
- Interoceptive

For most readers I anticipate you will understand those first five. However, it feels sensible to expand on the final three.

Vestibular

Our vestibular system is that which processes and regulates our balance. It is the system that comes online to ensure you don't fall over when you get off a roundabout, that stops you from falling over when you're stood on one leg at the top of the ladder trying to get the Christmas tree out of the loft.

Proprioceptive

Proprioceptive sense refers to the way our bodies work out where they are in space, it is the sensations in our muscles and joints that enable us to use a pencil without pushing so hard the lead breaks, that can allow us to walk up and down stairs without carefully watching each step to work out where it is spatially compared to our feet, that will allow you to sit down on a chair without feeling where the seat is and moving to it slowly.

Interoceptive

The interoceptive sense is that which manages our internal sensations, such as recognising when we are thirsty, or hungry, tired or need to go to the loo. It can also provide challenges with tuning in to how our bodies change when we experience different emotions, such as that butterflies in the tummy feeling, or the flush to your face when embarrassed. It is particularly important for speech and language therapists to have an awareness of this sense, when we have lots of goals set around communicating for food, or drink or communicating emotions. These challenges can lie much deeper than just not having a way to communicate the feelings, there may be challenges tuning in to notice the changes.

So we must consider two things:

1. reasonable adjustments to individuals during their therapy input, and within our recommendations to enable them within their environments and occupations.
2. how a sensory processing difference might cause challenges for communication in the way it takes up space in the brain for processing and limits the access to language processing parts of the brain not only when dysregulated but potentially throughout the day.

Fluctuations in Language Ability: Harriet Richardson

The following information is a description of fluctuations in my experience of autism and ADHD. I feel that there is not enough spoken about how ADHD can influence language and it needs more consideration!

There are some days where I can engage in very complex discussions, with high levels of language and large chunks of language. Then there are days where I cannot engage in less complex conversation. My emotional regulation has a significant impact on my communication, as I cannot access higher-level language if I am not regulated. During conflicts, I am completely unable to advocate and will generally agree with whatever the other person is saying because I cannot process the information quickly enough. Following directions is something I find extremely difficult because of my neurotype. I struggle to retain information, understand things that aren't completely specific and process larger chunks of language and sequences. On some days, I can present to hundreds of people about complex topics, where people comment on my skills in expressive language. On other days, I can barely string together a sentence or find the words I need to use. On some days, speech is not available, and I cannot formulate sentences to write them down. On those days, my communication is solely gesture and vocalisations, not being able to process what others are saying to me.

There are many contradictions in my language skills, which often left the adults in my life very confused. This was especially evident at tennis coaching, where coaches would comment to my parents that they could not understand how I was achieving so well academically, and how I was very affluent but could not follow a seemingly 'basic' set of instructions. I have been unable to get my medical needs met or taken seriously as a result of my language difficulties. Many doctors' appointments have been left without the required tests and support because I couldn't express myself clearly. In situations such as these I now use the following strategies:

- Write down what I want to say and the outcome of the appointment I need before the appointment. I then hand this to the professional for them to read themselves.
- Email the professional ahead of time to let them know about my communication differences and state what I need them to know.
- Take a trusted person with me to help communicate my needs, process and retain the information.
- Ask the professional to write things down or send me an email of the important information to support my processing.
- Request online meetings where I can use closed captions.

I can write and read very complex diagnostic, legal and medical reports for my clients, but I cannot process my own medical, financial or legal documents. I rely significantly on my family and partner to help me understand and sign contracts, in relation to work opportunities, solicitors or terms and conditions for example. I must place a lot of trust in other people, which makes me very financially and socially vulnerable. A lot of this is due to having an interest-driven attention style, as I can process things in relation to my interest but not much outside of this. ADHD has a significant impact on my language and literacy skills including:

- Difficulty processing large chunks of information, especially when it is unrelated to my interests.
- Becoming overwhelmed by large chunks of written information and avoiding reading them or scanning through very quickly and losing focus.
- Skipping words in my writing or joining words together. Skipping over words in reading or skipping lines.
- Word finding difficulties.
- Narrative difficulties, where I am unable to sequence a story and miss out bits and go off on tangents. Many times, during a narrative, I will forget what I am talking about.
- Saying the wrong words in sentences and not being aware, which means I don't self-correct or clarify.
- Difficulties with the concept of time. This means that I will give unreliable accounts of things that happened, for example how long things lasted and when they happened. I **generally use** the term 'a few days ago' to talk about something, which could have happened years previously.

The Nervous System and Polyvagal Theory

Dr Stephen Porges created the Polyvagal Theory, to explain and highlight the role of the autonomic nervous system, particularly the vagus nerve, in life. You may have heard of this theory, you might have heard of the concept of a fight/flight response, which is grounded in Polyvagal Theory. What we can see out in settings is the impact of vagus nerve activation in the neurodivergent population we support. It is an important lens to help shape our perspective and narrative of the way we see individuals and their participation and engagement with the environment around them.

For example, that child who when asked a question in class, refuses to answer. This might be described, as difficult, defiant, refusing to comply. When we apply a polyvagal lens, with our knowledge of sensory and communication, could that be a child in fight mode, because they are feeling scared? Their sensory system is processing a whole load of things that a neurotypical teacher or peer isn't, plus the way they understand language is different, so the question wasn't easy to understand and work out a response to, and now the whole class has turned to look at the individual to see what they say in response to the question.

We see this particularly with a Pathological Demand Avoidant (PDA) profile. Where perhaps an individual's nervous system is in a constant state of activation, and this can play out in a few different ways. We might, as above, get a fight response. We might get a freeze response, where an individual shuts down and is unable to respond or engage at all. We may also see a flight response, when an individual is seeking to escape the situation, this might be by physically leaving a space or trying to shift and detract attention and focus from the situation in hand, such as 'playing the fool' when the nervous system creates what might be deemed silly or inappropriate behaviour as its response to the stressor. We can also see a fawn response, where the nervous system creates an apologetic and people pleasing persona, that might result in a meltdown later on the day or week due to the pressure of this response.

All of these things are important to us a profession, as we know, communication cannot happen in a silo. Effective communication will happen when an individual feels safe and secure, so we must consider this during our assessments and observations and get curious if there are disconnects between communication skills in different environments. Is the nervous system being activated, for example, say, in a busy dining hall, as opposed to a quiet classroom?

Practice Example

Report Excerpt

> X experiences the impact of a heightened response of their autonomic nervous system, this can take one of several paths, into fight, flight, freeze or fawn. For X the world appears confusing, and they can shift between these states regularly within a short period of time. X may mask, and people please via a fawn response, become still and mute within a freeze response, begin to run away, or run around, or ask people to leave in a flight response or become aggressive

> in a fight response. They experience periods of intense restraint collapse, particularly after interactions with new or unfamiliar people. They can seemingly be excited to see family and miss them when they have gone, during their visits they will engage in positive interactions, but these also cause fatigue and challenge for them and they need time to regulate after these and can still experience periods of dysregulation.

We must also consider the implications for any assessment sessions we run, or on-going therapy sessions. How can we calm the individual's nervous system, to enable the best outcomes from both assessment and therapy sessions?

This theory and the example given speak to how important our language and lens are when we are observing and commenting on neurodivergent individuals and the way that they show up in their environments. It is also important we can incorporate this lens into our conversations, training sessions, supervisions and reports to enable others to create an affirming narrative. Our role is to advocate and uplift the individuals we support and knowing about these things enables us to do so.

Attachment Theory

Attachment Theory is key to child development, and what we know about how children thrive when they experience secure attachments in the early years of life. Equally, that if they do not experience a safe and secure attachment in the early years, it can lead to less positive outcomes.

Several researchers over the years have expanded on Bowlby's early theory to create four different attachment profiles, each that come with a list of traits that we may see and once again have a negative narrative about, that with the right understanding and lens are viewed differently and supported in a different way.

- Secure Attachment, those individuals who experienced distress and whose needs were met by their parents/caregivers consistently.
- Anxious Attachment, those who experienced significant distress when their parents/caregivers were away, and while being comforted would also seek to punish the adult.
- Avoidant Attachment, those who show little or no distress at being moved away from their parent or care giver.
- Disorganised Attachment, these children have mixed profiles and may present with traits from all three categories above.

Putting It Together

In the first instance Dundon's list is clear about how we shift our lens and adapt what we do. But, for speech and language therapy it becomes complex when we delve into the ways that we work, the expectations of how the profession supports neurodivergent individuals and map out the ways that we enable individuals to meet their goals. So, these principles while incredibly helpful for looking at things at a service-wide level need to be expanded in order to truly challenge how we work, and importantly what we use and do when we work.

For a lot of children and young people who are neurodivergent they will have access to some sort of speech and language therapy, this may be at the point of diagnostic assessment or following a referral before or after this point. For a lot of systems this will look like an assessment, with recommendations and points of follow-up, for others this may be regular therapy or regular support with the key adults in the individual's life.

For adults this is unlikely to be quite so straight forward, diagnosis assessments, first, can be hard to come by, coupled with health inequalities and privilege to access independent services, for example being a barrier. Some neurodivergent adults will access therapy through services they already access, such as inpatient mental health care, community learning disabilities and the criminal justice system. Diagnosed adults may seek out independent speech and language therapy to support them with communication, but in my experience a lot of this support is sought out through neurodiversity-affirming coaching, which is now very accessible, cheaper and more specifically tailored to the challenges that a neurodivergent adult may face.

Broadly speaking, for children or adults the process by which they enter speech and language therapy services is the same. This is where we first come into 'contact' with that individual, whether it is a self or other person referral, there is a set of information and criteria that we will get. This level of information will differ depending on who is referring and which service they are referring into. There are also differing amounts of capacity within

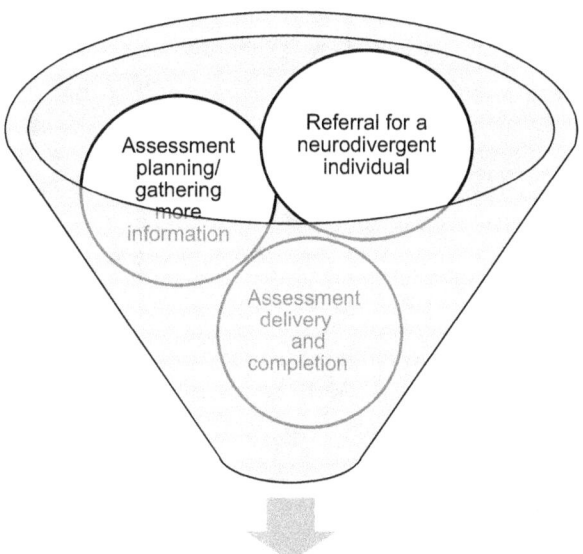

the varying spaces that speech and language therapists work to gather further information before planning and completing an assessment. Generally, though, the process will look something like the diagram above.

During the assessment process we can consider what and how we deliver a meaningful and neurodiversity-affirming assessment, we can challenge the current status quo of what is expected from a speech and language therapy assessment and what tools are used. We are in a powerful position within our profession during our assessments and conversations to challenge ableism and society's views of what communication should feel like and be like. What we know is that to be affirming we have to honour the differences and shift to a more strengths-based approach, and this has to start within the process of assessment.

> **REFLECTION**
>
> What are your assessments? Why do you use them?

Let's face it, for a lot of speech and language therapists the same assessments will get pulled out if you have a referral of an individual with a particular age and a particular diagnosis or neurotype. It will be explored more, but consider are they honouring or perpetuating a narrative of a specific type of processing and communicating being the 'best' and anything less, ultimately within those assessments individuals are then scored as 'bottom' percentiles or 'below average' and other negative narratives, that their communication is the problem.

Following that assessment, how are our goals and recommendations and support strategies and therapy tools used to be neurodiversity-affirming? We must surround this with the language we use, the narrative we share with others to embed and enhance the work we do through therapy too. Changing a goal, or a support strategy to be more neuro-affirming cannot exist in a silo. We must ensure that our whole way of working changes otherwise we may be developing progressive strategies within our therapy work, that then are not supported and integrated by others around the individual because we are not having those conversations to offer challenge for others to come on board and accept that there are better ways of doing things to enhance the participation and quality of life outcomes of neurodivergent individuals.

The concept we have to take on with this is the process of challenging ourselves, our practice, the systems within which we work. For this next walk through, I put my best speech and language therapy head on, with a bit of Occupational Therapy in terms of task analysis! So, what follows is an attempt to break down the task of questioning the tools and strategies that are in place to give a framework to put through different assessments, strategies, and tools that we may use.

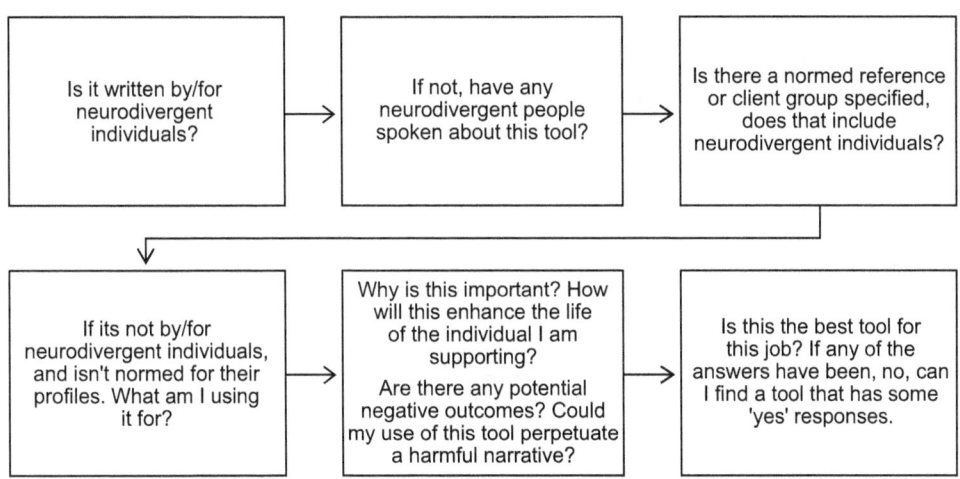

There are a range of different blogs and social media accounts that speak about speech and language therapy tools, so we can gain information on the lived experience of neurodivergent individuals that way. In doing so, we are, as per Raelene's principles, seeking to be informed by neurodivergent voices.

A core part of working in a neurodiversity-affirming committed way is to consider the impact of any tools that we use for the individual. This means thinking about things such as inaccurate age equivalents in an assessment score, or promoting a neurodivergent individual to mask their true selves to fit in. These kinds of practices, while often unconscious, can cause challenges and negative outcomes for individuals.

At the first point of contact with a speech and language therapy service, chances are this will involve assessment and information gathering; we have a wealth of tools available to us to inform this process. There are some go-to tools that speech and language therapists use, and I am sure if you are a therapist reading this you would think of a few core things you would never go anywhere without!

REFLECTION

For an assessment, what are we aiming to do? When we are working with a neurodivergent individual, what is the purpose of the process?

These individuals are wired differently, we are not working with them to get them to meet the neurotypical developmental norms of, say, language development or grammar. We may want to explore how they process and use language, to enable others around them and to comment on their use of language, we may agree with the individual this is an area they would like to work on, there may be a requirement for them to use language in a certain way for a certain process, such as exams.

(Although that is an entirely different conversation about how we are testing neurodivergent children within our education system, with tools that do not play to their strengths or their very valid ways of seeing and experiencing the world and then leading them to negative academic outcomes, perpetuating their negative narratives and sense of self … just going to climb down off that soap box.)

Although I may just climb on another soap box here … There is this area within our profession too, where perhaps we sit a bit too silent. I speak here about legal frameworks related to Education Health and Care Plans, and funding for services. Therapists ultimately are told about how to write and what to assess, and formal assessments are seen as the gold standard. I don't know if anyone has ever felt they 'have to' use a formal assessment? I wonder what thoughts showed up for you?

It seems to me, that as qualified therapists, we are the ones who can use our critical thinking skills and experience to pick the right tools to assess neurodivergent individuals. Yet, we seem quiet and silent as opposed to challenging this. I wonder if you have ever tried, and what your experiences were? It seems that as the 'experts' we should be trusted to autonomously assess, complete our reports and be able to rationalise for our decisions on goals, provision and recommendations without needing numbers to back them up.

REFLECTION

How does that thought land for you? Do you perceive yourself as an expert?

Here, too, we can introduce some of the complexities that neurodivergent individuals can experience accessing services and the perception of those services. What we hear a lot of are challenges from services as to the content and recommendations of independent therapy reports, perceptions that can drive a wedge between different therapists that seem unproductive and combative, and ultimately impact the access of individuals to the right support. The SLTs on the Same Team Clinical Excellence Network (see website in the reading list) strive to support therapists working within the independent sector, and those working for the National Health Service and other employers to explore some of the barriers to effective collaboration across sectors by promoting best practice, provide tools for problem-solving and increase commitment within the professional to work together to overcome the barriers. As discussed above, this is another more political area of our work, and one where recognition has to be that all therapists are equally qualified to do their role and are held to the same standards whatever setting in which they work. It is complicated based on services, resources and many other factors, at the centre of this though is an underlying question often over ethics and practice, which can often feel personal and challenging. We are all here for the same aim, and bound by the same guidelines to practice, we can disagree professionally, of course, there can be healthy debates and discussions. But with this, please, a healthy dose of kindness and curiosity.

A Walk Through

It feels helpful at this point to walk through a well-known tool to consider how we apply these steps of thinking. Clinical Evaluation of Language Fundamentals (CELF) - I choose you!

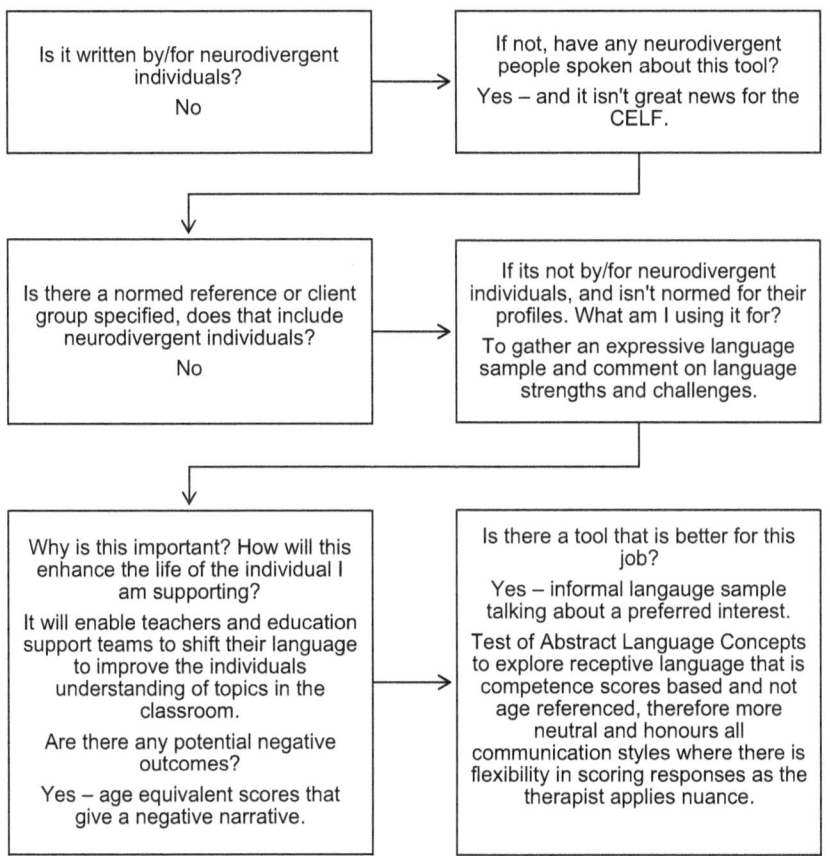

In this worked example, we can see that the tool is not written by or for neurodivergent individuals, and while in principle it meets the therapists' needs to gather a language sample and explore receptive language to enable teachers to better communicate with the child in their classroom, there may be negative consequences. There are moments I spend wondering if there is space or need for a holistic neurodiversity informed SLT assessment, but then equally moments of thinking we can use the tools we have to compile a profile of language and communication that is affirming.

- Take for example an observation, we can speak to an individual's way of being in the environment, their language understanding and use. For those who can, we can use tools such as a Talking Mat to offer chances for them to feed back on their language and areas of communication they find challenging.
- We can explore through informal questionnaires and tools how an individual's language and communication is enhancing or challenging their life and outcomes.
- We could employ learning on conversation analysis, to comment and unpick a neurodivergent individuals communication. Yu and Sterponi (2022) talk about how conversation analysis can offer a new approach to social communication assessments, where we can offer a meaningful and neurodiversity-affirming lens to assessment, and we can explore communication breakdown in real-life, which often is a barrier to a 1:1 speech and language therapy assessment anyway.

Affirming Assessment Spaces

To take a step back, before we are picking the assessment tools, we can revisit Dundon's list and consider how we offer a space that is neurodiversity-affirming. If we must complete a 1:1 assessment, how do we:

- check in with an individual before, during and after the assessment, do you know the signs to look for of dysregulation?
- promote autonomy; do you have cards to ask for a break, or drink, or the toilet?
- offer sensory accommodations; have you considered noise and lighting?
- make reasonable adjustments to how much we do, or for how long we work to complete an assessment?
- honour all forms of communication, do you have a range of communication tools available?
- offer options for a variety of communication supports within the assessment?
- take a strengths-based approach, incorporating and exploring preferred interests and activities during the assessment? Is this information included in a case history for you to prepare ahead of time?

Even before that, how are you engaging and informing the neurodivergent individual what might happen during the assessment? In order to assess an individual effectively, there has to be consideration of how we support and enable them and do not set them up to fail, such as giving them no information which may cause anxiety, and then not considering the environment in which we assess them, or the sensory and regulatory accommodations we make.

- Does your service have information for children and individuals that can be sent ahead of the assessment?

Putting it Into Practice 89

- Are there a range of access methods for this information? Things such as a video of how they find your rooms, or what tools they will see? Could you send a photograph of the therapist's face ahead of time?
- A social story to explain what will happen during the appointment, written in a range of different language and visual support types.

Here are a few points to consider to make reasonable adjustments to the sensory environment as a practical starting point for you.

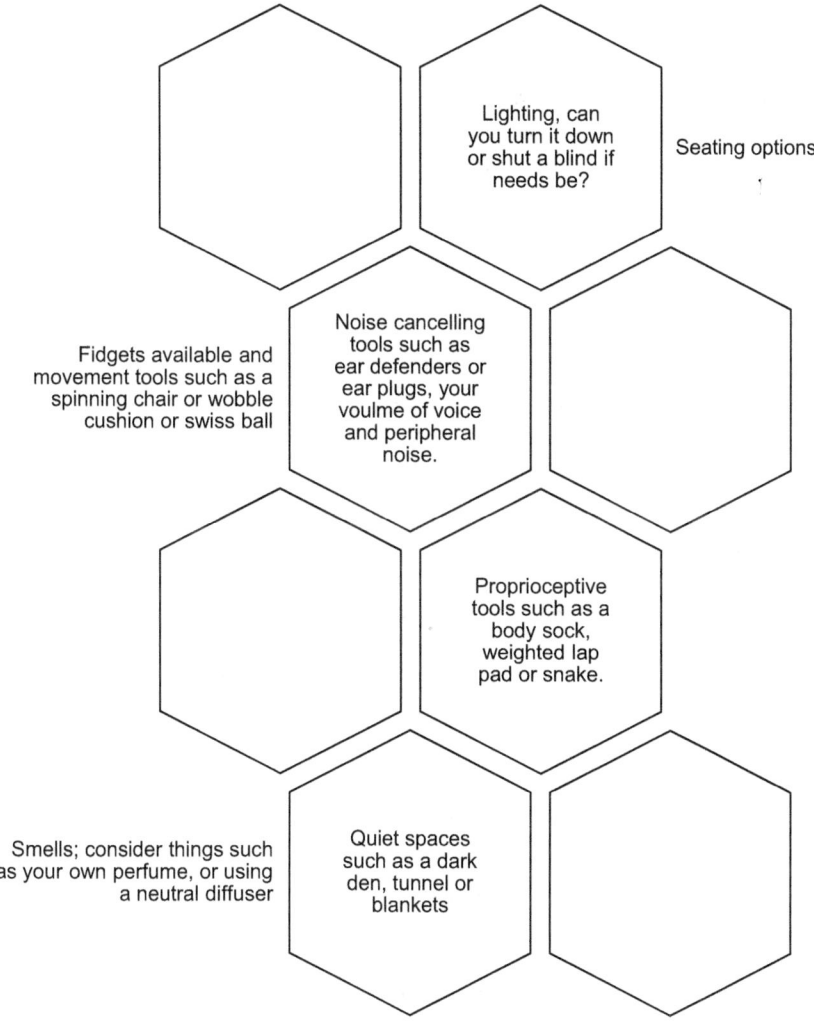

But now, let's get the lived experience perspective from Harriet.

The Limitations of Standardised Assessments: Harriet Richardson

If I was to complete a CELF assessment myself, I would be identified with a language disorder. That does not mean that I need speech therapy, and it does not mean that I don't have effective functional communication. I learnt very early on in my career that standardised assessments for a great number of people are not reflective of their language profile. That is mainly because standardised assessments are not designed to test language development outside of white, middle-/upper-class, non-disabled people. Standardised assessments are not appropriate for use with neurodivergent people. I often liken the comparisons drawn to developmental norms to different breeds of dogs (area of passion for me), where you wouldn't compare the height of a Labrador with a cockapoo, because they're different breeds. If you analysed the cockapoo's height development with larger breeds, you might refer to them as a 'disordered' Labrador. If you analysed the cockapoo's height development with others in their breed category, you might see their growth as the 'norm'. The same can be applied for neurodivergent people (loosely). Neurodivergent minds are wired differently to neurotypical brains, so why are we continuing to measure their language levels and development based on a different measure than their brain is wired for?

Unfortunately, we are often taught such a narrow view of language, behaviour and communication and it's heavily influenced by white, middle-class, non-disabled people. Anything outside of these parameters becomes 'disordered'. When we complete assessments, we do not account for cultural differences in terms of vocabulary for example. As a neurodivergent person who is monotropic and significantly interest-driven, my vocabulary is mostly based around my passions. If I did a standardised assessment based around vocabulary, it would likely label me 'disordered' because I do not fit into the expectation to label items, I'm not remotely interested in. Some people may never have experienced situations where they have seen or come into contact with a stethoscope or specific musical instruments, that doesn't tell us their vocabulary is 'limited'.

It is very rare that I have done standardised assessments, because I tend to get more valuable information from informal assessment, listening to the person's experiences and just spending time with them. In many cases, there is no better measure than asking the person what they think of their communication and what they want some help with. An SLT might highlight that I need some support with following directions and receptive language because I scored very low in the Concepts and Following Directions part of the CELF, actually I need more working memory supports for success. I need my communication partner to break down the instructions and give me visual strategies. I need to take instructions at my own pace for success. There are no language 'interventions' that will improve my ability to follow instructions because my brain just processes language differently.

But, within the constraints of certain services, it is hard to be able to gain such information and have the time and resources for observations and relationship building. In these times, I have conducted some elements of standardised assessments and asked the young person their views on the assessment. For example, I will ask about the Understanding Spoken Paragraphs subtest: 'what was difficult/easy about that activity?' providing prompts, such as 'complex vocabulary' 'too much to process at once' 'hard to focus on and retain detail'' 'remembering the information'. As a neurodivergent person, I know that processing information that isn't of interest to me is incredibly difficult so when I assess neurodivergent young people, we discuss how stimulating the information was, whether they 'zoned out' during the activity also. At times, I will offer the written information alongside speech and write the questions down for the client to see if they are better able to process the information when there is visual support and less language demand. The main focus of my standardised assessment is getting a read on what made the activity difficult and what strategies they have to support functional communication. I want to listen to what they think, not just what they score or what I observe. Generally, my autistic and ADHD clients tend to express the same reasons for finding aspects of the CELF difficult, mostly that it was difficult to listen to and process the information provided due to motivation, amount of information and memory.

Talking Mats has been a great resource to use alongside assessments, with a focus on the person's perceived strengths and needs and what they feel supports them in their education environment. I always start with the same script to introduce the discussion around their perceived communication: 'I would like to know what you think about your communication. This is not about what I think or what your parents/teachers think, only what you think. There are no right or wrong answers.' Most children I spend time with don't want to sit in a room and complete an assessment, they want to be heard, listened to and respected and treated as the person who knows most about their own communication. When I share similar experiences, this really helps them to open up about what is tricky, for example when we talk about eye contact, I always state that it's something I 'absolutely loathe' because 'why would I want to stare into people's eyeballs?' usually the young person will relate and share their own experiences. I find these activities a great way to share a laugh about the neurodivergent experience and get insight into whether the person fulfils the criteria for autism or ADHD due to their experiences of communication for my diagnostic assessments.

How Do We Support a Neurodivergent-friendly Session?
Harriet Richardson

I recall at university being taught how to manage a session with a child with 'challenging behaviour', including putting your foot behind their chair so that they cannot move and keeping them furthest from the door so that they have less chance of leaving. That certainly isn't neuro-affirming, neither is it ethical or respectful of boundaries. Entering into a session with my neurodivergent clients I use a social story to let them know what to expect and who I am. The most important part of that social story is a list of things that I'm interested in and like to talk about, because this really helps ease a lot of anxiety. My clients have discussed how it made them relax knowing what things they could mention to make conversations easier and script their interactions. It certainly helps that I have a lot of interests, which seem to be common for neurodivergent people! (Star Wars, dogs and dinosaurs usually being the shared interests.)

The beginning of the session is an overview of what we are doing in the session and why we are here as well as setting boundaries. These include: I do not expect eye contact from you; I will not touch you without your consent, such as tapping you to get your attention; if you zone out that's fine, just ask me to repeat myself; if you don't want to do something I suggest just let me know and we can move on; I love listening to people's interests so feel free to talk about them if you would like. I then like to make sure the sensory environment is okay, such as whether they want the lights on or off, if there are any distracting noises or smells they would like me to remove etc. I always find it really important that I give them an example of my own sensory needs so that they don't feel like they are alone in their differences, for example, stating that I want to ensure that the lights are okay for them because I find bright lights really difficult to manage. On one occasion, during an assessment, we moved three different rooms due to the background noises affecting the young person's communication. They really valued being able to move as many times as they needed and a bond was developed by me sharing my similar experiences with auditory processing and tuning out noises. This meant I got a very helpful insight into their experiences for the assessment report.

Next is seating arrangements, personally I am a floor sitter but I offer different seating where I can, such as a chair, cushion/beanbag on the floor or a rug. I try to meet the young person at the level they request and sit at an angle, rather than face-to-face, to limit pressure of eye contact. I find most clients are comfortable when we sit side by side. After this, I ensure that they know they have freedom to move, stating that some people learn better by moving so if they need to get up and walk around, stim, or make noises, they can do this. I also offer fidget toys and sensory experiences within sessions because I know that keeping your hands busy whilst talking can ease the anxiety of having to look towards the person and read all the non-verbals.

I have always found it very helpful to make mind maps throughout sessions, both for my clients and for myself. When engaging in discussions, I will write down everything we are talking about in little summaries, which are connected to our overall topic for the session. This helps for many reasons, as ADHDers, it helps us to keep track of the conversation and prevent ourselves from going off on tangents, as well as reminders of the topic of discussion to return back to. It also supports memory during the session and afterwards and enables a clearer reflection and summary of the session. For those with processing differences, written and visual information can be very supportive to ensure more accessibility. The other aspect is that it reduces demand on non-verbal communication, such as eye contact because we are both looking at and adding to an object in front of us.

How Do I Support a Neurodivergent-friendly Session?
Harriet Richardson

Ideas for a one-off assessment: As we start an assessment session, I like to offer the person some choices of things they would like to do first and repeat the point that if they don't want to do something we can move on. I explain the purpose of the subtests and what they will tell me. During each subtest, I keep relating back to their interests, such as using visuals of football when I know they like football and have conversations in between the questions. At the end of the subtest, I ask for some feedback on how they found it and discuss a similar activity they might do in school and request information on what helps them during those activities.

We then look at their perceived strengths and needs and I state that there are no right or wrong answers, as it is not what anyone else thinks, just their experiences. During the assessment, I always give items that I would place in the "I need help with" section so that they don't feel as vulnerable speaking about things that are difficult for them. Sharing my own experiences has helped me connect with young people during their assessments and have more honest conversations about what they would like help with. For example, I discussed with a young person in their initial assessment that I have difficulties with processing language when information isn't stimulating for my brain and he proceeded to tell me that he could not listen to anything unrelated to his interests in school but has developed a strategy of relating everything his teacher tells him to his interests in Pokemon, which helps him focus and retain information. This gave me a wealth of information about his learning and language skills for writing his report. For this chunk of the assessment, I use a Talking Mat of strengths and needs.

We also look at the things that support the person, which include sensory aids, environmental changes and communication partners adapting their communication. This activity takes the focus off the things that they find difficult and what they want to improve on and focuses more on what other people can do to support them. This is the basis for my report because when working with neurodivergent clients, most of my recommendations are based around environmental and communication partner adaptions. Following all this information, I provide a summary for the young person of their strengths, areas of need and what other people can do to support them and propose some goals based on what they have said they want some help with. These goals will be a mixture of things the young person can be supported to develop, and environmental and communication partner adaptations to support their communication and accessibility. For this chunk of the assessment, I use a Talking Mat of things that do and don't help.

During the assessment process, I ask the young person how they would like to be identified in the report, including pronouns, name and neurodivergent identity (e.g. autistic/with autism). It's really important that we respect their individual ways of identifying and do not assume how they would like to be spoken about. Generally, when we write reports as neuro-affirming practitioners, we automatically favour referring to the person as an 'autistic person' and it can feel uncomfortable to go against this pattern, going back to writing person-first language 'with autism'. However, if this is how the person wishes to be identified, it is important that this is respected. A person may also wish to identify as both and therefore, the report should reflect this, interchangeably using both terms as requested, rather than solely using the one that we prefer or feels more comfortable for us.

Goal Setting

Following on from beginning to think about affirming speech and language therapy practice, it is important to consider how we set goals for neurodivergent individuals. There are set formulas that we often think about in terms of goals; particularly common amongst speech and language therapists is the favoured SMART system: specific, measurable, achievable, realistic and time bound.

In the following chapters we will look specifically at goals for different areas of communication, but here we can touch on the challenges with goal settings and some general themes that you can explore and weave into your goals irrespective of what they are around.

Kerry Murphy shares an alternative option through her SHARE framework for goal setting: Suitable, Holistic, Adaptable, Relatable, Engaging and Enjoyable (Murphy, no date). Within this framework Kerry considers alternative ways to focus on play, in particular in the early years to support development of skills. I would argue that actually this can be transitioned across to all models, if we think about play in its broadest sense; to engage in an activity for enjoyment. Ultimately that is what therapy should be about!

We can also look to SCRUFFY targets, developed by Penny Lacey (2010), which is a welcome alternative to SMART targets in my view. Let's face it, there is likely merit in having systems and structures to the way in which we work, as this can enable consistency for service users, it provides clear expectations from them and the support they are getting. SCRUFFY targets focus on goals that are student led, creative, relevant, unspecified and fun for youngsters. Imagine here, we can switch out student to 'service user', and youngsters for 'your client', and suddenly this has breadth across all age ranges. Which sounds really quite marvellous, and it seems that this is a way we can give structure to our goals and how we write and talk about them, without them seeming to be too scatter gun. Bryony Rust has a wonderful video (2022) explaining these in the context of working with young children. It seems to me that these could be a lovely way to go to be affirming, while still giving clarity and direction to the support we offer.

Conclusion

We have talked about theories that include a wide range of topics, that are part of a holistic profile we must think about when we are working with neurodivergent individuals, it is important that you seek more information on these topics and consider how they might impact your work going forward.

We have explored goal setting, and while it feels strange to be suggesting to 'go against' what everyone tells us is best, but really, who is everyone? Where did you learn about SMART targets? Do you believe they are helpful tools, and if so, why? Does that feel affirming to you?

There is no right answer, just take this as a moment to pause and reflect: when did you last think critically about your goal setting, what additional factors do you consider and where have your skills and ways of working come from, and who 'said so'.

Chapter Summary

- Your reflections matter: question everything you do, it's time to think critically about all your practice with neurodivergent individuals from the point of referral onwards.
- Your critical thinking matters: really dive into the assessment process and the tools you use. We can be the change in the expectations of others around us.

- Your actions matter: reasonable adjustments can start in therapy, and do not just form recommendations following assessment.
- Your goals matter: and don't necessarily have to be SMART, and once again we can start a ripple here of change, challenging processes and systems in the way we work.

References and Resources

Ayres, A.J. (1972) *Sensory Integration and Learning Disorders*. Los Angeles, CA: Western Psychological Services.

Bowlby, J. (1988) *A Secure Base: Parent-child Attachment and Healthy Human Development*. New York: Basic Books.

Chapman, L. and Mears, K. (eds) (2024) 'Ways of being, knowing & doing: An anthology for neurodivergent informed practice'. https://autismbooksbyautisticauthors.com/ways-of-being-knowing-and-doing/ (accessed on 30/07/2024).

Dundon, R. (2023) *A Therapist's Guide to Neurodiversity Affirming Practice with Children and Young People*. London: Jessica Kingsley Publishers.

Lacey, P. (2010) 'Smart and scruffy targets'. *SLD Experience*, 57, 16-21.

Maslow, A.H. (1943) A theory of human motivation. *Psychological Review*, 50(4), 370-396.

Murphy, K. (no date) 'Share framework: Developing connection over compliance'. SHARE FRAMEWORK.pdf (eyfs4me.com) (accessed on 25/08/2024).

Porges, S.W. (2021) *Polyvagal Safety: Attachment, Communication and Self-regulation*. New York: WW Norton.

Rust, B. (2022) 'Speech and language targets: SMART or SCRUFFY'. www.youtube.com/watch?v=oEOOcgKTmCE (accessed on 25/08/2024).

Sumpter, T. (2021) *The Seeds of Learning: A Cognitive Processing Model for Speech, Language, Literacy and Executive Functioning*. Elk Grove, CA: ELH Publishing, LLC.

Talking Mats. (no date) 'Improving communication, improving lives' (accessed on 20/05/2024).

Yu, B. and Sterponi, L. (2022) 'Toward neurodiversity: How conversation analysis can contribute to a new approach to social communication assessment'. *Language, Speech, and Hearing Services in Schools*, 54(1), 27-41.

6
Expressive Communication

Presuming and Honouring

Expressive and receptive language are the bread of butter of speech and language therapy. (Total aside, but super honesty here, in my first post having had a job as a learning disability support worker and some time travelling following qualifying, I was so unaware of my incompetence and on my first day had to Google expressive and receptive language as my colleague spoke about them! I'd like to think that I am a tad more aware of these basic concepts now ...)

So, expressive communication and receptive language are areas that many neurodivergent individuals can experience challenges with, not least because of the double empathy problem. This chapter will explore expressive communication specifically, and there are some core values that we must integrate into our thinking if we are to truly deliver support for expressive communication in a neurodiversity-affirming way.

First, that we presume potential. Just take a moment and say that out loud. Listen to those words when they hit your ears and think about what they mean. Historically, within the deficits-based model, we have presumed a lack of competence and expected individuals to take steps to prove themselves to us. Their potential has been limited by the lens through which they were viewed, and opportunities diminished because of that.

As experienced therapists, we can certainly apply our experience to help guide us and others in terms of what are realistic expectations for an individual's expressive communication. However, there are often times narratives that suggest an individual might have 'maxed out' their communication potential, or that they must hit a certain list of skills before offering different types of support.

Second, that we honour all forms of communication. Historically, I am certainly guilty of pushing a communication tool and not honouring a child who is communicating in a perfectly valid way. All forms of communication are valid, and we can support individuals to use spoken words, and alternative and augmentative forms of communication (AAC). For a lot of individuals, we must seek a toolbox of different things that can support them in different situations, with different regulation levels and that can match their energy and capacity for communication flexibly.

This shift moves from some of the highest support needs individuals, through to those with low support needs, who might still need some forms of AAC for example during periods of burnout, or heightened processing moments when language is a cognitive function that might be too tricky. No longer is the phrase 'use your words' justifiable. Speech is quite quick and efficient, yes? So, if someone could use their words, they would. If they can't then we need to look at other ways to support them, and honour that.

Additionally, this includes honouring spoken words as they come, for some neurodivergent and particularly autistic individuals they may use echolalia as a meaningful form of expressive communication. We must honour this language, we might have to do some detective work to understand what it is they are communicating, but we honour and acknowledge those words.

We must consider that the type of language used by neurodivergent individuals may be different to neurotypicals, for example the grammatical structures might be different for someone with a specific learning difference, or their tone might be different for example if a person is autistic. When supporting these differences, we are not in a place now to say those differences are deficits and as such be working on changing that language within therapy. We may, if the individual seeks that as their goal, and this difference is having a negative impact of their functioning and quality of life support them in some way, but that might be to understand and advocate for their differences, as opposed to trying to teach them a different way of using language.

Expressive communication is part of our identity, and within this we also have to consider how our communicative identity might not be shared with the individuals you are supporting. Consider for example an expressive language sample, taken from an individual who is from a different cultural background to you as a therapist, and how you analyse that. Would you be commenting and scoring differences in grammar as negative? When perhaps they are very much culturally appropriate. With the evolving diversity within communities and the range of different cultures and languages that we might be supporting, we have to cast the net wider in terms of what is 'acceptable' use of language. Bring your awareness to any potential judgements that you might have because of someone's tone, use of language or social interactions. And, when supporting expressive communication take into account those cultural differences, both in language you might be teaching and things like programming of AAC.

Within all this work and development, we must take an intersectional approach, and this is no different with expressive communication. We must consider an individual holistically, understanding how intersections might impact access, safety and preference of communication support tools. It we embrace and explore these complex concepts, we can tailor our recommendations to be not only accessible and effective, but also respectful, safe and empowering for each individual.

How to Communicate with Autistic People: Harriet Richardson

One of my dreams in life is to teach neurotypicals how to communicate with neurodivergent people. I hope that one day this becomes part of the Speech & Language Therapy course and SLTs, as students, are trained in how to differ their communication to support autistic clients they will support in the future. Instead, we enter the world of work ready to teach neurotypical social skills to neurodivergents, believing that neurotypical communication is the only correct way to interact. Instead, why don't we focus a little on how we can communicate better with autistic service users and how we can make their experiences more comfortable? Here's a just a few ideas (based on my own experience and discussions with my autistic/ADHD clients):

1. Be aware of the communication environment.

    As sensory beings, communicating isn't going to be easy if we have to constantly be processing and be overwhelmed by the sensory environment around us. Check that the person's sensory needs are being met to ensure best access to a conversation.

2. Provide alternative forms of communication

    During sessions, try to ensure that you have your language supported by visual information, so that there is less processing demand for the autistic person. I usually tend to write things down as we go along and demonstrate using gesture or picture support.

    Alongside this, I also encourage clients to explain themselves through alternative means, such as drawing what they are referencing or showing me on their device and so on. I've spent a lot of time on YouTube researching their areas of interest in order to structure the conversation. Technology can be really helpful! During assessments, I always make sure that the person knows they can use the 'chat function' in remote sessions or use AAC on their phone etc in face-to-face sessions, if this is easier for them to express themselves.

3. Allow for processing time

    Medical appointments and similar situations have always been extremely difficult for me to process and use language in. I usually need a supportive person with me to help process the information and ask the questions I need to ask. Generally, I will try to get out of the appointment as soon as possible so will tell the healthcare professional what I think they want to hear. It's really important that we identify that for many autistic people, times of stress, new environments and unfamiliar people can make language processing even more challenging.

When we have neurodivergent clients, we must ensure accessibility in communication. Sometimes the client may need us to write down the key points of a session and hand it to us at the end or send a summary of what we talked about. The client might need visual formats for our explanations, such as social stories or video demonstrations. They may need additional time between asking questions and them answering. They may need time to answer questions you might have outside of the session. For example, I tell the adults who I assess that if they think of anything they didn't say or wanted me to know after the assessment, they can email it over to me afterwards, or I can send any questions I might ask before the session so they have chance to process it all.

4. Consider Auditory Processing Disorder (APD)

   There is not much known about APD generally, however it is something that time and time again comes up for the clients I spend time with and other people I interact with in the neurodivergent community. APD can create communication difficulties, especially for things like phone calls, big social events and in multi-sensory environments. I spent most of my life wondering why I couldn't take a phone call with someone else being in the room and hated to ever call someone. Now, I can identify that any background noise on either end of the call is too distracting, and I cannot tune it out and listen to the speaker or formulate what I want to say. Many of the clients I spend time with discuss feeling drained after going to restaurants because they weren't able to tune out the background noise and had to strain to hear other people the whole time.

   For this reason, we have to ensure that our environments are quiet and accessible for those who experience APD. It's important that we observe when the client might be having difficulty focusing if there is background noise around us. During assessment clinics, I have noticed that when there are people outside of the room, myself and my clients cannot pay attention to the assessment or the conversation. As a result, I now pause the interaction until the corridor is clear before resuming the conversation. Things like ticking clocks and traffic noise nearby can also have an impact on the client, and is likely to impact assessment data, if this is being collected.

5. Please be literal

   Many clients I speak to feel that they can understand sarcasm and non-literal language with more familiar people, but with those they don't know, this is very hard to read. This is something I relate to. I'm a very sarcastic person, but if someone uses sarcasm, I find it very hard to read this, especially if they are unknown or I am in a new or stressful environment. As neurodivergent people, we are going to experience people speaking non-literally all the time, so it is important that we can identify when this is happening. This is why I suggest to parents that they still use non-literal language, but they always explain what they mean when they do. It's really important that we pick times when we use non-literal language, because neurodivergent people's capacity for understanding and processing this kind of language can fluctuate. For example, it is not a good idea to use idioms and sarcasm when the person is stressed or in a meltdown, as well as when they are experiencing new transitions.

6. Direct and specific communication

    Lots of autistic people are direct communicators, meaning that often we can come across as abrupt because we say what we mean and mean what we say. I often appreciate other people being direct and honest with me, so that I don't have to spend energy that I don't have trying to figure out the person's intentions and what they really mean. When I go to doctor's appointments, I want them to give me key information that's specific and easily processed, such as what will happen, when and how.

    It can be extremely frustrating when people don't say what they mean, especially around time concepts. So often, we use phrases like: 'I'll be with you in a minute', 'see you later', 'let's do that later', 'maybe we could do that soon'. For a lot of autistic people, that uncertainty of time concepts can be difficult to manage, and we can take them literally. In healthcare settings, if a doctor tells me that they will be with me 'soon' my perception of 'soon' is within the next five minutes and if it gets extended past that period of time, I start to become very restless and irritable. Specificity is so key to supporting autistic clients.

7. Skip the small talk

    Whenever I run assessment sessions for teenagers, we have the same conversations again and again about how much we loathe small talk. 'Why are you asking me about the weather when you can see it for yourself?' one client once laughed with me. Many autistic people find social chit-chat confusing or unfulfilling, however there are other autistics that like it because they can develop set scripts for this. Personally, small talk is the bane of my life and exhausts me.

    During sessions, I like to jump straight into conversations with my clients about their interests and passions, rather than waste time speaking about their weekend. I work on this theory: if something is interesting to the other person, they will tell me about it. When I return home from work and my partner asks me how my day was, I often feel infuriated because he should know by now that if there was something I wanted to share, I would have infodumped about it already.

8. Information share, reduce questions

    So many times, my neurotypical colleagues comment on how difficult they found having a conversation with the client I just had a session with. I will often respond saying that we had a wonderful chat, and each time my colleagues can't get their head around it. Really, it's quite simple, I communicate 'neurodivergently', they communicate 'neurotypically'. The divide between our communication styles creates a breakdown in communication (see 'The double empathy problem' – Dr Damien Milton).

    From observing my neurotypical colleagues, I have found that there is a certain pattern to their conversations with the clients. Initially, they will ask the person questions, which are very general: 'what did you do at the weekend', for example. They will then ask further questions when the client gives them a brief answer before then speaking about their own experiences, briefly, expecting the client to comment on what they said with interest. As a neurodivergent person, I approach these conversations differently. I first enter the conversation with lots of expression, facially, tone of voice and ensure that I am the one taking on the language demand, talking about random things to ensure they don't have to initiate the conversation. I either gather information about their areas of interest before the session or try to guess their interests based on their belongings that they bring to the session. Then I use the phrase 'Ooh, that's interesting. Tell me more' and allow them as much space as they need to infodump about their passion. In turn, I will comment about my knowledge of the topic or discuss my own interests, providing more than just brief detail. I ask questions that are meaningful, rather than just to continue the conversation. I show enthusiasm and genuine interest in what they are speaking about, because I'm fully aware myself of when people are just humouring me. For many neurodivergent people, we will have been told not to talk 'too much' about our interests and will feel unsure of whether it is safe to share our interests, so our interest needs to be genuine.

The most important thing I always advise people communicating with autistic people is comment more than question. There is nothing worse than being asked a series of questions, especially about a very uninteresting topic or social chit-chat, like my most recent holiday. As a person with intense passions, I want us to get to that topic so I can feel comfortable in the interaction and share all the information I have in my brain. I will not get there by being asked direct and conversational questions, but by the other person making comments and sharing their own experiences.

Here's an example of how neurotypical clinicians may handle a conversation with an autistic client and how I would handle it differently:

Clinician:	What did you do this weekend?
Client:	Not much, just stayed at home really.
Clinician:	Oh, what did you get up to at home?
Client:	Read books.
Clinician:	What books did you read?
Client:	(frustrated) Nothing interesting.
Hat:	I had the worst weekend, my sink started leaking and I was cleaning up the whole time. I hope you had a better time than I did!
Client:	Probably not, I just spent the weekend at home
Hat (notices the client doesn't have an interest in discussing their weekend):	Ooh those are cool stickers on your lunchbox, what are they from?

Client: Well ... (leads into infodump).

9. Converse while doing other things

Sitting down to speak to even some of my best friends can be incredibly uncomfortable for me. My partner plays cricket and I will go to watch and talk to our friends while we are there, all facing the direction of the cricket rather than looking at each other. This is much more comfortable for me and I think people will notice I'm much chattier and more relaxed during these times. In therapy sessions, I was never comfortable sitting directly in front of my therapist and talking to her. Instead, I now have remote sessions, sit there with my fidgets and my assistance dog on my knee and talk with ease. When meeting friends, I usually opt for a walk and talk or some sort of activity that keeps my body occupied while conversing. For this reason, I find it just as uncomfortable as my clients to sit across from each other in a clinic room and discuss their experiences and have a conversation.

To support these uncomfortable interactions, I bring fidget toys in the sessions, ask them to bring things with them that are of interest to them, and they'd like to talk to me about, and have games and activities at hand. There is often so much emphasis placed on a client coming to a session and just talking and this can be very difficult for autistic people, as language can be overwhelming for us and conversations with unfamiliar people can be uncomfortable.

Expressive Language Assessments

NEWSFLASH – there are basically no assessments that are written for neurodivergent people in relation to expressive language. So, we have to make the best of what we have. There are two challenges with current assessments for expressive language: one is that where not written for neurodivergent individuals those types of questions might be difficult for a person to process and respond to and understand what the expectation is and therefore they score low. Additionally, the scoring systems do not take into account potential differences in the language use of a neurodivergent individuals, and again they score low because they have not got the 'correct' structures to score.

Expressive language samples can be a neutral way of looking at an individual's strengths, differences and challenges. Here, comment can be offered without a negative lens. Particularly for children and young people, a label of 'disordered' language, alongside low percentile ranks, can have a highly negative impact on the narrative surrounding them, both with parents and family members as well as with education professionals. These individuals may score low because their understanding and use of language is different, but that does not mean they are less, which let's face it a 9th percentile rank certainly carries.

When we consider formal assessments of expressive language, they are most often used to look at neurotypical children, either in support of differential diagnosis but more often than not as a way to identify their challenges and create a package of support to enable them to develop their skills along a developmental pathway to get them to the age equivalent, or percentile rank more within normal limits.

In addition, some of our expressive language assessments (I am thinking here in particular of vocabulary tests) are such a question of semantics often linked to experiences. If a child refers to a picture with a semantically accurate but 'incorrect' response then they may score down, and if we use the assessment to score them against developmental norms, this child is now 'below average'. However, this does not take into account the unique way that a lot of neurodivergent children see the world, and their application and understanding of language.

Speaking with speech and language therapists, there is often a desire or a request from local authorities and similar bodies for percentiles. But we must be the change makers, we have studied hard, we continue to meet our HCPC standards in continuing our professional development, and if all therapists share the same narrative that a language sample is enough or that we can use these tools to explore language but not score their percentiles, we can make the shift. The change can be led by us, we are the experts.

It seems that speech and language therapists apply the same process for neurodivergent individuals as they do for neurotypical children, and that is simply not fair. These individuals' brains are neurologically different, holding them to account along a developmental pathway that they might not be following is disabling. If we consider for a moment a child with a hearing impairment, we would comment on their language use, we would put in reasonable support strategies to enhance their expressive communication and develop their use of language, and we would not be trying to get them to not wear hearing aids anymore and be a hearing person.

We have to consider what we know for a lot of neurodivergent individuals and that is the concept of a spikey profile. These individuals may not follow those typically linear pathways of development in relation to their speech, language and communication. They may have some serious strengths way beyond 'their years' developmentally, and other challenges that place them way 'behind' developmentally. If we see it as a comparison that narrative shifts, as opposed to seeing it as their individual profile.

When supporting a neurodivergent individual, we are not trying to get them to where their neurotypical peers are developmentally with their expressive language. While for some this might very much be the trajectory they have naturally followed, it should not be our aim for those who haven't; it is likely if they have not, it is because their brain wiring has meant that they cannot or have not responded to the support they have been getting so far. So, we can seek to understand that wiring, and build on its strengths.

This may be feather ruffling. It might feel a bit scary to question these assessments we often hold so dear. However, progression and change are scary.

> **REFLECTION**
>
> How do you use assessments for neurodivergent individuals? Can you disrupt the systems within which you work to make sure assessment is more meaningful? With the tools that you have to assess neurodivergent individuals can you shift their use to be a more neutral way of capturing their expressive language profile?

Gestalt Language Processing

A final point to explore in relation to expressive language assessment is the concept of echolalia, which is prevalent particularly in the autistic population. This is a form of expressive language that can be immediate or delayed. An individual using immediate echolalia may repeat back things they have just heard, and it is very common in question-based situations.

Example:

Adult: Do you want a biscuit or fruit?

Child: Biscuit or fruit.

This is an example of immediate echolalia. In this form we usually see it for a few different reasons. It might be a way of processing what has been said, thinking about the language and remembering it to respond to. It might be a way of engaging in turn taking in a conversation when they don't have the language to respond, or comment or extend. We can also see immediate echolalia as a sign of dysregulation, or an indication that what has been said has not been understood.

In its delayed format echolalia can sound like scripts, which may be taken from a variety of places, including things they have heard someone in their world say, lyrics from songs, phrases from stories or programmes and films. This is an area with lots of research that has been going on since the 1970s, led by Anne Peters (1983) and Dr Barry Prizant (1983). (Who incidentally is the author of an amazing book, and co-host of a brilliant same titled podcast, 'Uniquely Human'. If you haven't got it, buy it and read it!)

Their research pioneered a new way of looking at those individuals who use echolalia and where previously it was felt to be meaningless behaviour, they sought to explore that it holds a deeper meaning and communicative function.

Fast forward to 2012 when Marge Blanc (2012) published her book surrounding support strategies and a framework for assessing these individuals, and a speech and language therapist in America named Alexandria Zachos (no date) read the work in 2016, and began implementing these strategies and seeing huge success and launched an online platform and marketed it through social media to grow a huge following and make the work of Prizant, Peters and Blanc better known and widely used. Delayed echolalia is now more commonly referred to as a gestalt language processing style, where a child is learning language in chunks, that hold a meaning for them, that may not always be clear to those around them. The first step is being curious and doing the detective work to understand where these chunks have come from, what was going on at the original point this language 'stuck' to enable us to model a broad range of language in a way that is suitable and interesting for these individuals' brains to hook onto.

Marg describes a framework known as Natural Language Acquisition that enables individuals to understand echolalia in the context of six stages; her book covers assessment, through to goals and support strategies. If you are working with a child who is appearing to use echolalia to communicate, reading and understanding this several decades-old piece of research and accessing current thinking around the topic will be pivotal for effective support of individuals whose expressive language is mostly in this format.

While we speak about expressive language it is important to also note that gestalt language processors don't have to be speaking, and therefore a few points to consider are if you have an individual present with:

- Rhymical humming, that sounds like words or songs
- Long, unintelligible strings of jargon
- Repetitively watching the same clips from programmes or films
- Using lots of single words, that have not progressed into short phrases or beyond
- Implementing typical language development tools via spoken language or AAC use have been unsuccessful

Again, this is where that language sample in a natural way can only serve as a great tool for seeing how a neurodivergent individuals use of language is showing up, whether it is echolalia or other features to note. For more information I would signpost you to the book *Gestalt Language Processing: Supporting Autistic and Neurodivergent Children with Natural Language Acquisition*.

My Experiences as a Gestalt Language Processor: Harriet Richardson

As a child I used to spend most of my summers in Spain, on a complex where my grandparents lived. We would often visit my uncle, who was Spanish, so I would listen to a lot of people speaking Spanish and was very motivated to learn the language. I picked up on phrases that were helpful to get by while in Spain, such as 'I need a table for four people' and 'I would like a tomato and tuna pasty'. I remember listening to my brother make random phrases in Spanish, including 'what a disaster, my pottery donkey is broken', and would repeat these over and over to myself. Now that I reflect back on it, I realise that I learnt Spanish in a Gestalt pattern. Instead of assembling the individual words, I memorised the peaks and troughs of the intonation patterns and the words blurred together as one long script. I knew what it meant as a whole, initially, but was unable to understand and separate each individual word. After using the phrase many times, I begun to separate the sections of the phrase into 'what a disaster' and 'pottery donkey', trialling them in new sentences. After this process, I started to dissect each individual word so that I could use it more naturally when constructing sentences in real time. I didn't realise until recently when I discovered Gestalt Language Processing, that it explained how I learnt the language.

Unfortunately, I don't recall how I learnt language as a child, so I would never have known I was a GLP without learning Spanish later in life. My language profile in Spanish is very similar to other GLPs, I was always drawn to the sound of the language and copied the intonation patterns, so much so that I developed a southern accent and dialect and people thought I was fluent in Spanish based on my accent. However, whilst learning Spanish in the classroom, I was often told 'the penny just wasn't dropping'. I couldn't learn the vocabulary in single words and put sentences together that were grammatically correct. My writing was never reflective of my spoken ability and was littered with grammatical errors. I couldn't get my head around verb tenses or for the different pronouns. In fact, my Spanish teacher often commented that she couldn't get her head around how I could be doing so well expressively but not be able to transfer the skills to writing, actual conversation or understanding. Now it very much makes sense!

Although I progressed through language development without need for support in English, I still have times where I am only able to access the earlier learnt and more accessible vocabulary. When I experience heightened emotions, I tend to return to set scripts and repeated language. My partner has often commented that I use the phrase 'five hundred times' when I'm upset and trying to explain things. I have no idea where that gestalt originated but I would suspect it was heard when I was upset and frustrated. During these times of heightened emotions, I find it extremely difficult to understand and process language and it can be very painful to process what people are saying to me. I start to get confused and only understand and retain certain chunks in what people say to me. We've found that I need clear and simple language during meltdowns as a result of this. I also use communication cards, which have set scripts on them when I do need to communicate during these times.

More recently, I have noticed how the way I learn language impacts me in adulthood. I find learning more complex vocabulary, which is highly contextual very difficult. For example, when learning neuro-affirming language and anti-racism concepts, I have needed to watch lots of videos of people speaking about and using the language to be able to understand terminology more completely and be able to use it myself. When words are not used in a variety of contexts across my life, it can take me a very long time to incorporate terminology in my own language and be able to understand what others are saying in relation to this. I am not able to rely on reading definitions, I need real-life examples and listening to people using it in context and in speech.

After my autistic identification, I didn't see myself as experiencing echolalia and it's taken me a long time to get my head around what is echolalia for me. The more I process my way of learning and processing language, the more I identify my echolalia, which is different from what I was ever taught it was at university. For example, I find myself drawn to song lyrics particularly and will repeat these over and over, often writing them down. My high school diary being filled with sections of Taylor Swift songs and my walls at university were covered in my own song lyrics that I would get enjoyment from reading and saying repeatedly. When I'm listening to songs where I really enjoy the lyrics, I have to say them out loud or whisper them if I'm in public. I feel intense joy from listening to the sound of my favourite lyrics and the patterns between the words, the music and their correlation to each other is such a magical experience. I could listen to music all day every day for this reason. I also experience more stereotyped echolalia and have begun to notice these the more my understanding of echolalia expands. I recognised many of my childhood and lifelong gestalts when rewatching the Star Wars trilogy only recently. Apparently, Jar Jar Binks' language was the basis for many of my gestalts, I never understand why I referred to myself as 'Mesa' until recently! I was also at work recently when someone referred to 'the triad of impairment' and my brain immediately began to recite the script of language from my brother's childhood video game: 'remember the difference between a triad and a triangle. A triangle has three sides, a triad only two'. I couldn't help myself laughing and needed to leave the room so that I could go and mutter the words to myself over and over just to get the feelings out.

Something that is so wonderful about being echolalic is the connection it brings me to other people. My dad and I are both echolalic and will repeat sequences of phrases to each other of Monty Python or Star Wars. We have so much shared enjoyment and connection through this interaction, which many other people do not understand. The fact that programmes aim to reduce echolalia for some individuals is something I find so upsetting because echolalia is so special to me and my family members.

Expressive Language Goal Setting

So, first we assess and then we make our recommendations and set our goals. This becomes a complicated and challenging shift, because what we are saying is that neurodivergent individuals may use language in a different way. If you are not a neurodivergent therapist, how can you know what that different way is? If you haven't worked with many neurodivergent individuals, where will your knowledge come from about communication styles?

When we begin to think about goals for expressive language we can think broadly about two different levels of support needs, those with AAC needs and those with spoken language needs. There will of course be individuals who cross over both of these profiles and we can use the information here to enable and support.

First, the biggest thing I would ask once you have assessed an individual and are thinking about setting a goal, as those goals come to mind consider the following:

- Why is that a problem?
- Who is this goal for?
- What tools might I be using to support this goal?
- Are those tools neurodiversity-affirming?

It feels helpful at this point to do a few 'walk throughs' of different individuals that may show up on your caseload.

Individual 1:

Age 3;07 (years; months), white male, diagnosed Global Developmental Delay, experiences sensory processing differences, not yet speaking.

Assessment has identified that they can follow simple instructions within context and the provision of objects and symbols supports their understanding. They vocalise and engage in people games, and enjoy running, jumping and climbing. They particularly enjoy bubbles, inset puzzles and repetitive games like posting and ball runs.

They can hand lead adults to what they want and will use objects to communicate, for example, get their shoes when they want to go out. They experience frustration and distress and adults around the child believe this is due to their lack of communication skills and being able to say what they want, or what they are experiencing.

They will let an adult join in their play alongside them when regulated and will initiate by giving an adult an item to ask for help or their participation.

> **REFLECTION**
>
> Pause for a moment before reading on, challenge yourself to spend a minute or two, scribble in the margins or note down your thoughts. After reading this information consider:
>
> - What are this child's strengths?
> - What might impact on their communication skills? What reasonable adjustments might be needed?
> - What would your goal focus on?

What do you do?

Well honour their current communication first, this is a strength. Commenting on their skills to be able to lead an adult shows a lot of cognitive processes, it also highlights their skills to initiate, focusing on their strengths. That they have a range of different interests and engage with people in play, all of these will offer this child opportunities for communication. They already have some means, but can we extend those? What about their reasons?

So, if we are looking to work on their means and reasons, a goal around extending play-based communication would be meaningful and fun. 'More' is functional and can be transferred across many different activities and settings, both for regulatory and basic need items such as 'more' food/drink, 'more' cuddles, tickles, bouncing, oral chew tools, squashing, it can be used for meaningful engagement 'more' singing, chasing, bubbles, and so on.

Our goal might read something like 'Child to be able to communicate more consistently when offered meaningful opportunities, with unrestricted access to regulatory strategies and inclusive communication tools by the end of the half-term'.

Individual 2:

Age 10;09, Black, female, diagnosed ADHD.

Assessment identifies when in a quiet space with unrestricted access to movement, this child can follow complex instructions, understand abstract concepts and hold engaging two-way conversations. Observations in the classroom saw the child unable to engage in a lesson for longer than 10 minutes, at which point their need for movement meant they engaged in seeking behaviours that were punished by the teacher after repeated reminders to sit still, with all four chair legs on the floor, resulting in a detention and having to stay in from their break for 10 minutes.

> **REFLECTION**
>
> Pause for a moment before reading on, note down your thoughts. After reading this information consider:
>
> - What are this child's strengths?
> - What might impact on their communication skills? What reasonable adjustments might be needed?
> - What would your goal focus on?

What do you do?

My less professional response here would be to throw a copy of *The Explosive Child*, by Ross W. Greene at the teacher, swiftly followed by Alfie Kohn's book *Punished by Rewards*. But in all seriousness, this kind of experience is all too common for neurodivergent children, particularly those ADHD profiles.

The assessment highlighted this child's potential, so there are a few things to consider here. The environment and how it might be able to be more enabling – in particular at this age in primary school where the child is likely in one classroom with one teacher for most of their time. Exploring with the child what movement do they like, and then teaching them how to express their needs to move in a way that works with the teacher and ensures that movement is unrestricted; this could be an exit card to go for a quick walk, it might be a space in the classroom to retreat to for a quick bounce, or some alternative seating options, things under the desk to wiggle feet on, or TheraBand to bounce their legs off.

The goal might be something along the lines of 'Child will recognise when their body needs to move and express this in an agreed way with their teacher to seek unrestricted access to movement throughout their day'.

This goal, while based on expressive communication, does hold some deeper cognitive requirements in terms of self-awareness, interoceptive understanding and connection and planning. We will explore this further in future chapters.

Individual 3

Age 21;07, white female, diagnosed Dyslexia, sensory processing differences and self-diagnosed autistic.

Assessment identifies challenges with language processing, in particular spoken language and lengthy instructions. Has experienced difficulties in making and maintaining relationships and has self-referred due to challenges in their place of work and concerns over their capacity to complete the workload. Additionally, it has been noted to them in a recent review that their blunt communication style is causing other colleagues and clients to feel upset and uncomfortable.

> **REFLECTION**
>
> Pause for a moment before reading on, note down your thoughts. After reading this information consider:
>
> - What are this individual's strengths?
> - What might impact on their communication skills? What reasonable adjustments might be needed?
> - What would your goal focus on?

What do you do?

Well, here we have to explore the impact of the differences in communication on the individual's goals for life. We can explore with them what they would like to achieve, and also their understanding of themselves and views on disclosing and advocating for their differences.

In order to work in an affirming way, we would ideally explore identity and challenges within their profile through therapy, and enable the individual to feel confident to disclose their challenges within the workplace, and to friends. In turn, then, we might work with them as to what they feel are reasonable adjustments in the workplace that they can speak to their employer about: this might include written instructions, or spoken instructions are followed up with an email to confirm. Perhaps having an email footer that says 'I am Dyslexic and Autistic, my communication style is ...' to notify and enable others to understand, with increased understanding comes a different perspective. This too can then cross over into relationships; if the individual has an understanding of themselves and their communication style, they can advocate for this with friends and partners, what their love languages are, what they need to regulate, how best to communicate with them, and other key things.

Our goal might read something like 'Individual will be able to list a set of reasonable adjustments to explore with their line manager at their next review'.

Individual 4

Age 9;03, brown male, profound and multiple learning disabilities, wheelchair user and ambulant with a walking frame, sensory processing differences, exposure to both English and Chinese languages, currently minimally speaking.

The case history identifies that this child has had restricted access to communication tools. Informal basic assessment highlights understanding of routine instructions, and concepts, but equally has engaged in simple conversations and interactions around sharing joy and humour with AAC supports offered during assessment. Both their parents and education team feel this child has potential for communicating more with the right tools.

> **REFLECTION**
>
> Pause for a moment before reading on, note down your thoughts. After reading this information consider:
>
> - What are this child's strengths?
> - What might impact on their communication skills? What reasonable adjustments might be needed?
> - What would your goal focus on?

What do you do?

Here, we have to consider cultural and bilingual aspects when we are thinking about goals and expectations. We can recognise from the description that he will need access to some form of AAC, what elements of privilege might impact on their access? Does this individual's parents need language support to access the health care systems? When we are advising, how do we consider bilingual family communication needs?

Our goal might read something like 'Individual will have unrestricted access to communication supports across all settings and adult communication partners will have accessing training in teaching communication tools by the end of the term'.

Expressive Language Supports

When we are thinking about how we support expressive language skills it seems sensible to consider a few different things as we delve into this topic.

1. We have a cohort of neurodivergent individuals who use AAC to some extent and this is a large topic we will cover.
2. We have a cohort of neurodivergent individuals who are speaking and in education and therefore there are some expectations around literacy and language use for education purposes.
3. We have a cohort of neurodivergent individuals who may exist across both these groups.

So, the tools we have at our disposal for supporting language are vast. Some are more structured resource-based tools, others are more about adult language modelling and others are AAC tools.

How do we know which ones to use? Are some 'not allowed'? Well, there is no secret answer here. The considerations are complex, but ultimately not outside of our critical thinking skills as speech and language therapists. There can be a lean into 'off the shelf' packages of support for neurodivergent individuals, a regular set of support recommendations that do not differ vastly from child to child. Attention Autism, Social Thinking and the Picture Exchange Communication System, are the kinds of approaches I am talking about.

And while having specific tools to recommend can be incredibly helpful, where for a lot of individuals regular bespoke therapy is just not available, they miss the nuance of neurodivergence and the flexibility that might be required. They do not (for the most part) have a neurodiversity-affirming lens and can be delivered by well-meaning practitioners in settings following a speech and language therapist's recommendations to the letter which again does not leave room for a bespoke, flexible and nuanced approach. These are also approaches that without proper training can result in practices that do not follow affirming practice and become more punitive. I have seen this particularly with bucket time, where practitioners haven't had training, and deliver 'buckets' and children are made to sit down, remain seated and it becomes a battle.

First point here is that we need better training for support staff and this is something as therapists we must seek to do more of. If we can impact the process of being neurodiversity-affirming committed on to our health, social and education colleagues, for those who might be supporting our recommendations we can enable better outcomes.

If a list of recommendations at the end of a report ends up with a teacher who has an understanding of the critical thinking skills that need applying, we can hope for more for that child in their care.

> **Practice Example**
>
> An Autistic individual who has a recommendation of Attention Autism, who can be dysregulated at times but is still 'made' to return to their seat for the bucket is likely to get quite frustrated at this experience. But if there is a Teacher with an ND-affirming lens leading that session, who respects that individual's need for movement and thinks flexibly, their participation may increase in the session if, for example, they can move and stand at the back of the classroom to engage.
>
> A child within a mainstream group who is entering a secondary English Language class, where the speech and language therapist's recommendations were to integrate word maps for less frequent or more complex language, but the Teacher applies their understanding of the child and knows that today's lesson, while having language that fits the recommendations, is language that the child in fact has understanding of and skills so that recommendation is not taken up at that point in time.

Question everything. When it comes to developing our practice to support expressive language it is about questioning everything we put in place and thinking critically. This includes consideration of our recommendations through an intersectional lens. Access to things like robust AAC are impacted on by an individual's level of privilege and financial support. Or language skills to navigate the systems for referrals or charity supports. The expectations of expressive communication can differ from culture to culture. Some recommendations might mean an individual becomes unsafe in their communities if we are encouraging them to unmask their expressive communication preferences and styles.

If we return to our examples from goal setting and take Child 1, who we are going to work on 'more' with using their meaningful activities and preferred games and interactions, we might start to think about how we are going to teach 'more'. Symbols, signs, technology?

Importantly, if we listen to neurodivergent individuals, what we won't be doing to practice this is withholding items until they have said 'more' in whichever way we are teaching, and we won't be using physical prompts to move their body to point to a symbol in order for them to get 'more'. We can teach language naturally, in the moment in a time that is meaningful and engaging. Honouring their bodily autonomy while offering a child-led opportunity to practice this skill. So a teaching moment or part of a therapy session might look like several of their preferred activities laid out, and seeing which they want to engage with.

The Picture Exchange Communication System

Here comes the complicated conversation about the Picture Exchange Communication System (PECS). This child would be a 'classic PECS' child: frustrated, several motivating things that they enjoy. First, PECS is an evidence-based approach for supporting children with expressive communication difficulties, particularly autistic individuals. I have done my training, and I have used PECS for many years within my practice. Now, I do not. But should we throw the baby out with the bath water?

PECS can work beautifully, and I have seen some wonderful cases. However, I have also worked with many children who have not enjoyed, or even really tolerated the physical prompting, who have learnt a behavioural exchange but not to discriminate pictures and therefore take any piece of laminated card they can find and exchange it in a bid to get what they want. I have worked with children who believe communication can only be 'win or lose', that it is about asking only for what you want and there is a right and wrong. Communication is to be rewarded, not used for the pure joy of it.

There are two things here that are helpful to aid the thought process and clinical decision making in relation to using PECS with neurodivergent individuals: one is our practice-based evidence around communication supports; the other is the lived experience of individuals who can speak on the topic.

Practically when we are thinking about AAC, we want to explore:

- Access to robust language
- Motor planning
- Linguistic competence (Light, 1989)
- Social competence (Light, 1989)

If we think about the Picture Exchange Communication System, first it is not access to robust language. The system teaches a behavioural response and has only access to the symbols available in the book at that time, and equally requires a focus on requesting in the earlier phases before exploring other reasons for communication. So, it does not offer robust language.

In that though, not everyone will have the privilege to access robust communication aids, technology-based, but equally for paper-based systems with the relevant training too on how to implement them. This may be an important factor when recommending systems, while core communication boards are often free, these are not, by definition, robust.

When we move to consider motor planning, the fact symbols move and change within the book, rather than having the same thing in the same place causing challenges. While this does aid discrimination in a sense, it provides a challenge that our communicators don't need adding to their load. If things stay in the same place such as within a core board or a device, or push button with a symbol attached, there is a reduced cognitive load required to access communication.

Considering linguistic competence, what language is available to an AAC user when we are teaching? What range of different reasons for communication can be taught with the tools? Yes, you might be focussed on one particular word, BUT if we presume potential then a tool that offers opportunities for modelling more language in an individual's day, and has 'space to grow' without needing to meet thresholds, is going to be a good place to start.

PECS teaches via a process of exchanging and if we consider social competence this is an important skill, to teach an individual that other people are a core part of communication and ultimately that communication is an exchange.

The downfall of PECS is that it is teaching an exchange for a reward, as opposed to, for example, an exchange for fun. As I write, I realise that fun in itself is a reward, but that is an intrinsic reward, something that just feels good. Extrinsic rewards, such as a motivating item taught using PECS, is not a child enjoying the process of communication, but the end point.

I will introduce here a point from Raelene Dundon (2023): she discusses how, generally, therapy approaches that are very prescriptive and have a structure that cannot be deviated from are unlikely to be neurodiversity-affirming, as we must maintain some flexibility in our approach to supporting neurodivergent individuals. For me, this applies to all areas of our work from start to finish with a neurodivergent individual, flexibility is such a core part of how we have to work and support our colleagues and families to understand and apply in their interactions and support of neurodivergent individuals too.

Communication itself, while complex can be a joy in the art of doing it, and sharing experiences, therefore looking at strategies that can enable these skills in a more natural way of exchanging interactions feels more meaningful.

> **REFLECTION**
>
> Pause for a moment and consider the difference for this child between being taught to hand over a picture and getting a ball for their ball run, or using the ball run with an adult modelling alongside 'like it', 'fun', it's good', and using language to share in their enjoyment. This is still teaching communication and interaction, and when they go to put the next ball on modelling 'more' to fit in with their goal.
>
> During this pause, think, if that child wanted the ball and it was available, would they just get it? Is that communication? Should we just honour that? If the ball wasn't there, could they lead an adult's hand to the cupboard it is kept in? Should we just honour that? Could we model using a core vocabulary board at that point 'more ball' to integrate their goal, or have a symbol keyring with more on that matches a core board that we can get out to engage with the ball run in shared play?

We have to take each child and weigh up and consider the best tools for them. We have to look at their strengths and how we can build on these. In addition, we have to consider the least invasive ways to extend and ensure they have access to meaningful communication and think about who the goals are for.

Child-led Approaches

For some individuals they might not be at the stage of having interests or showing a desire to interact with others. First, we must consider and honour that if it is their choice. I have worked with several older autistic children who have spoken about not wanting friends and finding more comfort in their preferred interests and items than social interaction.

But, we can seek to explore with all individuals if this is a preference or a connection and skills difficulty. Again, presuming potential becomes important and finding the right method to support connection and interaction is key.

Child-led experiences offer a wonderful opportunity for developing a means to interaction, this can include things like gross-motor activities, preferred toys or figure games, puzzles, books, drawing and colouring, iPad and screen-based games. It might also look like messy play or being still together in a calming sensory space exploring light and tactile toys and tools.

For so many with higher communication support needs when we are seeking to enhance their expressive communication skills, child-led enables attention building and Intensive Interaction (2020) is, honestly, like gold dust! Intensive Interaction works on early interaction abilities – how to enjoy being with other people – to relate, interact, know, understand and practice communication routines.

Again, with Intensive Interaction we have to use critical thinking skills and ensure it is affirming and honouring. Some individuals really don't want to have someone join in their vocalisations and movements; some may love it, but only at certain times, some just for certain vocalisations or movements. We have to be led by the individuals we are supporting – and again, this can be very nuanced.

Spelling to Communicate

A final word on supporting expressive communication with higher support needs individuals is that we cannot have the conversation without introducing spelling to communicate. This is a long and complex history, and this book is not the place to explore this in depth. But it is a form of support that needs speaking about so you can go and do your own research. Spelling to Communicate (S2C) is a form of alternative communication, where an individual is taught to spell with a communication regulation support partner. So while we listen to the community about bodily autonomy and hand over hand prompting to offer a challenge to the use of PECS, others in the community speak to their challenges controlling their body due to complexities in their motor planning and say they need physical support and prompting to be able to communicate.

S2C is a form of communication that has been developed to support individuals particularly with sensory-motor challenges that can impact on their use of reliable speech. It was developed in 2015 by Elizabeth Vosseller. Historically, other forms of spelling for communication have been used to support neurodivergent individuals, including Facilitated Communication and Rapid Prompting Method.

There are strong arguments both for and against these support tools and it is important that you as a clinician seek out your own information to enable you to weigh up and make decision about spelling as a communication support for the individuals you are working with. There are positions papers on this, and inclusions within guidelines such as the National Institute for Clinical Excellence (NICE).

What we know is that there are some methods with an evidence base, there are some with less so. There are some with great track records of opening up communication for those who were presumed to have no means or reason to communicate, and their quality of life has vastly improved. Seek out information on these approaches with an open mind, there are several recommendations for reading/listening/watching at the back of the book and some included are on this topic.

There are some things with the journey to being neurodiversity-affirming that I feel I can speak to with certainty and a sureness, this, however, is not one of them. I have some opinions and I have some experiences, but they are not enough that I have formed an opinion on the validity and use of these tools.

Honouring Communication Styles

When we are thinking about some of our individuals who have lower support needs, we might be thinking about their use of language. There are several things to consider here, in particular the culture of some neurodivergent profiles in terms of communication. In particular, ADHD and autistic individuals who recognise their neurotype can create a specific way of communicating, and if they are gestalt language processors, who have moved through the stages of Natural Language Acquisition, they can often have some more unusual forms of expressive language use.

So, yes, we can support, IF the individual feels they need that support, or perhaps if it is impacting on their well-being. For example a difference in expressive language is meaning that they are struggling with academic tasks and falling behind in their potential achievements; while there are many things wrong with the education system for neurodivergent individuals, and the assessment formats for them (see earlier section on speech and language assessments, and you will know where my thoughts are in terms of academic assessment too) they are here to stay for a while – but fight the fight, please, people! – so we might be supporting individuals to develop their expressive use of language in order to achieve the grade they desire in a particular subject. This is affirming, this is listening to the individual and enabling them in an environment where advocating for their differences will not enable them. We can totally support them in reasonable adjustments to exams, but we cannot have exams re-written or scored differently based on neurotype, so this might be a goal. Another angle is that instead of where we might have historically looked at someone's expressive use of language and started to encourage them on what they 'should' say in certain situations, and how it should be said, we just embrace their unique way of using words. We might help them should they wish to advocate and share their neurotype with others so neurotypicals can have the right lens through which to view this use of language, but the end game is well-being and quality of life through good communication skills, so do what is necessary in order to support that from the individual's perspective.

Some of our more common expressive language supports outside of AAC tools might be:

- Colourful Semantics
- Shape Coding
- Narrative therapy tools
- Language modelling
- Specific language targeting activities
- Word Maps
- Semantic activities
- Vocabulary Enrichment Programme
- Word Aware
- Social Stories

Often therapists will take these approaches and create a variety of activities for therapy based on the process that these approaches give us. However, what often happens too is that these approaches will be handed over to colleagues in the education system, or to parents and families to implement, and this can be where for our neurodivergent individuals the effectiveness diminishes.

When we are working with neurodivergent individuals, so much of what we have to think about is building on their strengths and using their interests. Be mindful here to not ruin their favourite thing by turning it into work! In particular, listening to autistic adults who share experiences of adults taking their favourite enthusiasms and using it for work and learning that then totally hindered their enjoyment of their favourite thing and access to the learning being offered. This was one of those moments in my journey when I read that and thought, whoops. Time to reflect and consider how I do use those interests!

So while planning a fabulous set of language activities to embed grammar into the history of microwaves (actual lived experience of mine from some therapy sessions) or how to make the best Minecraft-based colourful semantics kits can feel like you are bossing it at being a neurodiversity-affirming committed and meaningfully engaging therapist, just think about your favourite thing. If someone tried to turn that into a work-based learning activity, how would that feel? For some it might be great, and for others it would put a real downer on things, and this is just the case for our neurodivergent individuals. So, if you can, check out with them what they would prefer, and if they can't engage in that conversation, tread lightly until you get to know them a bit better.

All our good language tools are not wasted here, the conversation is not throw it all out! But more thinking about what are the goals you're setting. Are they in line with the individuals' ways of thinking? Have they said they'd like to work on it, or was it someone else? Do they build on their strengths? If they don't meet a certain box on an assessment, ask yourself, before commenting and preparing recommendations to help that challenge, so what?

Speech

I will now touch here on two topics related to expressive communication that can be thought of specifically related to speech:

- Apraxia
- Mutism

It is important that I note neither of these are my areas of clinical expertise so I will not speak to the complexities of these topics in terms of therapy. But in terms of neurodiversity-affirming practice, a few points to consider and think about when meeting and working with neurodivergent individuals.

Apraxia is classified as a motor speech disorder and viewed very much with a medical model lens. Assessment is complex particularly for those with higher support needs and therapies can vary in terms of how they are accessed; for those with more language understanding we might look to therapies such as the Nuffield package, or for those who it is relevant for or we might look to something such as Prompt therapy. Questions here might be raised about physical prompting, and consent and allowing bodily autonomy. In all cases, looking at a robust AAC tool to support while therapy around the motor planning aspects of apraxia is on-going, is recommended as affirming and supportive.

Mutism is more complex; we know it as an anxiety-driven difficulty with producing spoken language. For a lot of neurodivergent people, it can be part of their communication profile. However, we have to get curious here, because there are so many factors to consider if we revisit the list at the beginning of this chapter. Is it a nervous system response to a stressor? Is it an executive functioning overload? Is it due to the sensory and social challenges the environment is placing? Could it be a combination of them all?

We also have to explore that individual's holistic profile, and cultural expectations of others on their communication style, their safety to advocate for themselves and, for example, use AAC when required.

In particular, considering the profiles that we might see mutism sit within, it is particularly common among autistic individuals and those with a Pathological Demand Avoidant (PDA) presentation. Here, that curiosity is key and thinking about creating an environment that minimises the demand for interaction, and most definitely speech, but also how to foster a space that can create safety and security for those individuals is the foundation for any assessment and therapy moving forwards.

Signposts here would be to the work of Libby Hill and the PDA society which are included in the reading list of this book, and individuals of the global majority, such as Kaishawna (@kaishawna_music).

More generally for neurodivergent individuals who experience speech difficulties, such as stammering or developmental phonological processing differences, we can look to the evidence-based approaches, but need to supplement these with the reasonable adjustments, and ensure that we take time to foster a sense of safety and security for these individuals more so than their neurotypical peers. This might look like leaning into relationship building before entering 'therapy activities'.

My Experiences of Being Semi-speaking: Harriet Richardson

The term 'semi-speaking' is something new to our profession, but something that is essential for us all to be aware of. As a semi-speaking person, I wasn't even aware of my own periods of mutism. But what do we mean by 'semi-speaking'? My working definition is: someone who experiences periods of mutism, where it is effortful, tiring and sometimes impossible to speak. It is characterised by forced speech and is different from selective mutism in that it is not anxiety based, but capacity based. As a result of being semi-speaking, I have to use AAC part-time, including a variety of different modalities of communication: text-to-speech, communication cards and gesture.

My identity has always been assumed by others as a speaking person and, therefore, I have been pressured and forced into speech when it wasn't my most effective or comfortable form of communication. As a child who was very articulate and chatty for the most part, I was deemed defiant and difficult when I 'chose' not to speak. Since understanding semi-speaking experiences, the number of clients I have come across who, like me, are extremely chatty but have a lower capacity for speech output, is huge. Our expressive language level and content does not determine a lack of need for AAC.

Forcing semi-speaking people to speak and not providing alternative supports to manage periods of mutism can be extremely harmful. I attribute a lot of my burnout accumulation to forced speech, it can be horribly painful, tiring and counterproductive. We must honour all forms of communication regardless of the person's primary means of communication.

Conclusion

Expressive communication is rich and varied, it has many factors that influence how we show up expressively with the world around us. As speech and language therapists, we have to consider our expectations of expressive communication and honour all forms. It is important that we consider the implications of our approaches and apply critical thinking to how we support communication development in an affirming, safe and authentic way.

Chapter Summary

- Your thoughts matter: question everything, the why and how of the work you are doing to support expressive language.
- Your approach matters: think about how to foster the sense of safety and security that a neurodivergent individual experiences when within your presence.
- Your reflective skills matter: apply your knowledge of affirming concepts to support strategies in order to think critically about whether or not they are the right approach for the individual.

References and Resources

Blanc, M. (2012) *Natural Language Acquisition on the Autism Spectrum: The Journey from Echolalia to Self-Generated Language*. Madison, WI: Communication Development Center.

Dundon, R. (2023) *A Therapist's Guide to Neurodiversity Affirming Practice with Children and Young People*. London: Jessica Kinglsey Publishing.

Intensive Interaction Institute. (2020) Intensive Interaction Institute – Fundamentals of Communication. www.intensiveinteraction.org/find-out-more/fundamentals-of-communication/ (accessed on 12/07/2024).

Light, J. (1989) 'Toward a definition of communicative competence for individuals using augmentative and alternative communication systems', *Augmentative and Alternative Communication*, 5(2), 137-144.

Meaningful Speech (no date) Echolalia Education – Gestalt Language Processing. www.meaningfulspeech.com/ (accessed on 12/07/2024).

Milton, D.E.M. (2012) 'On the ontological status of autism: The "double empathy problem"', *Disability & Society*, 27(6), 883-887.

Peters, A. (1983) *The Units of Language Acquisition*. New York: Cambridgeshire Press.

Prizant, B. (1983) 'Language acquisition and communicative behavior in autism: toward an understanding of the "whole" of it', *Journal of Speech and Hearing Disorders*, 48, 296-307.

7

Social Communication

What Is Social Communication?

This is a term that is thrown around a lot in our field, often children in particular are on the 'social communication pathway' or in specialist schools in the 'social communication classes'.

By definition:

> Social; connected with activities in which people meet each other for pleasure, connected with society and the way it is organised, connected with your position in society, enjoying spending time with other people.
>
> *(Oxford Dictionary, no date)*

> Communication: the activity or process of expressing ideas and feelings or of giving people information, methods of sending information, a message, letter or phone call.
>
> *(Oxford Dictionary, no date)*

So we can take that it is about connecting with others, it might be enjoyable or not and it is a process of expressing oneself. We have spoken in the previous chapter about how different neurodivergent expression of self might be, and in previous chapters about societies expectations of how communication should look, and sound, and make other people feel.

Social communication first needs to be honoured, so when what we know is that for a lot of neurodivergent people their social communication expression can be different, to a neurotypical person, though, this might feel uncomfortable. We might experience things like info-dumping (Autistic SLT, no date), a term that describes where an individual might speak lots on a topic of their preference and not follow neurotypical convention of asking questions, making comments and allowing space for others to join in the conversation, or switch the topic. We might see lots of clarifying questions that seem unnecessary and irritating to a neurotypical person, or very specific direct communication that can appear rude to a neurotypical individual. These individuals might experience a literal understanding of language, and perceived good intentions in social situations.

> **REFLECTION**
>
> Are these ways of communicating wrong? Whose problem is it if a direct comment is felt as rude? What even is rude? Who decided?

We will come back to the theory of double empathy within this chapter, what can and should social skills support look like, and how can we offer therapy that improves outcomes rather than potentially encouraging masking, that can cause distress and reduce well-being.

Masking as an AuDHDer: Harriet Richardson

I can't begin to explain the complexities of masking within this chapter of the book, but a great place to start is *Autistic Masking* by Amy Pearson and Kieran Rose. Instead of speaking about masking generally, I will share my own experiences of this, as everyone experiences this differently. Firstly, I want to state that I have privileges in being able to mask because it has saved me at many times throughout my life, including the avoidance of bullying, isolation and unsafe situations. Holding privileges as a cisgender, white woman means that it is less dangerous for me to unmask in public and it is important to keep that in mind when working with people of the global majority. For more information around the experiences of people of the global majority with regard to masking, please have a look at the resources provided at the end of this book.

I began masking from a very young age. I have always been very aware of people's non-verbals (in some domains!) and their emotions, which meant that I quickly realised when people didn't like me or what I had said or done. Even though I was able to tell that something had gone wrong, I never knew what it was, and this continues to this day. It seemed that whenever I let out a bit much of my personality, children would walk away or end our play. Of course, there were other neurodivergent children who were drawn to me when I was being myself and we'd often just go off on our own with the rest of the children confused. Most of my childhood I spent time with the boys, because girls were very confusing for me and a lot of the time didn't want anything to do with me. As I got older, I realised that I was different for being around boys all the time and I needed to fit in with the girls too. I understood that for the girls to like me I would have to act like them, so I learnt facts about horses and asked my parents to buy me horsey things. I would wear my hair like them and try to sit like them in the classroom. It would work for a while but eventually the mask would slip, and they'd see the 'real me' and the cycle would repeat.

At high school, masking became even more necessary, and I would return home absolutely exhausted, in hour-long meltdowns. I moved from group to group not quite fitting, getting stuck in conflicts and being vulnerable to toxic friendships. My mum reminds me that I cried almost every day about some situation that happened where someone was unkind or angry with me because I did something wrong that I couldn't understand, all whilst highly masking. I learnt how to ask people questions, show concern when they were upset, talk to them about the boys in the year, pretend I understood their banter and it didn't make me want to cry and on and on. My social skills were completely analytical. It felt like I had a blueprint in my mind of what each facial expression and verbal response could mean in each different situation and then I would have an action plan of a 'socially appropriate' response. Each night, I would take a confusing situation home to my mum and together we would problem solve it and figure out how I could respond to it next time. There wasn't much about my social interactions that was natural.

When I was first identified as autistic, my mum asked me how come I could interact with such a broad range of people with confidence. My answer was that I had spent the first ten years of my life standing back and observing other people to the point that I learnt the nuances of social behaviour that even adults didn't pick up. I realised quickly when people were uninterested in what other people were talking about. I spent lots of time with adults during my breaktimes and learnt how to communicate with them, which felt so much easier than it did with my peers. I could converse with a wide range of ages and personalities because I had learnt what was expected of me and I could mould myself to suit the situation and person each time.

During a social interaction with people outside of my family and closest friends, here is what runs through my head as an AuDHDer:

- Am I speaking at the right pace? Do I need to slow down?
- Are they bored? Do I need to change the subject? Have I been speaking too long?
- Are they having to work hard to have this conversation? Do I need to ask more questions? When was the last time I asked them a question?
- Am I making enough eye contact? Do I need to use less gesture? Am I using my hands too much? Am I standing close enough?
- What am I going to say next? What topic should I bring up next? Did I move on too quickly from that topic? What are they going to think if I go back to the previous topic? Are we going to have enough to talk about?
- When is a good time to end the conversation? Have they finished the conversation? Do we just stand here now we've finished talking or do we move? How can we get involved in the conversation the people next to us are having?
- Am I being too smiley? Does my facial expression match the topic they are talking about? When should I stop smiling after the joke?
- Did I laugh too loud at that joke? Why did no one else laugh? Why is everyone else laughing? Are they laughing at me?
- When would be a good time for me to share what I want to say in this group chat? I really want to say it but they're going to think I'm rude if I don't say it at the right time. Am I talking about myself too much? Am I not talking enough? Does my disinterest show?

And on and on it goes. As you can imagine, social interactions like these are so exhausting, constantly. These things occur automatically, and I can't switch off the running commentary. It means I don't have the energy to be around people all that often.

Through all that exhaustion, masking is also extremely helpful for me to cope with life and relationships. To perform in my job, I must mask. In my closest relationships, I must mask. Although we shouldn't encourage children to mask, we also have to be careful about taking the option away from them. A couple of years ago, I spent some time with a young person who had a lot of reliance on masking due to trauma. In our sessions, we had lengthy discussions about the impact of masking but also the benefits of this. We discussed that for both of us, masking had protected us from further trauma and in some situations, it wasn't safe to remove the option to mask. Instead, we talked about safe spaces to unmask and connecting with more people outside of school, who helped him be comfortable enough to be himself more often. There are some situations where masking is vital for survival and it's important that neurodivergent people have the strategies available should they need them.

It's not as black and white as 'we shouldn't teach children to mask'. We do not yet live in a society where people are safe and free to be different. Until then, conversations around this have to be more nuanced.

The History

We have covered in earlier chapters the role of the medical model and ableism, and this plays a big role in how neurodivergent individuals have been supported historically. Social skills training, to work on eye contact, to work on turn-taking in conversations and games, to learn to talk about others interests more and your own less. How to sit still in a classroom and behave, how one should be playing, how to show good listening skills and ultimately fit societies' expectations of how a child should be in a classroom, and how an adult should be in the workplace. Anyone viewed as different often became a victim, either by standing out or by shutting themselves away.

Some of these skills are without a doubt important to function in current society, and this is where the challenges begin to lie with neurodiversity-affirming practice in relation to social skills and communication. Neurodivergent people will have their own communication identity, and we should not encourage them to mask that, but to advocate for it. But is the world ready? How can the systems within which we work enable this where historically it has disabled? Are all individuals across all intersections safe to communicate authentically within society?

It is important here to introduce the concepts of code switching and dialling down.

Code switching is the ways in which a member of a less dominant culture (consciously or unconsciously) adjusts their language, syntax, grammatical structure, behaviour, and appearance to fit into the dominant culture.

'Code-switching can be so damaging for members of minority populations. If the dominant culture runs counter to our own, we might feel like our "natural" selves are unacceptable, unprofessional, unpalatable, and undesirable' (bypnetwork 2023).

These terms refer to a kind of masking that marginalised communities feel they have to do in order to fit in and ultimately be safe. This feeling of 'should do' is part of the on-going historical impacts of ableism and societies' expectations of how communication should sound. This might show up for example as an ADHD dialling down their energy in interactions because, historically, they have been told they are 'too much'. It could be a Black African individual switching from their usual language use or 'code' to a more White English way of communicating. Netta Selene (2022) explains this well with some good examples in her video in the references.

When individuals previously accessed therapy the goals would have been to focus on developing ultimately their white neurotypical social communication skills, and oftentimes there is still this practice going around, when we are providing support we have to consider all areas of an individual's identity to ensure we are enhancing their communication identity not encouraging them to shift it into our unconscious expectation of what is 'best'. We must consider the situation through varying lenses.

'Communities are key', writes Warda Farah, 'at the heart of new ways of thinking' and 'innovative and life changing experiences' are found within them (in Chapman and Mears, 2024). So, we must lean into the communities of the individuals we are supporting to understand what is social communication to them, how does it look and sound? Our role is to enable individuals to achieve their communication best, which means being able to effectively connect with others, and if we are working with individuals to teach them the same white neurotypical communication skills, and that is not their community, we actually will be doing more harm, than good.

Social Skills Training: Harriet Richardson

When I first started out as an newly qualified therapist I was working in an SEMH school for children who had experienced developmental trauma and/or were neurodivergent. I was nervous as anything but so excited and keen. One of my first duties in the school was to deliver a Social Skills Programme for a group of teens guided by a pre-planned social skills training session plan. The first couple of weeks I observed another therapist delivering to the group and ran a few of the activities, after that I was left to my own devices. As a person who struggles with anxiety, running groups and sessions is hard work, it exhausts me because I'm constantly worrying about things that will go wrong and the social dynamics of it all. I didn't have much confidence in my skills in this area, which didn't help. I had never run a social skills group before, we'd never really covered it in lectures. I was totally dependent on the session plan to guide me. Some of the activities were great, the children enjoyed them, and we all had a good laugh together. There were also some parts of the sessions that I felt completely out of my depth with. On one week, we were to complete a task whereby we would talk about what makes a good friend. Not knowing that I was autistic at the time, I thought this was quite straightforward, we would all talk about what we like about a friend. I scripted my answers, drawing pictures of a good friend and a bad friend, labelling aspects about them that were good and bad traits. All the children took some time creating their own and everyone had a good understanding of what made good and bad friends. I started to wonder why we even needed to do this; they already knew. The teacher of the class I was supporting then began to give real-life examples of social situations involving friendships. I was at a loss; I couldn't explain to the children why those things weren't 'socially appropriate'. I couldn't explain to them how to handle the situation. I couldn't even tell if the intentions of the people in the examples were true or untrustworthy. Yet, the teacher stood there at the front of the class and explained perfectly what we could do to prevent certain situations and what the person might be intending. I came away from the session deflated, feeling that I couldn't explain to children how to handle social situations. Reflecting back on this, the truth was the social situations made as much sense to me as they did the other neurodivergent children in the group. Sure, I could say whether the situation was good or bad but I couldn't explain it, I couldn't tell someone how to deal with the situation. I was speaking neurodivergent, not neurotypical.

The weeks progressed and some of the activities didn't sit right with me. One included sticking coloured dots on our faces to practice eye contact. I felt so uncomfortable walking around that room looking at other people's faces as I spoke. As I sat in my own discomfort, I saw similar discomfort on the faces of the children in the room. After this, I started to modify the activities. I started to do less talking about how other people might feel when we do certain things and how we can make it better or communicate better. Instead, I started to teach the children to read neurotypicals, not knowing that's what I was doing. We would take turns making expressions and guessing how the other person was feeling. We would play games centred around guessing sarcasm and idioms. We developed scripts for social situations and different ways to express and understand emotions. After I changed my method, I felt much more confident in what we were doing and what we were achieving for the young people. This led to some more 1:1 sessions with members of the group who professionals highlighted as having difficulties socially out in the community. We spent some time going to the local shops together and planning what we might say to the shopkeeper and what we needed for the trip. The young person coped well with the shop, getting everything he needed and feeling confident in his interaction with people whilst out there. I couldn't understand what the 'difficulties' were when he was out and about with other adults. Really, the difficulties were more likely differences in the way he interacted with people in the community and his confidence to do so. Sure, he was direct in the way he talked but he was successful!

I remember having conversations with professionals outside of my work, where I would say that I believed that social skills training just doesn't work. Without awareness of my neurotype at this point, I identified that people didn't learn social skills just by explicit teaching, as this wasn't natural. I suggested that people needed to learn these skills in real time and designed a sports social skills group, which featured things like watching the body cues of a goalkeeper to identify where they were going to lunge to when kicking a football. I looked at communication in the context of movement, teamwork and people's interests. Somehow, I knew that people needed to be doing motivating activities to generalise these skills. Reflecting back now, I realise that this was how I learnt social skills, through playing sports. I learnt to read body language by watching the angle of someone's body position in relation to the shots they played in tennis. I learnt how to read eye gaze through communications with teammates in hockey and netball. I subconsciously recognised that I didn't learn how to communicate and interact with others by people coaching me through it, instead I learnt through careful observation and the motivation of my special interests. My social communication skills have therefore never been natural, everything I do has been learnt through an analytical process. Instead of naturally knowing how to communicate with people and understand their behaviour, I almost have a collection of blueprints for social situations based on my previous experience.

As a young child, I spent almost all of my early years watching other children play rather than joining in. I would sit at a distance and take it all in. I was learning how other people interacted and how other people responded. I learnt from the mistakes made and skills other people had and when I was confident enough that I could replicate these behaviours, I would then join in. This has been similar for all new situations in my life, I will always be the last person to have a go at new things because I have to watch what other people to do first to be sure of what is expected socially. I have developed a lot of compensatory strategies like this throughout my life, which have enabled me to look 'socially competent'. Although this has been a very helpful skill throughout life, it has also meant I am exhausted quickly by social situations.

Assessment of Social Communication

Here is a list of a few assessment tools I have used over the years to find out about an individual's social communication style:

- SCERTS
- DASEL
- Language for Behaviour and Emotions
- Talkabout
- Pragmatics Profile
- Narrative Assessment
- CCC-2
- Merrimaps
- Social Skills Improvement System
- Observation

It isn't exhaustive and as speech and language therapists we will use clinical decision making, but also our own experiences and preferences when it comes to choosing assessments. As with expressive language it can be argued that speaking with an individual and observing them, using tools such as reflective questionnaires and talking mats to gain their views on their social communication strengths and challenges is the most affirming way to go. Most of the time that is the method I would advocate for.

There are times where something a bit more structured might be helpful, and for some of the listed above tools I would use them now and adopt an affirming lens when then reporting on them and goal settings from my findings; primarily this means avoiding scores and using qualitative information. However, they are still mostly from the perspective of scores against some norm, or the perspective of often neurotypical adult assessors, or contributors.

We have to consider when assessing social communication, the society that individuals are communicating within, what are the cultural expectations of communication? Can these impact on an individual's safety if they are communicating in a way that is authentic to themselves? What challenges might an individual face if part of their social communication is perceiving genuine intention?

> **REFLECTION**
>
> What are you trying to find out? Which assessments allow this? Are the assessments affirming of and representative of the intersectional experiences of your service user? When we assess social skills, who defined the assessments as skills that are essential, quantifiable and 'right'?

The Nuances of Neurodiversity-Affirming Practice: Harriet Richardson

When I first learnt of the neurodiversity paradigm and began to shift to neuro-affirming practice, I was very literal in my interpretation of this. The more time I have spent developing my practice, the more I have learnt about the nuances of neuro-affirming practice. At first, I believed that we should never write turn-taking goals and then I came across a situation in clinical practice, which shifted my thinking.

I was working with a young girl who struggled with waiting for her turn (and by struggling with this, I mean her internal experience – it was uncomfortable for her). She was at times, motivated to join in with her peers and play turn-taking games and at other times she was not. Often, when she joined in, it resulted in conflict because others would become frustrated when she would rush in to take her turn before them. I related SO much to her experience, and I reflected on my own journey with turn-taking, which helped me think of a solution.

Instead of 'making her better' with turn-taking, I wanted to help her feel more comfortable with it. I also wanted her to be able to opt out of turn-taking when she needed to. Instead of forcing her to suppress her feelings of discomfort and patiently wait for each person to take their turn, supposedly 'building her tolerance', I took a different approach. We discussed together situations where she might be more motivated to engage in turn-taking activities and when she would not. In situations such as queues or supermarkets she did not want to engage in waiting, so we talked about using disability aids, such as wearing a sunflower lanyard so she could go to the front of the queue. Then we talked about which activities would be more suited to our differences in turn-taking, including different sports, which doesn't involve waiting. I recognised that as a child I would only engage in single sports because I couldn't cope waiting for my turn to come around.

Finally, we talked about situations where she wanted to join in games and we learnt different ways to manage waiting. There will be situations where we don't have any control over waiting, such as being in a traffic jam or waiting for our food in restaurants, so we can find stims to help us manage our restlessness. We can engage in games with the people around us, such as I Spy. We can use fidgets and movement. We have to make sure we carry things with us that keep us entertained whilst we wait, such as pocket games or a book to read. These are skills that help us during our adult life and it's important that young people are supported to have scripts for opting out of waiting and have the strategies to manage their discomfort with this should they choose to opt in.

What my clients wanted others to know

'I don't want to change who I am, I want people to accept how I communicate. I want them to accept me for who I am.'

'Speech is sometimes so hard for me. It actually hurts to force myself to speak. I wish people would just let me communicate in other ways.'

'I think autistic people are awesome. It's a shame other people can't see that.'

'People with autism can be really clever and creative.'

'I hate small talk, I wish people would talk to me differently.'

'Everyone is different, some can cope with things and others can't. Realise that.'

'It makes me happy when people encourage me to talk about things I'm interested in.'

'We're full of really cool information about our favourite things. Ask us about them!'

'I'm very different from the mask you see.'

'I often feel like people don't accept me.'

'People are always making decisions for me. I want to decide what is best for me.'

'I feel like people don't always accept me.'

'Some things that are easy for other people are really difficult for me.'

'I feel left out a lot but I really want to have friends.'

'Things that you think aren't a big deal can really be important to me.'

Supporting Social Communication

Pete Wharmby (2024) writes: 'if you want to teach autistic children "social skills" be explicit that they're neurotypical social sills: useful when dealing with non-autistic folks, but not the "only, correct" way. Autistic social skills should be valued too'.

So, when we begin supporting social skills we have to consider the contexts and environments in which the individuals we support are living, what are the expectations? Are there reasonable adjustments? Are the individuals they are interacting with neurodivergent informed? Are their peers neurodivergent too?

We can think about this with children and young people in education, and youth group environments, through to adults in the further education and workplace environments. Their deficits are perceived as such because of the power imbalance within society and the perspective that there are 'better' ways to be in terms of communication.

As with all areas of neurodiversity-affirming practice, I suggest applying the 'so what' question to any areas of social communication that are showing up as challenging here.

> **Practice Example**
>
> For example, someone who struggles with transitions. Well, that might be having a huge impact on their quality of life and then does become a goal.
>
> What might your goal be? What support strategies would you recommend?
>
> It could, for example, become a goal for the individual to advocate for their challenges, work with you and the people who know them well to come up with strategies that support their transitions, review progress and reflect on further barriers once those strategies are in place. We might introduce scripts, affirmations and coaching social stories.

Advocacy, and self-advocacy in particular are a great way to shift from previous practices around social communication. If a neurodivergent person finds a particular skill difficult, we can look at how to teach them to find it easier of course, and one of those ways might be to just say they find it hard to people. I wonder how many times you have just said 'it's hard' and asked for help, rather than battled through or masked the difficulty? Or if you did mask the difficulty, what was that experience like for you?

For a lot of individuals their world will likely mean lots of interactions with neurotypical people, so do we need to therefore consider how we support the other people with understanding the neurodivergent communication style? There are so many great pieces of work going on with companies beginning to train their staff better, but I do wonder what our early years, school and further education facilities can do better too.

One resource I recommend is the LEANS curriculum (Learning About Neurodiversity in Schools, 2022) which is a tool that can support understanding and accepting environments within schools. In addition, there are many books that can be included into libraries, and reading corners that can show a wide range of differences and also have intersectional representation. This is not all about working with the individual, goals can also be set to develop their environments.

> **REFLECTION**
>
> When did you last visit a library? What books were there displayed or available on neurodiversity? How do neurodiversity-affirming spaces show up in your local community? Is there a way you can support some of these environments to develop?

I recall working in a small town, where students from a local specialist provision would often visit and use local businesses, and how as a therapy team we would support trips to those businesses and work with them to develop their understanding and tools. A school worked with the local pub, not only for the students to get some work experience, but also to promote symbol use by developing inclusive communication tools. These are the kinds of thing that can enable an inclusive communication environment for neurodivergent people in wider society, and begin to reduce some of those wonderings we might have; if we are supporting neurodivergent individuals to unmask, is the world ready? Perhaps not, but then how can we make it ready?

When we think about social communication skills for the individual we would likely explore:

- Attention and listening
- Waiting and turn-taking
- Conversation skills
- Play
- Understanding of non-literal or abstract concepts
- Use of and understanding of humour
- Negotiation
- Managing communication breakdown
- Making, and maintaining friendships and relationships
- Understanding and expression of emotions and regulation

These are all foundations of effective communication, and we need to investigate how they are effective or not for the individuals we are assessing.

There are several 'core' approaches that have been at the heart of neurodivergent support to name a few: Talkabout, Social Thinking, Social Stories, Attention Autism, Autism Level Up, Lego Therapy. We might also consider resources written by Joel Shaul, or *Teaching Children with Autism to Mind Read* by Simon Baron-Cohen. Again, as with expressive language let's not throw the baby out with the bath water here.

But it is how we use these tools or recommend them if we are working within a more consultative model. What are the goals you are setting? It all boils down to this, if the goal is affirming and led by the individual the methods of getting there often will be too. Which goes back to good-quality assessment that is led by the individual, offering them a safe space to explore their challenges. If this is not possible, it is where you as the therapist are observing and offering informal assessment opportunities and then creating a narrative and goals that affirm than individual.

> **Practice Example**
>
> For example, if an assessment highlights a child as enjoying play by lining up toys, spinning them around by windows or lights and jumping up and down. How would you write that up? What might your goals be?
>
> Remember these children will be developing differently. So, do we need to set a goal for them to join in play with others? Whose expectation is that? Would trying to work on this cause distress? Can we instead work with the peers around that child to offer some understanding of their play, and model how they might observe the child and comment, rather than try to take turns in the lining up, or join in a more neurotypical way?

When we think about neurodivergent play, we have to honour how it shows up. Kerry Murphy (no date) writes: 'most of us were trained to identify concerns in how children play and to use this as evidence that they require assessment, intervention and diagnosis. The dominant idea is that play should "look" a certain way to be considered successful, purposeful and of value to broader development'. This is what as speech and language therapists we have been trained in and why we need to challenge the developmental model when we are thinking about neurodivergent individuals.

> **Practice Example**
>
> For example, an adult is referred to your service, having difficulties in the workplace because of their challenges with reading others' facial expressions and understanding their own and others body language. What do you do? What might the goals be?
>
> Do we give them lots of 'training' in body language recognition through watching videos and looking at photographs? Or can we work with them to advocate? 'I find reading your body language tricky, can you tell me what you are thinking about what I just said?'

In a recent conversation with Amy Cats, Speech and Language Therapist, she reflected on a few terms that I found interesting instead of social communication difficulties: she used the term vulnerabilities. She described more of a likelihood to perceive intentions as genuine. This to me underpins what it is to talk about a communication profile in a strengths-based way, we are not ignoring the challenge, simply taking the challenge away from being that of the person and talking about it more within the context of the communicative environments within which the individual exists and functions.

When we think about attention, we are often thinking about attention development through the stages from fleeting, through to integrated skills. We explore how individuals share and gain attention from others, and this is particularly relevant to neurodivergent profiles.

Listening looks different for a lot of neurodivergent individuals, in order to regulate their energy levels and sensory sensitivities. They are unlikely to sit still, with their eyes and body focussed on the person speaking. If they are, it is likely they are masking and this will cause them a lot of fatigue, so we as individuals can offer that space safely to listen how they feel most comfortable. We can support developing attention, but we have to think about how we do this, what the goals are and why. Should we expect an individual whose body seeks movement to sit still and attend for a long period of time? Why would we say for three minutes as a goal?

If an individual doesn't seek to share eye contact, does that matter? Can they connect and listen in other ways? In my experience no matter the level of support needs, shared attention and connection can always be found, if we tune in and look hard enough.

Joint attention can look different in neurodivergent individuals, and we can link back to Dundon's book (2023) that part of being affirming is respecting all communication styles and honouring neurodivergent culture.

How We Can Support Neurodivergent Emotions as SLTs: Harriet Richardson

I hadn't heard of Alexithymia until after my autism diagnosis. Neither was I aware of how differently I processed my emotions, how much longer it took for me to realise I was feeling something and understanding the body sensation that came with it. Alexithymia is common amongst autistic people and something that's not well understood. I like to explain it as a disconnect between my awareness and my emotional state; sometimes I'm completely unaware of my emotions, other times they're very intense but I can't put my finger on what the emotion is in that moment. Alexithymia is something that ranges and looks different for each person, almost a spectrum in itself.

A few reasons why neurodivergent people may experience differences in emotions:

- Invalidation of our emotions
- Difficulties with interoception (body awareness)
- Different intensity of the emotions (some experience huge emotions, others smaller changes)
- Difficulties understanding other's emotions or being hyperaware of other's emotions
- The sensory world impacting our emotions

What do emotions have to do with SLT?

In order to progress in our learning, social relationships and language processing we have to be regulated. I've spent many years trying to engage a child in therapy who was still struggling to process their trauma and had a baseline of fight or flight. There was no impact and there will continue to be no impact without first helping the person feel safe and regulated.

Emotions are part of the communicative experience; they underpin all our social interactions. That's why emotional support is part of the SLT role. We need to provide the person with the tools to express their emotions in whatever way feels right for them. It might not be about having a rich emotional vocabulary, but more giving the person a dictionary of their own to identify and share what they are feeling. Words aren't everything and the phrase 'name it to tame it' as Dr Daniel Sigel11 describes, doesn't necessarily mean labelling with words.

Unfortunately, many of the strategies out there, such as Emotion Coaching and the Zones of Regulation, are centred around the neurotypical experience, as with most things. We are neurodivergent, we don't experience our emotions neurotypically and so those strategies don't always work for us. Often, I'm asked 'well if we can't use the outlined strategies, then what do we use?' And most of the time my response is: 'we have to understand how the person experiences their emotions first'.

During sessions, I have worked with children who for decades have struggled to express their emotions. Many times, neurotypical emotion strategies have been used and they've plateaued in progress. This happens so many times with the Zones of Regulation, because children think that the Green Zone is the target, so they will check in as 'happy' at every check in. Over the past year, I have been working with a client who has always experienced difficulties with emotional expression. We spent the first few sessions getting to know each other and engaging in their interests and connected really well. In the next few sessions, we explored different ways of "checking in" with our emotions. This included:

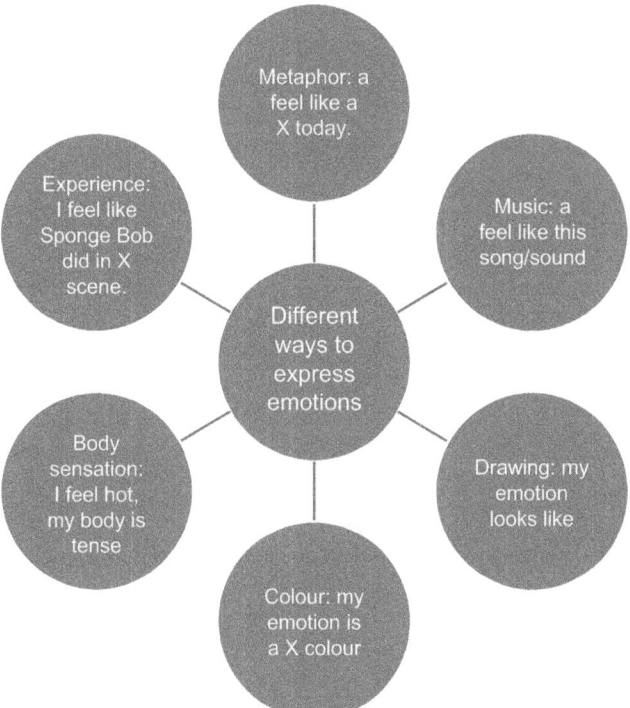

Through this, they chose to check in with music, as this was one of their passions. We had a flick through all the different playlists I have made on my iPad, which help me to process and express my emotions.

Quickly, we discovered a shared interest in Ed Sheeran and discussed a range of emotions in relation to the songs being played. He identified that when there have been big changes in his life, he will listen to a song, which centres around the feeling of loss and uncertainty. When he has hope and positive experiences, he listens to an uplifting track about things getting brighter. At the start of each session, we checked in with a song that connected with our current emotional experience. More recently, this has developed into him creating his own songs on the Incredibox app to share his emotional experiences more individually. The pitch, rhythm and duration of the songs tell a story of exactly what is happening internally for him on each session and it's such a privilege to be let into his world in such an honest way. He now goes home and shows his parents how he is feeling with a song or tune on the piano.

My experience of emotions

Emotions aren't necessarily always words for me, in fact unless they're glaringly obvious, they aren't ever connected with words. I experience emotions deeply and I'm hyper empathic at times, meaning that I pick up on other's emotions and feel them as if they are my own. However, there are other times that I don't feel empathy to the same extent that others might. I feel excitement so intensely that I feel like I'm going to explode, every part of me is buzzing with energy. And likewise, I experience sadness with crushing depression. It's both a blessing and a curse to experience such a range of emotion.

But, I don't feel the full range. I feel opposite ends of the emotional continuum. It's very rare that I experience happiness or relaxation. I jump almost immediately from frustration to anger. I'm either excited or sad and my excitement tips so easily into anger. I don't tend to feel the smaller feelings in between, instead I'm just unaware of my emotion. I recently started to use a 'light switch' analogy with my clients to explain this. It can feel like the emotion is either on or off and there doesn't feel to be an in-between.

During ADOS assessments, the person will be asked to explain how the emotion feels, what are our body sensations in relation to that emotional experience. I genuinely have no idea because of my difficulties with interoception. I am totally unable to detect raises in my heart rate unless it is extremely significant. I don't realise when I'm hungry or thirsty until it's extreme and that can often lead to large spikes in my emotions. Usually, other people have to cue me into my emotions and suggest that I may be hungry for example. I don't realise my emotions often until it is too late to regulate and manage them, which leads to meltdowns.

Strategy!

Something that has really helped me to develop my awareness of emotions and the body sensations in connection, has been the use of check-ins. This is something I suggest to all of my adult clients and what I work with my young people to practice. A check in varies dependent on what best suits the person, but the general framework is:

Every three hours, I will set an alarm on my phone and think about the following:

- Do I need the toilet? Am I thirsty? Do I need to eat?
- Is my attention on the task it's supposed to be on?

- How does my body feel? Any pain etc. (to do this, I try a quick body scan)?
- Dependent on my needs – either five regulation breaths or get up and move around.

This also helps me and my clients with monotropism and making sure we have regular breaks to meet our needs during hyperfocus. This way, I am regulating my emotions and my attention at the same time.

My experience of intense emotions

Growing up, I was always told that my emotions were 'too much', they were 'too big' for the situation. I was often told that I was being 'silly' or 'too sensitive'. Unfortunately, the more we tell our children that their emotions aren't appropriate, the more damage this does. Being told that my emotions were incorrect meant that I learnt to distrust my internal experiences, body sensations and emotional responses. I learnt to suppress how I was feeling and not show it to other people. Even now, I will not cry in front of people outside of my family, not even my friends. I save everything that I feel and wait for it to result in a meltdown when I get home. I've been taught that my emotions are too much for others to handle.

The problem with invalidating someone's emotional experience is that it doesn't help in any way. Just because we are being told that we're overreacting doesn't magically make us stop feeling how we feel inside, it just makes us hide it. Being told that we're overreacting does not reduce the emotion, it remains the same and often becomes more intense because we've not been seen. Instead, if people validate our emotions, it can help us to regulate and affirm our emotional experience. For many autistic, ADHD people, life is painful because we can absorb the emotions of others and feel things more intensely.

Conclusion

Similarly to expressive communication, social communications way of showing up for each individual differs and as speech and language therapists we have to challenge society's expectations (and in all likelihood some of our own) to support and advocate for the neurodivergent individuals we support. This will lead to skill development in a bid for better outcomes across all areas of life.

Chapter Summary

- Your assessment and the lens matter: how you think about and assess the individuals social communication can create a total shift in their experiences.
- Your consideration of what social communication entails matters: emotions are complex and are grounded in cognition and communication.
- Your critical thinking matters: historical tools don't necessarily need avoiding but offering with an affirming lens. Check for lived experience feedback on the tools if you're not sure.
- Your perception matters: social communication looks different for different people, in different situations and this has to be considered when we assess and make recommendations.

- Your systems matter: if we are working in a consultative model, staff training and understanding of affirming practices has to underpin any recommendations made for the long-term well-being of the individuals we are supporting.
- Your approach to the wider context matters: the environments within which neurodivergent individuals are communicating, can be a good place to target to enable belonging.

References and Resources

About the LEANS resources (2022) https://salvesen-research.ed.ac.uk/leans/about/resources (accessed on 24/08/2024).

Autistic Communication. Autistic SLT (no date) www.autisticslt.com/communicationfeatures (accessed on 25/08/2024).

bypnetwork (2023) *Code Switching*. [Instagram]. 22/03/2023. Available from: www.instagram.com/p/CqGDm7Qr3tX/?utm_source=ig_web_copy_link&igsh=MzRlODBiNWFlZA== (accessed on 24/08/2024).

Chapman, L. and Mears, K. (eds). (2024) Ways of Being, Knowing & Doing: An Anthology for Neurodivergent informed practice (ebook handout).

Dundon, R. (2023) *A Therapist's Guide to Neurodiversity Affirming Practice with Children and Young People*. London: Jessica Kingsley Publishers.

Murphy, K. (no date) 'A beginner's guide to self-directed neurodivergent play'. https://tapestry.info/wp-content/uploads/2023/12/A-Beginners-Guide-to-Self-Directed-Neurodivergent-Play-Dec-2023.pdf (accessed on 25/08/2024).

Oxford Dictionary (no date) social adjective–Definition, pictures, pronunciation and usage notes. *Oxford Advanced Learner's Dictionary* at OxfordLearnersDictionaries.com. www.oxfordlearnersdictionaries.com/definition/english/social_1?q=social (accessed on 24/08/2024).

Oxford Dictionary (no date) communication noun – Definition, pictures, pronunciation and usage notes. *Oxford Advanced Learner's Dictionary* at OxfordLearnersDictionaries.com. www.oxfordlearnersdictionaries.com/definition/english/communication?q=communication (accessed on 24/08/2024).

Selene, N. (2022) How code switching fuels white supremacy. Available at https://youtu.be/H6vETfcy_6c?si=u16-O_nLU4hkrgNj (accessed on 24/08/2024).

Siegel, D. J. and T.P. Bryson (2012) *The Whole-Brain Child: 12 Revolutionary Strategies to Nurture Your Child's Developing Mind*. New York, NY: Random House.

Wharmby, P. (2024) *Social Skills* [Instagram]. 11/08/2024 (accessed on 24/08/2024).

8
Relationships and Sex Education – A Speech and Language Therapist's Role

Kate Boot

I would like to thank both Fatimah Bint-Hanif and Amy Cats for their time and energy in helping review and influence aspects of this chapter.

Sensitive content warning:

It makes sense that this chapter should have a sensitive content warning, as it addresses subjects like safeguarding, sexual abuse and intimate partner violence. It also emphasises the need for an intersectionality-affirming approach to neurodiversity-affirming Speech and Language Therapy and Relationships and Sex Education.

Navigating changes and growth towards neurodiversity-affirming practice as a profession will undoubtedly be met with resistance, for example, there may be tension within the system or individual practitioner biases. While it's important we each move through this journey at our own pace, with compassion for one another, we need to do so with boundaries and accountability to reduce harm to historically and systematically oppressed communities.

Throughout the chapter I have provided pause points and, inspired by the work of Layla Saad's (2020) adapted 'circle way', I have offered questions to support you to process and reflect, allowing you to work with, rather than against, any personal discomfort.

Positionality:

You have read positionality statements throughout the book and this chapter is no different. In writing this chapter and contributing to the wider efforts of this book to support neurodiversity-affirming practice within Speech and Language Therapy, I do so from the perspective of a white British, late discovered AuDHD, queer, cis-gender woman, with middle-class privileges. I also bring lived experiences of navigating friendships and intimate relationships pre- and post-diagnosis and having had personal experiences of involvement with the Criminal Justice System as a teenager witness to sexual offending.

Limitations statement:

In writing this chapter, my aim has been to introduce the idea of Speech and Language Therapy having a role within Relationships and Sex Education (RSE), specifically within the framework of intersectionality and neurodiversity-affirming practice. I acknowledge that while I address the inherently ableist nature of existing systems, this chapter does not dive deeply into deconstructing broader systemic structures like capitalism or white supremacy. I made this choice deliberately to stay focused on the core purpose of this work.

I also recognise that it's not possible to explore every way RSE might need to be adapted to meet the diverse needs of the people we support. By highlighting these limitations, I hope to emphasise the need for ongoing dialogue and critical reflection in our profession. I believe there is power in naming these challenges and in using this chapter as a starting point for broader discussions within Speech and Language Therapy.

Introduction

When I decided to go back to university to pursue a career in Speech and Language Therapy, I had no idea that one day I'd be supporting 16–25-year-old autistic students (some with other co-occurring neurodivergence) through Mental Capacity Act assessments on their capacity to consent to sex, or that I'd be supporting the police to deliver information regarding safeguarding matters. I couldn't have anticipated running a self-advocacy group session, with an RSE theme, where we ditched our session plan in response to our learners needs to, instead, practice putting condoms and lube onto penis demonstrators. But hey, here we are, and I wouldn't change any of those experiences, in fact, I feel incredibly privileged to have been able to support those individuals and to champion the Speech and Language Therapists (SLT) role within Relationships and Sex Education.

RSE is a fundamental part of supporting individuals' growth and well-being, equipping them with the knowledge, understanding and communication skills necessary to navigate relationships, boundaries and their identities. For neurodivergent individuals, accessing and participating in meaningful RSE can present unique challenges due to differences in communication, processing and social understanding, but also how well designed the RSE curriculum is to affirm neurodivergent identities and lived experiences. SLTs are uniquely positioned to play a pivotal role in ensuring RSE is accessible, inclusive and empowering.

This chapter explores the role of SLTs in RSE, focusing on neurodiversity-affirming approaches through an intersectionality lens. It considers how therapists can support neurodivergent individuals in developing the skills and language needed for healthy relationships, personal safety, and sexual health, while respecting their identities, processing styles and sensory preferences.

Why Is RSE Important for Neurodivergent Individuals?

When you grow up undiscovered or feeling misunderstood or overlooked, you often lack the support necessary to fully understand and embrace your identity. In that absence of support, narratives about yourself begin to form – narratives that are often neither fair nor accurate, and too frequently unkind. Many of you reading this will likely relate, whether through your own experiences or those of neurodivergent people you've worked with, whether on your caseload or as colleagues.

As humans, our connections with others are foundational. Relationships shape our sense of self-esteem, belonging, and self-worth. For those who have completed trauma-informed practice training or work in services grounded in this approach, the transformative role of relationships will be a familiar concept. Relationships have the power to either perpetuate harm – through invalidation, misunderstanding, or exclusion – or to heal and empower, fostering safety, trust, and affirmation of identity and experience.

Neurodivergent people navigate a world that often marginalises them. For those who experience multiple neurodivergences or belong to other historically oppressed groups, this marginalisation is further compounded. Relationships can serve as a sanctuary of safety, joy, and connection – but they can also become sources of harm, isolation, fear, and othering. These risks are heightened for those who exist outside socially dominant groups. (Refer back to Chapter 2, where Fatimah Bint-Hanif and I explore this in greater depth.)

This is where RSE becomes vital. RSE offers a structured framework to explore the complex intersections of relationships and identity, particularly for neurodivergent children, adolescents, and adults. In an era where our profession increasingly debates the role and purpose of 'social skills' work, I would argue that RSE provides a much-needed alternative – a lens through which to understand the breadth of human experience. It equips individuals with the language to articulate and reflect on their experiences, usualises human diversity, and challenges stereotypes and unconscious biases through accurate representation and lived experiences.

As our profession continues to grow and diversify, we are slowly breaking away from its historically homogeneous mould – a predominantly white, cisgender, heterosexual, non-disabled workforce. With the increase in diverse voices, we are better equipped to represent and affirm the identities of the people we work with. Representation matters, and as we shift toward inclusion, our work becomes not only more relevant but also more impactful for those we serve.

> **Did You Know?**
>
> The terms 'usualise' and 'actualise' were coined by Dr Sue Sanders (2021), the founder of Schools OUT UK and a key figure in the establishment of LGBT+ History Month. These terms are used in the context of education and representation to advocate for:
>
> - ***Usualising***: Making the presence and contributions of diverse groups (such as LGBTQ+ individuals) part of everyday teaching and culture, rather than treating them as exceptional or separate.
> - ***Actualising***: Providing accurate, truthful representations of these groups to challenge stereotypes and offer authentic narratives.
>
> Dr Sanders uses these concepts to emphasise the importance of inclusive practices that foster belonging and acceptance. To 'usualise' something is distinctly different to 'normalising' it, which when used, still infers that what you are describing isn't 'normal' and therefore perpetuates harm to those within the group(s) being described and risks othering them.

RSE is fundamental for everyone, however, while the evidence base remains limited, and not without its own growth edges in terms of how aligned with the neurodiversity paradigm it is, we do know that neurodivergent individuals often face systemic barriers to accessing RSE effectively (Smusz, Birkbeck and Bidgood, 2024). Misconceptions about their capacity for intimacy, relationships or autonomy and a lack of focus on intersectional experiences can lead to an education that is either inadequate or patronising. Without appropriate RSE, neurodivergent individuals are more vulnerable to misunderstandings, exploitation, and difficulties in forming healthy connections (Pearson, Rose and Rees, 2023).

The Sex Education Forum have undertaken several surveys since RSE became statutory in 2020. While their latest survey findings suggest that children and young people are experiencing better RSE now compared to when their polling began, still only 50% of young people report their RSE provision to be good or very good (Sex Education Forum, 2024). In terms of inclusivity, only 43% of young people felt personally represented in their RSE with many turning elsewhere to find out information and learn about under-taught and represented experiences. For example, 22% shared that online options are their main source of learning on pornography, with 15% saying that their main source is pornography itself.

Incorporating discussions about pornography into RSE is vital, particularly given its pervasive influence on perceptions of relationships and consent. For neurodivergent individuals, tailored RSE can address the challenges posed by online pornography, such as unrealistic portrayals of intimacy, gender roles and consent. Research indicates that excessive or uncritical exposure to pornography can affect self-perception, sexual competence, and relational satisfaction, which highlights the importance of equipping neurodivergent people with critical thinking skills and media literacy through RSE frameworks (Calderdale and Huddersfield NHS Foundation Trust, 2020).

While there are reportedly improvements in how RSE is meeting the needs of all children and young people, poll findings still suggest that RSE is not addressing sensitive topics which impacts the effectiveness of RSE, such as sexual pleasure, power imbalances within relationships, pornography, gender identity and cultural and faith perspectives on relationships and sex (Sex Education Forum, 2024).

A strengths-based, neurodiversity-affirming approach could explore consent, boundaries and respectful relationships while countering harmful narratives. By integrating accessible materials and neurodivergent communication styles, RSE can empower individuals to navigate digital influences with agency and self-awareness. The absence of appropriate RSE not only increases vulnerability to exploitation and challenges in forming healthy relationships but also intersects with broader societal narratives that place undue blame on neurodivergent individuals, as seen in discussions of intimate partner violence (IPV), where victim-blaming and systemic factors are often overlooked.

Research indicates that framing IPV primarily through the lens of, for example, autistic social differences is both reductive and inherently ableist. This perspective unjustly places the responsibility on the individual for not recognising manipulation, thereby perpetuating victim-blaming (Fardella Burnham Riosa, and Weiss, 2018; Pearson, Rees and Forster, 2022). Such an approach neglects critical contextual factors, including systemic inequities and relational dynamics, that contribute to vulnerability in IPV situations.

This underscores the importance of adopting a more nuanced understanding, for example, intersectionality theory, originally coined by Black critical race scholar, Kimberlé Crenshaw (Crenshaw, 1998) and the Disability Justice field, pioneered by queer, disabled activists of colour, Patty Berne and Mia Mingus (Mingus, 2011; Berne, Morales, and Langstaff, 2018) which consider environmental, social, and systemic influences rather than attributing vulnerability solely to perceived deficits.

These systemic gaps emphasise the necessity for neurodiversity-affirming RSE that accommodates diverse communication styles, learning needs and social contexts to foster safety, autonomy and healthy relationship-building for neurodivergent individuals. This approach also helps challenge stereotypes and provides a foundation for empowerment and self-advocacy.

We know from a growing body of research into intimate partner abuse and sexual victimisation that themes from the above factor into participant feedback. It is estimated that 50-89% of autistic people have experienced IPV (Papadopoulos, 2016; Griffiths et al., 2019). Cazalis and colleagues (2022) found that while sexual violence affects about 30%

of women in the general population, it is between two to three times as much for autistic women. Furthermore, they are more likely to become victims of sexual assault earlier, with many in their study reporting being victimised for the first time before they were 18 years old.

What has struck me, largely from the work of Dr Amy Pearson, is how for many autistic people, their earlier experiences during childhood contributed to a feeling of normalcy when it came to being victimised or being hurt by another person. Her 2023 paper with Kieran Rose explores the unique vulnerabilities of autistic individuals to IPV. It highlights how autistic traits, such as an assumption of good intent and a desire for acceptance, can be exploited by abusers, making autistic individuals more susceptible to manipulation. The study also notes the significant issue of internalised ableism, where autistic survivors often blame themselves for the abuse due to societal attitudes that devalue them. This self-blame, coupled with low self-esteem, can contribute to trapping them in abusive relationships.

The chapter discusses the barriers autistic survivors face when seeking help, including communication challenges, a distrust of services and the misinterpretation of their experiences. Relationships play a crucial role in the identity of autistic individuals, making them vulnerable to abusive dynamics, especially when isolated. Despite these challenges, many survivors develop coping mechanisms and stress the importance of advocacy and tailored support, calling for services to be more inclusive and better equipped to understand and assist autistic survivors of IPV.

While research specifically addressing the experiences of individuals with differing neurotypes, such as Developmental Language Disorder in relation to IPV is limited, existing studies on intellectual and developmental disabilities suggest that these groups are also susceptible to such abuse (McCarthy, 2017; McCarthy, Hunt and Mile-Skillman, 2017). For example, individuals with learning disabilities are recognised as being at heightened risk for IPV, mate crime and hate crime due to factors like social isolation, communication challenges and dependency on caregivers. As with Pearson's work, studies focused on the experiences of people with intellectual disabilities suggests that they are less likely to identify their experiences as abusive due to limited RSE and the de-centralisation of their autonomy and agency throughout life.

In terms of ADHD, a recent systematic review found that ADHD individuals are at an increased risk of both perpetrating and experiencing IPV, driven by factors like impulsivity, emotional dysregulation and communication challenges. Gender differences are notable, with ADHD women being particularly vulnerable to victimisation, underscoring the intersection of ADHD with gender-related vulnerabilities (Arrondo et al., 2023). Studies like this emphasise the need for targeted, intersectional supports that address specific ADHD-related challenges within intimate relationships, aiming to reduce IPV by considering the unique interplay of mental health, gender and ADHD needs.

Inclusive, neurodivergent and intersectional-affirming RSE recognises that every individual deserves to understand their rights, boundaries and identities. It can:

1. **Empower Autonomy**: Providing tools to help individuals understand their values, communicate their boundaries and make informed choices.
2. **Support Safety**: Equipping individuals with the language and awareness needed to recognise unsafe situations and assert their rights.
3. **Enhance Emotional Well-Being**: Encouraging self-awareness, confidence and the ability to build meaningful connections.
4. **Affirm Identity**: Celebrating diverse sexual orientations, gender identities and relationship preferences.

Neurodivergent individuals are as capable of forming fulfilling relationships as anyone else. However, they may need support and adaptations to understand abstract concepts like consent, social dynamics and emotional nuances that people from within socially dominant groups may not, because the systems, for example, education, are designed for the majority groups.

By leveraging their expertise, SLTs can play a vital role in empowering neurodivergent individuals through tailored RSE, fostering healthier and safer interpersonal experiences. This approach aligns with evidence-based practices that emphasise the need for specialised, accessible education to mitigate vulnerabilities.

Take a pause

Before we move on, I've provided some reflective practice questions designed to encourage reflection and growth:

- What personal or professional biases did this section challenge or bring to light for you, and how might these biases impact your practice as an SLT? Consider how recognising these biases can contribute to your growth and effectiveness in supporting neurodivergent individuals.
- How has your understanding of neurodiversity and its intersection with IPV evolved after engaging with this section?
- Reflect on the language you use in your practice. Are there terms or phrases that might unintentionally diminish the autonomy or humanity of the individuals you support?
- What practical changes can you implement to ensure that your practice actively resists dehumanising narratives about neurodivergent individuals?
- What growth edges do you recognise you have and what next steps could you take to learn more?

The Role of SLTs in RSE

SLTs are uniquely placed to support with RSE. I believe we have two distinct roles to play; working within systems and advocating for systemic change and helping individuals and the people around them develop what I often refer to as 'language for their experiences'.

In the context of RSE, the latter encompasses a broad spectrum of topics, all fundamentally rooted in language and the ability to understand and express concepts like self-advocacy, safety for oneself and others, perspective-taking, interoceptive awareness, emotional regulation and fostering self-determination and agency. By empowering individuals with the language to articulate their unique experiences, SLTs play a critical role in building protective factors, both for the individual and within their support networks.

This impact is evident not only in direct client work but also through collaborations with families and professional colleagues, such as therapists, educators and social workers. In my practice, I have witnessed the transformative potential of this approach repeatedly, whether supporting clients directly, guiding therapists and peers through supervision or working with key people or systems within an individual's community.

When SLTs collaborate within interdisciplinary teams – including with educators, psychological practitioners, support workers and other Allied Health Professionals – the outcomes for individuals and their families are even more profound, emphasising the importance of integrated, holistic care. However, giving people 'language for their experiences' requires us to affirm all intersectional identities, including but not limited to race, gender, sexuality, disability, class and ethnicity. To achieve this, we must draw on the theory of intersectionality and the Disability Justice literature to understand how to work towards anti-oppressive practice. While I'm not here to teach you about Disability Justice, if it is the first time you are being introduced to the term; in brief, it offers a broader and more inclusive approach than disability rights. It looks beyond legal protections to challenge the social, economic and political systems that create and maintain inequality. This approach recognises that a disabled person's experience is shaped by many factors, like race, gender, sexuality and class. Disability Justice aims to break down these intersecting systems of oppression, not just secure individual rights. It educates us on the intersectional underpinnings of ableism, as outlined in Talila Lewis' (2022) working definition of ableism.

These frameworks support us to ensure our services are working towards actively dismantling systems of oppression rather than perpetuating harm. This involves critically evaluating how our practices, policies and assumptions may unintentionally reinforce beliefs, stereotypes and practices that sustain inequality or silence the experiences of neurodivergent individuals from marginalised groups. We create space for these voices to be authentically represented and valued, addressing the compounded barriers they face and fostering true inclusivity.

It impacts your self-esteem when time and time again, you struggle to navigate the frequent Double and Triple Empathy Problems (Milton, 2012; Doherty et al., 2023) between you and other people, including those with similar neurotypes. The systems and environments around you further compound this. Simply put, it's Dr Luke Beardon's (2022) 'Golden Equation', or an adaptation of it, if we were to expand 'autism' to include any one or more neurotypes. The individual's neurodivergent and intersectional identities, navigating environments which may vary in terms of how supportive or affirming they are of the individual, influences the outcomes that individual experiences. Outcomes which may at times be helpful, supportive, provide a relational buffer and be affirming of difference, but which we sadly know are all too often harmful, traumatising and invalidating of neurodivergent, intersectional experiences and needs.

From my point of view, neurodivergent-affirming Speech and Language Therapy practice and how we facilitate and support RSE is about developing autonomy, agency, self-determination and, importantly, community. Regardless of neurotype, don't we all co-regulate with others? Aren't we all to varying extents, reliant on relationships to support us day to day? I mean, how many times have you made or had a hot drink made for you, in work, because things have been a bit stressful and either you have noticed a colleague in need, or had someone attune to your support needs? Put your hand up if you've accessed therapy individually, or perhaps as a couple, to navigate changes or differences within relationships, with the support of a qualified practitioner. Or think about the last time you chose to WhatsApp a message, therefore accessing Augmentative and Alternative Communication (AAC), to deliver thoughts that otherwise felt too big or uncomfortable to externalise verbally?

White supremacist society often prioritises independence as the ultimate goal, overshadowing the importance of interdependence – mutual reliance within communities. This focus can impose unrealistic expectations on neurodivergent individuals and those with disabilities, creating pressure to achieve independence while undervaluing adaptive strategies like assistive technologies or collaborative support. Recognising interdependence as equally valid shifts the narrative to affirm human interconnectedness, fostering inclusive systems that celebrate diverse needs and preferences. By moving beyond disproportionate independence goals, we can embrace more empowering and sustainable approaches to well-being.

For me, a huge amount of my neurodivergent trauma is inextricably related to my experiences of relationships across my life. Whether that be my attachment relationships, early childhood, teenage and adult friendships and relationships, my experiences of intimacy, or more recent relational experiences, including professionally, both online and in person. It influences my life, every single day. Navigating relationships often feels like walking through a forest filled with both beautiful paths and hidden traps. I have learned to tread carefully, but the echoes of past missteps shape every step I take, guiding my responses and reactions, whether I want them to or not.

At times, I've wondered, how different could this be if I were a child or teenager growing up now, whose neurodivergence had been identified earlier and I was able to access support from a variety of wonderful services who are committed to neurodiversity-affirming practice? What language and ideas could I have been taught much earlier on by an SLT committed to neurodiversity-affirming practice? How might this have provided me with a protective buffer for my adult mental health and well-being? I often leave supervision spaces with the neurodivergent therapists I supervise thinking: 'If I had had you as my SLT growing up, I would have had someone quite amazing to look up to'. Imagine being that difference to a child or teenager, even a neurodivergent adult. I believe that we all can.

Of course, while I'll never know the answer for my own lived experience, what I do know is that I have seen the difference SLTs can make in practice, to other neurodivergent children, young people and their families receiving intersectional, neurodivergent-affirming speech and language therapy input that truly affirms their lived experiences in relation to RSE and its many topics:

- It's the glance of a pronoun badge on an SLT's lanyard by a gender-curious teen, which, without knowing, helps to establish a degree of safety between the pair.
- It's the SLT who is providing differentiated, language-rich, accessible therapy to a young adult with a learning disability assessed as not having capacity to consent to sex (for which the Mental Capacity Act excludes Best Interests Decisions being made on).
- It's a young female autistic adult with Downs Syndrome who feels able to share with their SLT that they think they may 'like girls'.
- It's a young autistic male who feels safe to bring questions related to accessing porn safely to their RSE and MCA speech and language therapy session.
- It's the Detective Sergeant working with an SLT to try and 'achieve best evidence' following a safeguarding referral from the Designated Safeguarding Lead.
- And it is the Muslim family who collaborate with their son's SLT and teacher to ensure that the curriculum is culturally sensitive, respecting their religious beliefs, while developing their son's understanding and ability to self-advocate for his own safety, being a high support needs individual who will always require paid support.
- It's the work an SLT is doing with an adult male in prison and who is convicted of sexual offences.

Running a Community of Practice for SLTs doing RSE work, with Dr Claire Bates from Supported Loving, I know there are SLTs doing this work, in many settings, with very different client groups. However, what we don't have as a profession is enough emphasis, narrative, literature and resources to support this work, we don't see it taught in SLT training, nor the recognition given of how our role is imperative for giving people language for their experiences, safeguarding them and building mental capacity.

> **Take a pause**
>
> By now you may have already started to have some thoughts and responses to this chapter's topic. As is human nature, everyone is influenced by their own biases, beliefs, experiences and values. I already caveated at the start how my own lived experiences and values align with the role SLTs can have within RSE. It's therefore unsurprising

that I would be advocating for this. However, if you are reading this and feeling unconvinced that we have a role to play, I would encourage you to take a look at these reflective questions before moving on. Perhaps spend a few minutes in silent reflection, or maybe discuss in a team or peer supervision group:

- How do your personal biases, values, or assumptions influence the way you view the role of SLTs in RSE?
- In what ways could you expand your understanding of neurodivergent individuals' needs when it comes to RSE?
- To what degree do you relate to the concepts of interdependence and independence?
- If our lives and day to day activity are interdependent on ableist systems, then what 'brand' of independence are we even working towards?
- How can you ensure that your practice in RSE remains inclusive, empathetic, and affirming for individuals with diverse identities and experiences?
- How do systems shape our reflections and judgements around what we deem to be 'capacity'? Do we need to reimagine 'capacity'? Are we projecting neurotypical and white supremacist norms and cultures?

Beyond the Master's Tools: Embracing RSE for Meaningful Social Learning

As a profession, we have long been involved in supporting social skills development. While I'm not going to delve into this topic in depth here, I believe that RSE provides a valuable context in which social learning can be explored and applied. This exploration is particularly relevant to various life stages – childhood, adolescence and adulthood – and can be connected to meaningful experiences and occupations, helping individuals navigate complex social dynamics in a more holistic way.

For example, let's imagine I had been diagnosed as a child **and** neurodiversity-affirming approaches were available to me. I would have welcomed someone teaching me how some people expect eye contact from others, but that usualised differences in eye contact preferences among people. Alongside this, I would have been taught about executive functioning differences and given support to understand my individual preferences and support needs. Additionally, in this scenario, my parents and education providers would also have received some education on AuDHD experiences, too. Perhaps then I wouldn't have reached the age of 33 before having language to self-advocate to tell you the following:

While you talk to me, I will make eye contact as I'm listening. However, when I speak to you, I'm unlikely to make much eye contact. In fact, I'm most likely to look upwards, towards my left as I simultaneously try to process the conversation, and find my responses, plan them and execute them (which a colleague once described as being like watching Sherlock

Holmes and his 'mind palace'), while being acutely aware that I'm not making eye contact with you. This in turn produces a shame response, felt as a warmth throughout my head and upper body because I am very much aware that I am not making eye contact, yet I know it's an expectation from socially dominant groups perpetuated by oppressive systems, such as capitalism, which centralises productivity and limited inflexible conventions around social politeness, acceptability and professionalism. My own discomfort at struggling to make or maintain eye contact inevitably distracts me away from what I'm trying to say, and the already effortful exchange.

Perhaps, if I had been taught this at a much younger age, I'd have different internalised experiences of the following:

- Being told 'look at me when I'm talking to you', which literally compounded my difficulties and discomfort, with shame and a fight, flight, freeze response.
- Holding eye contact with partners while being intimate, thinking if I just do my best to hold their gaze, maybe it'll make me sexier and more desirable?
- If I could make eye contact like my friends could, during my late teens and early 20s, maybe my experiences on nights out might have felt different?
- If eye contact didn't feel as uncomfortable, my dating experiences would have felt more comfortable.
- If I could make and sustain eye contact upon entry to social or workspaces, even with people I know, maybe I wouldn't go away with rejection sensitivity and thoughts like 'I think I look unapproachable/unhappy/unfriendly'.
- It wouldn't be an influencing factor in my freeze response when in conversation with people in senior roles to me (loop back to example one above).

RSE could provide us as a profession with an effective framework for supporting meaningful social learning because it offers a structured way to teach essential aspects of communication, self-awareness and interpersonal interaction in real-world, meaningful contexts. That said, it is crucial to ensure that we are working towards dismantling oppressive systems and demands for conformity to neurotypical norms. As Audre Lorde reminds us in 'The master's tools will never dismantle the master's house', true liberation cannot be achieved by using the oppressive systems that sustain inequity. While it would arguably be harmful to not acknowledge the role we play as SLTs in being facilitators of the master's tools, we can commit to a transformative approach to RSE which critically examines these systems, celebrates neurodivergent diversity and empowers individuals to navigate relationships authentically, rather than reinforcing ableist or reductive assumptions about independence and social competence.

Here's how:

1. **Empowering Relational Communication and Reciprocity** RSE nurtures collaborative and reciprocal communication and reciprocity, emphasising skills like expressing thoughts, active listening and mutual understanding. These practices foster

relationships built on shared respect, dismantling traditional hierarchies in favour of equitable interaction.
2. **Redefining Consent and Boundaries** Consent extends beyond individual boundaries to encompass collective agency, advocating for environments where mutual respect and humanising people is a shared responsibility. RSE reframes consent as a dynamic, relational practice rather than a transactional concept, fostering shared accountability.
3. **Grounding in Real-Life Contexts** By exploring relational dynamics in everyday scenarios, RSE deconstructs rigid norms and supports individuals in navigating diverse social landscapes. For neurodivergent individuals, this contextualisation provides a space to reimagine connections outside dominant expectations.
4. **Centring Emotional Justice** Emotional literacy in RSE goes beyond regulation to challenge stigmas and power imbalances that affect emotional expression. It affirms diverse ways of feeling, processing, and relating as valid, resisting systems that pathologise, infantilise and dehumanise difference.
5. **Valuing Intersectional Narratives** Inclusive RSE celebrates a spectrum of identities and experiences, rejecting homogenised social norms. It fosters critical awareness of how power operates across race, gender, neurodivergence and other intersections, including dominant cultures and conventions within these, such as Ace (the umbrella term for asexual and aromantic identities). Therefore, creating space for collective liberation.
6. **Challenging Stigma in Social Norms** RSE validates diverse relational challenges without framing them as deficits. It encourages adaptive strategies that affirm individual agency and promote mutual respect, countering deficit-based perspectives of neurodivergent sociality.
7. **Advocating for Collective Agency** RSE promotes shared empowerment by prioritising agency within interdependence. It shifts from individualist models of independence to communal frameworks that value collaboration and support.
8. **Fostering Radical Collaboration** Through interdisciplinary approaches, RSE integrates perspectives from educators, families and therapists to co-create meaningful frameworks with individuals. It disrupts siloed systems and ensures relational learning aligns with diverse lived experiences.

By grounding social learning in the context of relationships and human connection, RSE goes beyond abstract teaching to provide meaningful, practical applications that can enhance well-being and interpersonal competence.

When I think about neurodivergent social communication preferences and lived experiences, there are a number of topics that come to mind, for example, monotropism, inertia, alexithymia, masking, stimming, and so on. When I contextualise this within intersectionality and Disability Justice theory (environments, socially dominant groups and systems of oppression) I am reminded that any input I may have as an SLT delivering social learning or RSE support to an individual or their family must prioritise the individual's autonomy, affirm their identity and be rooted in their lived experience, while navigating systems and societal norms which dehumanise and infantilise people, particularly those with learning disabilities.

It must also critically examine and address the broader systemic barriers and biases that shape their experiences, ensuring the approach does not inadvertently perpetuate harm or conformity to socially dominant norms. My role is not to 'fix' their social communication but to create opportunities for exploration, self-expression and connection on their terms, while also advocating for societal shifts that embrace and value neurodivergent ways of being.

Let's pause to consider some case studies:

Case Study 1: Supporting Autonomy Through RSE

Context: A 16-year-old autistic girl, Nia, struggles with understanding consent in relationships. Nia's monotropic processing allows her to intensely focus on certain topics, which can make shifting her attention challenging.

SLT Input: The SLT collaborated with Nia and her family to provide RSE sessions tailored to her learning preferences. By integrating visual aids and clear, repetitive language, the sessions broke down the abstract concept of consent into manageable parts. Discussions included using specific scenarios and role-playing activities to explore communication strategies that aligned with her processing style.

Outcome: Nia began to articulate her boundaries more confidently and recognised how to check for mutual understanding in social situations. The SLT also engaged with Nia's school to ensure her needs were accommodated in wider social settings. The approach celebrated Nia's strengths and validated her communication preferences, fostering self-confidence and autonomy.

Case Study 2: Supporting a Young Woman Navigating Honour-Based Violence Concerns

Context: Amira, a 17-year-old autistic young woman, was referred to a SLT due to increasing withdrawal and difficulty expressing herself in peer interactions. She confided in a teacher that her family was pressuring her to enter an arranged marriage, and she feared repercussions associated with honour-based violence (HBV).

SLT Input: The SLT adopted a neurodiversity-affirming and culturally sensitive approach, collaborating with Amira to support her unique communication needs. Visual aids and written scripts were used to help her articulate her boundaries effectively. Discussions focused on understanding consent, self-advocacy, and her rights within her relational and cultural context. The SLT also worked closely with the school's safeguarding lead and pastoral support team. Having sought out additional supervision and professional development, the SLT contributed to safety planning and equipping Amira for interactions with external services like the police and social workers. The SLT sought additional supervision in light of their growth edges around understanding how to navigate supporting within oppressive systems and institutions.

Outcome: Amira developed greater confidence in expressing her needs and understanding her rights. She accessed additional support from HBV specialists, reinforcing her sense of safety and agency. The collaborative, holistic approach respected Amira's autonomy and acknowledged the intersecting influences of her neurodivergence, gender, and cultural identity.

Case Study 3: Affirming Identity in Social Learning Development

Context: A 22-year-old ADHD and autistic person, Alex, faced challenges navigating workplace relationships, exacerbated by alexithymia (differences in identifying and expressing emotional experiences).

SLT Input: Using an intersectionality-informed approach, the SLT provided 1:1 sessions focusing on emotional vocabulary and self-advocacy. Stimming was incorporated into these sessions as a regulated means of expressing and managing emotions. The SLT also worked with Alex's employer to promote a more inclusive environment, highlighting their strengths and the need for structured feedback.

Outcome: Alex learned strategies to identify and articulate their feelings in specific contexts, such as workplace disagreements. Their manager adapted communication styles to reduce ambiguity. Together, this enhanced Alex's confidence and supported positive professional relationships, validating their neurodivergent identity while promoting understanding in their environment.

Case Study 4: Addressing Misogynoir in RSE for Neurodivergent Black Women

Context: A 19-year-old autistic and ADHD Black woman, Aisha, expressed feelings of alienation in her college environment. She often faced microaggressions related to her race, gender, and neurodivergence, such as being labelled 'aggressive' when setting boundaries. Aisha also struggled with internalised stigma around her natural hair and cultural expression, exacerbated by misogynoir – the intersection of racism and sexism uniquely affecting Black women.

SLT Input: Grounded in Disability Justice and intersectionality, the SLT designed sessions to validate Aisha's experiences while equipping her with the language and tools for self-advocacy. This included practicing scripts to address microaggressions assertively and integrating afrocentric cultural pride into self-identity discussions. Collaborative sessions with her family helped unpack and affirm her dual experiences as neurodivergent and a

Black woman. Additionally, the SLT facilitated peer education workshops in Aisha's college to raise awareness of misogynoir and the intersectional barriers faced by neurodivergent individuals.

Outcome: Aisha reported feeling more empowered to articulate her boundaries and address misunderstandings in her social environment. Her peers began to challenge biases, fostering a more inclusive culture. Aisha's increased confidence in navigating intersectional challenges contributed to a stronger sense of identity and belonging.

> **Take a pause**
>
> Here are some reflective practice questions to consider now:
>
> - How do your biases, assumptions, or cultural background shape the way you approach RSE and social learning support for neurodivergent individuals?
> - In what ways do you incorporate intersectionality and Disability Justice principles when delivering RSE or social learning support?
> - How do you navigate your professional role and working within systems and hard institutions which may lack safety for many people with intersectional identities?
> - How do we acknowledge our power within these contexts and balance being in a role where it is part of our job to prevent harm while facilitating the masters' tools?
> - How do you measure the impact of RSE and social learning support on the autonomy, agency, and emotional well-being of the individuals you support?
> - How do systems shape our reflections and judgements around what we deem to be 'capacity'? Do we need to reimagine 'capacity'? Are we projecting neurotypical and white supremacist norms and cultures?

These Considerations Are Not Just Theoretical; They Have Real-World Implications

As a profession, we have a duty to use research to inform our practice. However, we also must listen to lived experience. To only look to the research base assumes the people we work with have the privileges to be involved in research. We know that this is not always the case and that many important 'voices' remain excluded from the literature. This means following intersectional voices through other means, such as diversifying your social media following, buying books written by intersectional authors and paying to attend training developed and delivered by people with lived experiences.

The historical approach to neurodivergent care, particularly autistic care, within the SLT profession is often critiqued for its alignment with pathologising and deficit-based models of support. Historically, much of SLT 'intervention' for autistic individuals focused on 'normalising' communication and social behaviours to align more closely with neurotypical standards. These approaches often involved therapies aimed at reducing or eliminating autistic traits, such as echolalia, stimming and neurodivergent communication preferences, rather than celebrating and supporting neurodivergent ways of being.

This perspective has contributed to a broader societal narrative that views neurodivergent individuals as 'broken' or in need of fixing, which can foster feelings of inadequacy and vulnerability in people from a young age. For many, these early experiences within therapeutic settings may reinforce a sense of being fundamentally flawed. When a person's differences are consistently highlighted as problems to be corrected, it can lead to internalised ableism and a diminished capacity to recognise and resist abuse, both as children and later in life. Pearson's work highlights how these deficit-based approaches can contribute to a normalisation of victimisation, where the pain and mistreatment experienced by autistic individuals are seen as inevitable or deserved, rather than as violations of their rights and dignity.

If we look at the discussions around active infantilisation and dehumanisation of disabled people, especially those with learning disabilities, in the name of protectionism and paternalism, what we are talking about is a reflection of systems Talila Lewis refers to in the working definition of ableism, such as, eugenics, white supremacy and superiority politics. These fundamentally dehumanise, underestimate and devalue people, their ways of thinking, being and moving through the world. We must question and reflect together on how the very systems we work within, which are designed to protect people, may in fact be susceptible to manipulation, offering protection for services and professionals, over the quality of life and rights of the person being supported, or assessed.

I would encourage us as a profession to shift towards more affirming, strengths-based approaches that respect and celebrate neurodivergent, intersectional identities, rather than attempting to mould people to achieve socially dominant standards. By fostering self-advocacy, rather than compliance and conformity, SLTs can help dismantle the harmful narratives that contribute to the normalisation of victimisation in neurodivergent individuals.

The revised Health and Care Professions Council standards, effective from 1 September 2024, include several aspects that align with the critique of the historical approach to SLT practices. These standards emphasise person-centred care, respect for diversity and the need for practitioners to challenge their own biases – principles that are crucial for addressing the issues I've described.

SLT's have a unique role to play supporting with neurodiversity-affirming RSE, regardless of whether this is proactively, for example, informing curriculum development for children and young people, or reactively, for example, in response to an event, experience or crime which has already occurred. We can play a crucial role in giving people language for their identity and for topics pertaining to safeguarding and mental capacity. For example, consent, bodily autonomy, self-advocacy skills, vocabulary for body parts and understanding of concepts related to RSE topics, such as private and public body parts, access to appropriate

AAC supports, environmental supports, understanding sensory and emotion processing preferences and challenges and empathy gaps.

SLTs bring expertise in communication, social understanding and language development, making them invaluable in delivering neurodivergent-accessible RSE. Uniquely placed, our role includes:

1. **Supporting Language Development for RSE**: Helping individuals develop the vocabulary and pragmatic skills to understand and express their needs, boundaries, and feelings.
2. **Adapting Content for Accessibility**: Tailoring RSE resources to align with individual learning and processing styles.
3. **Fostering Self-Advocacy**: Empowering individuals to assert their needs and navigate interpersonal situations.
4. **Collaborating with Educators and Families**: Ensuring RSE is consistent and reinforcing across environments, holding people, systems and institutions to account.

> **Take a pause**
>
> - Reflect on any discomfort or resistance you felt while reading this section. What aspects of the content were particularly challenging, and how can this discomfort serve as an opportunity for personal and professional development?
> - Reflect on the systems you work within. In what ways might they be prioritising professional protection over individual rights, and how can you advocate for systemic change?
> - Consider the concept of compliance in your practice. How might it unintentionally reinforce disempowerment, and what alternative approaches could you adopt to foster true self-advocacy?
> - How do you actively seek out and incorporate intersectional lived experiences into your professional development? Reflect on any gaps and actionable ways to address them.
> - What strategies can you implement to ensure your therapeutic approaches promote autonomy and affirm neurodivergent identities, rather than aligning with societal norms of 'fixing' or 'normalising'?

Key Areas of Focus in Neurodiversity-Affirming RSE

Providing inclusive, neurodiversity-affirming RSE support as SLTs involves addressing specific areas crucial for fostering understanding, safety and empowerment. Each focus area builds skills and confidence, helping neurodivergent individuals navigate relationships and express their identities. I believe we can play a pivotal role in using our expertise to tailor these areas to individual needs, ensuring that all learners feel supported and valued.

Below I will outline some practical strategies and considerations for SLTs to deliver meaningful, affirming RSE that respects neurodivergent perspectives and fosters holistic development.

1. **Language for Relationships and Boundaries**

   Neurodivergent individuals may need adapted teaching of relationship vocabulary and concepts. SLTs can support by:

   - Building Foundational Vocabulary: Teaching words for emotions, relationship types, body parts (using the correct terminology) and sexual health.
   - Clarifying Abstract Concepts: Breaking down terms like 'consent', 'intimacy' and 'respect' into concrete, relatable scenarios.
   - Supporting Pragmatics within the context of the Double Empathy Problem. Teaching individuals about empathy gaps and exploring pragmatics through the lens of the neurodivergent person to understand and teach about healthy communication in relationships.

2. **Consent and Autonomy**

   Understanding and practicing consent is crucial for fostering respectful relationships and ensuring personal safety. SLTs can:

   - Provide Visual Supports: Use tools like social stories or visual scales (e.g., a traffic light system) to illustrate the dynamics of consent.
   - Role-Play Scenarios: Create safe spaces for practicing assertive communication and recognising non-verbal cues.
   - Teach 'Safe Yes' and 'Safe No': Equip individuals to assertively communicate agreement or refusal while honouring and affirming neurodivergent and intersectional identities and barriers.

3. **Identifying and Expressing Emotions**

   Emotional literacy is a cornerstone of RSE, enabling individuals to recognise their feelings and those of others. SLTs can:

   - Expand Emotional Vocabulary: Move beyond 'happy' and 'sad' to explore nuanced emotions like 'frustrated', 'nervous', or 'affectionate'.
   - Integrate Interoception: Support individuals in connecting physical sensations to emotional states.
   - Use Multi-Sensory Tools: Incorporate visuals, body maps or sensory aids to teach emotion recognition and regulation.

4. Social Understanding and Relationship Dynamics

Navigating the social nuances of relationships can be particularly challenging for neurodivergent individuals. SLTs can:

- Teach Explicit Social Rules: Address topics like personal space, appropriate touch, and social hierarchies, ensuring explicit teaching of green and red flags for safety within relationships.
- Develop Scripts for Social Situations: Provide frameworks for initiating friendships, resolving conflicts, or ending relationships.
- Practice Perspective-Taking: Use storytelling, comic strip conversations or role-play to explore others' feelings and intentions within the context of the Double Empathy Problem. Utilise intersectionally-affirming programmes, such as Heartbreak High and Heartstopper.

5. Affirming Diverse Identities

SLTs must affirm the diversity of sexual orientations, gender identities and relationship preferences. Neurodivergent individuals may express their identities differently or require tailored support to explore and articulate them. SLTs can:

- Validate Identity: Use inclusive language and visual aids that represent a wide range of identities and experiences.
- Provide Resources: Connect individuals to affirming media, organisations, and peer communities.
- Support Self-Expression: Help individuals find ways to articulate their identities, whether through mouth-produced language, AAC, or other creative outlets.

Strategies for Delivering Neurodivergent-Affirming RSE

Delivering RSE that affirms neurodivergent identities requires thoughtful strategies rooted in inclusivity, accessibility and co-production. By recognising and addressing diverse communication styles, sensory needs and lived experiences, SLTs can promote safer, empowering environments for learning.

1. Collaborative Goal-Setting

- Involve individuals in defining their RSE goals, respecting their autonomy and interests.
- Engage families, educators and multidisciplinary teams to create consistent support, holding institutions and systems to account.

2. Personalised Approaches

- Assess communication strengths and challenges to tailor RSE materials.
- Use sensory-friendly and accessible formats, such as videos, tactile resources, or simplified text.

3. Creating Safer Spaces (note the use of 'safer' and not 'safe')

- Foster trust by ensuring sessions are non-judgemental and empowering. Affirm intersectional identities.
- Use clear routines and predictable structures to reduce anxiety.

4. Developing Capacity and Self-Determination

- Teach problem-solving and coping strategies for navigating complex or uncomfortable situations.
- Provide tools for managing rejection, peer pressure, and internalised ableism.

Through these strategies, RSE can become a meaningful tool for equipping neurodivergent individuals with the skills and confidence to navigate relationships, safeguard their well-being and celebrate their identities.

Challenges in Delivering Neurodivergent-Affirming RSE

RSE is a vital aspect of personal development that equips individuals with the knowledge and skills to navigate relationships, boundaries, consent and identity. For neurodivergent individuals, the importance of RSE is amplified by unique challenges they face in communication, social interaction and accessing appropriate resources. However, these needs are often overlooked in traditional RSE curricula, which are typically designed with neurotypical developmental trajectories in mind. This oversight risks leaving neurodivergent individuals without the tools to advocate for their autonomy, recognise inappropriate behaviours or fully engage in safe and meaningful relationships. To ensure equitable RSE, it is crucial to identify and address the systemic, cultural, and communication-specific barriers that hinder access and efficacy. Below is an exploration of key challenges that must be considered to develop neurodivergent-affirming RSE practices.

1. Systemic Barriers

- Limited RSE resources tailored to neurodivergent learners, particularly those with medium to high support needs, with accompanying intellectual disabilities and who may be non or minimally speaking.
- Lack of training for educators and clinicians in delivering neurodivergent-affirming RSE.
- SLTs as facilitators of the master's tools and their role in dismantling these.

2. **Communication Barriers**

    - Difficulty in identifying or articulating experiences of abuse or discomfort.
    - Variations in non-verbal communication and its interpretation by others.

3. **Cultural and Societal Stigmas**

    - Misconceptions about neurodivergent individuals' capacity for relationships and autonomy.
    - Overlap of neurodivergence with LGBTQIA+ identities, often leading to compounded marginalisation.
    - The perpetuation of dominant cultures.

4. **Intersectional Barriers**

    - Neurodivergent individuals of the Global Majority may face heightened disparities in accessing culturally relevant RSE resources.
    - Gendered expectations and misogynoir can exacerbate barriers for neurodivergent women and nonbinary individuals.
    - Experiences of honour-based violence and intimate partner violence may go unrecognised or unsupported due to cultural stigma and systemic biases.

5. **Emotional and Sensory Processing Challenges**

    - Sensory sensitivities can make discussions about RSE topics overwhelming or uncomfortable.
    - Alexithymia, often present in autistic individuals, can make it difficult to identify or express emotions related to intimacy, boundaries, and consent.

6. **Educational Gaps**

    - A focus on mainstream developmental milestones in RSE curricula often excludes the unique developmental trajectories of neurodivergent individuals.
    - Lack of representation in teaching materials, may reinforce feelings of exclusion or inadequacy among neurodivergent learners.

7. **Reluctance to Discuss Sexuality**

    - A tendency to infantilise neurodivergent individuals can result in their exclusion from conversations about sexuality and relationships.
    - Fear of triggering discomfort among educators or families often leads to avoidance, perpetuating gaps in knowledge and empowerment.

8. Systemic Underreporting of Abuse

- Neurodivergent individuals are disproportionately at risk of sexual violence and abuse but often lack avenues to report incidents safely. Dominant systems limit growth of agency and autonomy.
- Caregiver or institutional gatekeeping can further silence neurodivergent voices in contexts of abuse or boundary violations.
- It is hoped that in providing this framework a more comprehensive understanding of the systemic, cultural and interpersonal factors that hinder equitable RSE for neurodivergent individuals is developed within the speech and language therapy profession.

The Future of Speech and Language Therapy in RSE

I believe that the future of Speech and Language Therapy in RSE lies in its potential to create more inclusive, empowering and holistic approaches for neurodivergent individuals. As RSE continues to evolve, therapists can play a pivotal role in bridging the gaps between traditional curricula and the unique needs of those with communication and social interaction differences. This involves not only supporting individuals with skills like vocabulary for consent, bodily autonomy and emotional expression but also addressing systemic barriers that impede access to meaningful, neurodivergent-affirming RSE.

To move forward, SLTs must embed intersectionality and neurodiversity-affirming practices within their work. This includes advocating for the development of accessible, tailored RSE resources that align with diverse communication preferences, such as visual supports, AAC, or sensory-based approaches. Collaboration with multidisciplinary teams, including educators, psychologists and social workers, will be essential in ensuring comprehensive, person-centred support.

Research and advocacy are equally critical. SLTs should contribute to the evidence base by exploring the intersection of neurodivergence, RSE and broader social factors, such as gender, race and disability justice. Additionally, empowering neurodivergent individuals and their families to co-create RSE content will ensure that the resources and strategies used resonate with their lived experiences.

Ultimately, the future of SLT in RSE depends on the profession's commitment to dismantling stigmas, promoting autonomy and addressing the structural inequalities that have historically marginalised neurodivergent voices in this vital area of education and personal development.

Conclusion

RSE serves as a cornerstone of holistic support for neurodivergent individuals, offering tools and knowledge essential for navigating relationships, autonomy and self-advocacy.

SLTs bring a unique perspective to this field through their expertise in communication and social interaction, enabling them to make RSE more inclusive and impactful.

Adopting a neurodiversity-affirming approach ensures that individuality, autonomy and dignity remain central to RSE delivery. By tailoring support to align with the strengths and needs of neurodivergent individuals, SLTs can help foster a sense of empowerment and confidence. This approach also reinforces the importance of co-production, involving neurodivergent individuals in the creation of RSE content to reflect their lived experiences authentically.

As societal understanding of neurodiversity continues to expand, SLTs have the opportunity to lead systemic change. Through advocacy, interdisciplinary collaboration and the development of accessible, affirming resources, they can work to dismantle barriers and biases that have historically excluded neurodivergent voices from RSE. In doing so, SLTs can help shape a future where RSE is an empowering, inclusive framework, supporting individuals to navigate their relationships and identities with dignity and autonomy.

As I end the chapter, I'll leave you with a quote that has impacted my perspective and hopefully will help you consider yours:

> The trouble is that once you see it, you can't unsee it. And once you've seen it, keeping quiet, saying nothing, becomes as political an act as speaking out. There's no innocence. Either way, you're accountable.
>
> *Arundhati Roy*

Chapter Summary

- Your awareness matters: of how SLTs can show up and support RSE in our practice.
- Your understanding of our role matters: think about the learning you have just done and consider how you might integrate it into your practice and advocate for the role of the SLT profession within this area.
- Your voice matters: when you feel you have an understanding, being able to then use your voice to shape the profession is key, exploring the topic through supervision, training and professional conversations.

References

Arrondo, G., A. Osorio, S. Magallón et al. (2023) 'Attention-deficit/hyperactivity disorder as a risk factor for being involved in intimate partner violence and sexual violence: a systematic review and meta-analysis', *Psychological Medicine*, 53(16), 7883-7892. doi:10.1017/S0033291723001976.

Beardon, L. (2022) *Avoiding Anxiety in Autistic Children: A Guide for Autistic Wellbeing*. London: Sheldon Press.

Berne, P., L. Morales, E. Langstaff, and S. Invalid (2018) 'Ten principles of disability justice', *Women's Studies Quarterly*, 46(1&2), 227–230. www.sinsinvalid.org/blog/10-principles-of-disability-justice (accessed on 24/11/2024).

Calderdale and Huddersfield NHS Foundation Trust. (2020) *What is the impact of pornography on young people? A research briefing for educators*. Sexual Health Calderdale and Huddersfield NHS. https://sexualhealth.cht.nhs.uk/fileadmin/sexualHealth/contentUploads/Documents/What_is_the_impact_of_pornography_on_young_people_-_A_research_briefing_for_educators.pdf (accessed on 2/12/2024).

Cazalis, F., E. Reyes, S. Leduc, and D. Gourion (2022) 'Evidence that nine autistic women out of ten have been victims of sexual violence', *Frontiers in Behavioral Neuroscience*, 16, 852203. https://doi.org/10.3389/fnbeh.2022.852203.

Crenshaw, K. (1998) 'Demarginalizing the intersection of race and sex: A Black Feminist critique of antidiscrimination doctrine, feminist theory, and antiracist politics', in *Oxford University Press eBooks*, pp. 314–343 https://doi.org/10.1093/oso/9780198782063.003.0016.

Doherty, M., S.C.K. Shaw, L. Carravallah et al. (2023) 'A triple empathy problem leads to adverse healthcare outcomes for autistic adults: A qualitative analysis', *ResearchGate*. www.researchgate.net/profile/Mary-Doherty-9/publication/370580252_A_triple_empathy_problem_leads_to_adverse_healthcare_outcomes_for_autistic_adults_a_qualitative_analysis/links/64566f705762c95ac378c9dc/A-triple-empathy-problem-leads-to-adverse-healthcare-outcomes-for-autistic-adults-a-qualitative-analysis.pdf (accessed on 1/12/2024).

Fardella, M., P. Burnham Riosa, and J.A. Weiss (2018) 'A qualitative investigation of risk and protective factors for interpersonal violence in adults on the autism spectrum', *Disability & Society*, 33(9), 1460–1481. https://doi.org/10.1080/09687599.2018.1498320.

Griffiths, S., C. Allison, R. Kenny et al. (2019) 'The Vulnerability Experiences Quotient (VEQ): A study of vulnerability, mental health and life satisfaction in autistic adults', *Autism Research*, 12(10), 1516–1528. https://doi.org/10.1002/aur.2162.

Health and Care Professions Council (2024) *Release of revised standards of conduct, performance and ethics*. www.hcpc-uk.org (accessed on 1/12/2024).

Lewis, T. (2022) *Working definition of ableism: January 2022 update*. www.talilalewis.com/blog/working-definition-of-ableism-january-2022-update (accessed on 1/12/2024).

Lorde, A. (1984) 'The master's tools will never dismantle the master's house'. In A. Lorde, ed. *Sister Outsider: Essays and Speeches*. Berkeley, CA: Crossing Press, pp. 110–113.

McCarthy, M. (2017) 'What kind of abuse is him spitting in my food?: Reflections on the similarities between disability hate crime, so-called "mate" crime and domestic violence against women with intellectual disabilities', *Disability and Society*, 32(4), 595–600.

McCarthy, M., S. Hunt, and K. Milne-Skillman (2017) '"I know it was every week, but i can't be sure if it was every day": Domestic violence and women with learning disabilities', *Journal of Applied Research in Intellectual Disabilities: JARID*, 30(2), 269–282. https://doi.org/10.1111/jar.12237.

Milton, D.E.M. (2012) 'On the ontological status of autism: The "double empathy problem"', *Disability & Society*, 27(6), 883–887.

Mingus, M. (2011) 'Access intimacy, interdependence and disability justice. Leaving evidence'. https://leavingevidence.wordpress.com/2011/05/05/access-intimacy-interdependence-and-disability-justice/ (accessed on 23/11/2024).

Papadopoulos, C. (2016) 'Autism stigma and the role of ethnicity and culture', *Network Autism*. www.researchgate.net (accessed on 24/11/2024).

Pearson, A., J. Rees, and S. Forster (2022) '"This was just how this friendship worked": Experiences of interpersonal victimisation in autistic adults', *Autism in Adulthood*. https://doi.org/10.1089/aut.2021.0035.

Pearson, A., K. Rose, and J. Rees (2023) '"I felt like I deserved it because I was autistic": Understanding the impact of interpersonal victimisation in the lives of autistic people', *Autism*, 27(2), 500–511. http://doi:10.1177/13623613221104546.

Roy, A. (1999) *The Cost of Living*. London: Flamingo, p.114.

Saad, L.F. (2020) *Me and White Supremacy: Combat Racism, Change the World, and Become a Good Ancestor*. Naperville, IL: Sourcebooks Inc.

Sanders, S. (2021) 'Visibilising and usualising the LGBTQ+ community', TED. www.ted.com/talks/sue_sanders_visibilising_and_usualising_the_lgbtq_community?subtitle=en&geo=es] (https://www.ted.com/talks/sue_sanders_visibilising_and_usualising_the_lgbtq_community?subtitle=en&geo=es) (accessed on 24 November 2024).

Sex Education Forum (2024) *Young People's RSE Poll 2024: Report.* www.sexeducationforum.org.uk/sites/default/files/field/attachment/Young%20Peoples%20RSE%20Poll%202024%20-%20Report.pdf (accessed on 2/12/2024).

Smusz, M., C. Birkbeck, and A. Bidgood (2024) 'Exploring the experience of romantic relationships and sexuality education in neurodivergent and neurotypical young individuals', *Sexuality and Disability*, 42, 735–764 https://doi.org/10.1007/s11195-024-09857-8

9
Flipping the Narrative on Behaviour

Curiosity and Narrative

At the heart of flipping the narrative is considering the lens through which we view the way that neurodivergent people show up in the spaces in which we support them. As we have discussed in previous chapters, the nervous system and sense of safety play a big part in this. In the way we consider this we can think about those basic needs being met, the sensory environment and energy and emotional regulation skills.

When we are supporting individuals either in therapy, or when working with the other individuals in their environments, such as parents, partners and other professionals we can shift how we support their views of the individual's behaviour.

> **REFLECTION**
>
> First, we need to look inward about the way in which we frame the individuals' behaviour in our minds, do we apply a narrative that is they are in control? Do we apply a narrative that they have an awareness? Are we thinking about their behaviour and wondering how we can change it to be more like a neurotypical person?

When we think about descriptions often used – lazy, defiant, manipulative, confrontational, challenging, weird, eccentric, manic – the list goes on, and these all stem from narratives about the individual, again stemming back to societies' expectations of how someone should be in particular situations. When we think differently, these words don't come out of our mouths, and when we hear others use them, we can offer a space to reflect with them 'I hear you, that sounds really difficult. I wonder why they did that?' as an example of a way to begin that curious conversation.

A group I am part of to develop our understanding and anti-racist practice recently shared a conversation, prompted by an Instagram post from Blair Imani (A Guide for Tough Conversations [Instagram] 1/10/2024). In this post Blair shares thoughts on how to begin these conversations about topics that can feel confronting, in a way that supports safety and exploration:

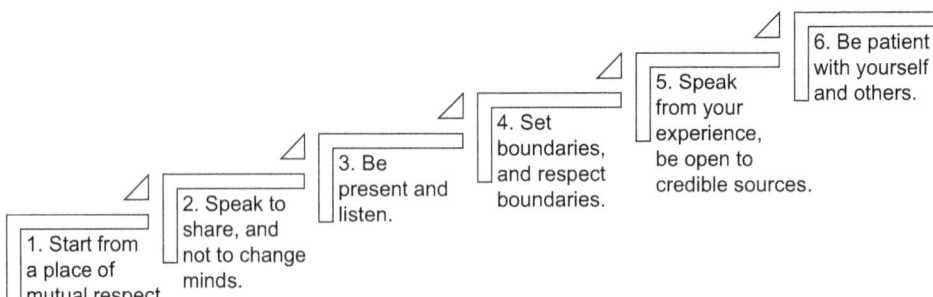

It feels useful to share this, as I had a particular reflection after reading and considering this. People can find change and neurodiversity-affirming practice leaves them vulnerable and challenged and these are uncomfortable feelings we have to sit with. Importantly, though, as we grow and develop, if we are the ones starting the conversation, we want to try and have those tough conversations in a way that creates safety to explore and reflect. My purposeful communication on this topic, I reflected, was often to try to 'win' someone over (see point 2 above) and that I am holding in mind much more now, that it is sharing, rather than trying to change someone's mind.

REFLECTION

How do you find having these types of conversations? Are there skills you have that you can share with others? Do you think you need to develop some skills to make these conversations easier?

Practice Example

Take for example a parent who is finding it hard to manage a child's sensory seeking behaviours of climbing, where things are becoming unsafe, and they are also damaging property climbing on things that they should not. A parent may want a quick fix, they might want a way to tell the child 'no', however, we could support a conversation 'I wonder why they are climbing?'. This isn't about trying to win the conversation, but exploring and encouraging curiosity. We might explore the sensory seeking nature of an under stimulated vestibular system and how vestibular input can be integrated into

> other activities throughout their day; we might write a social story to support and coach the child with other safer seeking activities that they can experience along with maybe some visual keyring tools the parent could use to show the child these options in the moment. This is honouring their need for sensory input and movement, while also ensuring safety and offering coaching to do that. It is also not about winning but offering a conversation.

When we think about how to support any differences in behaviour, first we must get curious about what is driving that. Be it an adult who is constantly zoning out during a meeting, a child who won't stop clicking their pen in class, or a young person who will just get up and walk out of a classroom. With all these situations, the start must be curiosity. 'Once you have seen it, it is hard to unsee' was said by Arundhati Roy; it was shared with me during supervision by Kate Boot. It feels very important to neurodiversity-affirming practice, and something we have to be aware of, that once we start this learning and mindset shift, it opens up an awful lot around us that does not align with the practices and the values that we might want to be championing. Therefore, having the skills, references and sources to support these conversations becomes an important part of our professional development.

For different support needs the way we explore this will also change, for some individuals we might get curious with them: 'I noticed you were clicking your pen a lot when I was in class, I wonder why?' They might not even be aware of doing it, but we can think about it with them, 'I wonder if it might be because your body needed to move? I wonder if it might have been distracting your teacher, I noticed they kept telling you to stop. If your body needs to move, what quieter things can we find for you to do that with? Here are a few things we could try and you can tell me what you think.'

It might be as above: we do that wondering with a parent or individual close to the child to explore and shift their narratives if the individual themselves has support needs that mean they could not access that conversation. This can be particularly helpful with parents and education staff, creating that space for curiosity and a way to shift their views and thoughts in safe conversations with you. As a therapist we can facilitate this thinking and support a shift from viewing these parts of a neurodivergent presentation as solely problematic and a problem of the individuals, to an expression of their neurodivergent identity that we can explore and support.

If the impact of the presentation is affecting safety, or access to important and meaningful opportunities and occupations, then we have to think about how we set goals, with the individual to enable them to find ways to honour and affirm their needs but also engage in the things that are important to them, be it school, work or recreational activities.

The impact of sensory and energy regulation here is key, and knowing and understanding these differences and having ways to support is how we can affect a positive change.

We have to explore these things with double empathy at the forefront of our mind and an understanding that sometimes individuals will show up differently in different environments for a variety of reasons.

Neurodivergent Capacity: Harriet Richardson

Neurodivergent people can experience the world much more intensely than neurotypicals. Our emotional experiences can be more intense. The sensory world can be more intense. For me, it's like everything is in ultra-HD constantly, every sound, touch, movement, feeling, it can all be very, very overwhelming! I recently went to London and suddenly remembered I'm autistic, after a few days of being in what I refer to as 'ADHD-setting', something that I find commonly happens as an AuDHDer. I was in the centre of Soho and stepped out of the venue we'd been to into chaos. There were people everywhere, flashing lights, traffic noise, people shouting, visual stimulation everywhere, bright colours, intense smells, people brushing past me; it was awful. In that moment, I made the decision that we quickly needed to go back to the hotel in a taxi and I didn't care how much it cost. I got in the taxi and experienced a low-level shutdown for 48 hours afterwards. I had intermittent periods of mutism for a day afterwards. Had I not got into that taxi at that point, I would have had intense meltdowns almost every day for potentially the entirety of the following week.

I was outside of my neurodivergent capacity. My cup had been filled earlier on in the day and the sensory overload of the environment had meant my cup overfilled and I was unable to cope with anymore. This happens a lot to neurodivergent people and it's something very hard to manage, especially for an AuDHDer who craves stimulation but can be quickly overstimulated. A lot of the time, it feels like I am either overstimulated or understimulated and finding the right balance is very difficult.

Coping with Change

So often, parents and professionals will ask me how to help a child cope with change. They want the child to get better at coping with changes and transitions. In fact, children often say to me that they would like to get better at coping with this. The strategy that I commonly recommend is:

To help Timmy to cope with change, give him advance notice of change and plans in time to discuss and check in with him after the change has occurred to problem-solve. When changes do occur, make sure that demands are lessened on Timmy following this and he has more time to process and recover from the difficulty of the change.

As an autistic person, I have fewer meltdowns now because I am mostly in control of my day and plans. If things change, I can make decisions to adapt things and give myself time to process the emotions which come with it. As a child, I did not have the option to do this and would constantly be stressed by my lack of autonomy with changes. Although the frequency has reduced, the intensity of emotions which come with changes is not any different. Difficulties coping with change is not something autistic people grow out of; it is not something that can be conditioned out of us. Instead, it's about validating how difficult changes are for the person and working collaboratively to resolve the situation. I know that I am much more able to cope with changes if I am emotionally regulated, my sensory environment is accessible, and I am with people I trust. That's why it is so important to work on autistic wellbeing to support autistic people experiencing changes.

When I moved house, I needed very low demands, reduced sensory stimulation and less social time. This meant that I reduced my working hours, spent more time exercising and engaging in special interests and did not have any social commitments. After the change, I gradually built up my working hours and social commitments at a pace I was comfortable with. Without these measures, my mental health would have been massively affected. Children transitioning to a new school, for example, need similar support to help manage their wellbeing during these times.

To me, change feels crushing, especially if it is something I had very specific expectations of. It can feel like being on a wobble board, where everything feels unbalanced, uncertain and unsafe. I feel uncomfortable and anxious and need lots of reassurance. During these times, I tend to eat lots of 'safe' foods and control my environment as much as possible. At times, this can look like needing people to act and talk to me in specific ways, because I need complete predictability. Changes physically hurt sometimes, and I am totally unable to move on from the emotion that comes with it. On a recent birthday, I was expecting to have an ice cream, go to a specific restaurant, and a specific park, with specific weather conditions. When the day did not match my expectations and plans, I became very stressed. Eventually, my partner told me we should go and get ice cream closer to home, I completely shut down and cried, asking him to take me home instead. He could not understand why I no longer wanted to have an ice cream. Unfortunately, too much had changed in the day that I could not cope with being outside of the house any longer and needed to go home and eat something that I could rely on to taste as I expected.

Burnout, Meltdowns and Shutdowns

As neurodivergent people, if we do not support and manage our capacity, we experience meltdowns and/or shutdowns. These two things present very differently, and shutdowns are seen as 'better' from an external perspective; however, the internal experience for me is very similar. Meltdowns are something that autistic people are commonly shamed for, especially as we enter adulthood, as it is felt we should 'grow out' of them, which is very damaging. As I have aged, my meltdowns have not become any less intense, though they are less frequent because I have more control over my environment and the demands placed on me. Having a meltdown or a shutdown is very traumatic, it's an intense emotional response to things that are outside of our capacity. Each meltdown or shutdown is scary, each and every time. Trying to stop a person having a meltdown when they are in one is not the goal, because once it is happening you cannot prevent it. However, it is about helping a person to find safe spaces and engage in less harmful stims when they are in a meltdown and preventing the person from experiencing the meltdown in the first place. We must shift our view from meltdowns/shutdowns being 'bad behaviour' or 'tantrums' because it is so far from this. Any person dealing with what an autistic person is dealing with before a meltdown, would end up in a meltdown but neurotypicals don't generally experience the same conditions and so it is hard for them to understand.

For many neurodivergent people, burnout is a looming cloud, which follows us around for most of our life. I constantly feel on the edge of burnout and have to walk the line between 'coping' and 'not coping' very carefully, which means managing my capacity. I have experienced periods of burnout from being a very young age. Burnout occurred for me at the end of the school day in primary and secondary school, where I would mask and be on high alert all day and then would go home without being able to speak, shutting myself in my room and putting some music in my ears to block out sensory stimuli and conversation. As a child, I generally went home to low demand and expectation and so I could recover my capacity for the next school day. As I got older, this became more difficult, and I would have days where I felt physically sick about going to school and could not get myself up in a morning because I was so exhausted. When I went to university, the demands on me suddenly shot straight up, as I was expected to mask and preform academically all day and then return home and manage my self-care, cook and clean for myself, socialise and organise myself for the next day. It was all too much, and I spent most days in bed, in darkness, not able to cook and feed myself, or shower and perform basic hygiene.

Burnout can have a devastating impact on a person and can co-occur with depression and anxiety. It's very different from the burnout that neurotypical people experience. Unfortunately, it is not yet recognised by the healthcare system, but there is more work and research being done on this to aid recognition. I am seeing children as young as six experiencing burnout symptoms, which is terrifying, given that demands and burnout only increase with age. Many of these children experiencing burnout are too exhausted to regularly attend school. As an adult, I reached a point of burnout where I was unable to continue as outside of my working hours I could no longer look after myself, verbally communicate or have any social interaction. The only thing that helped me to recover from that burnout was two months of unemployment and leaving my job to be self-employed. Now that I have more flexibility in my working life, social demands are lowered and I don't have to deal with politics in the workplace, I am in a much better place. We want children to learn and be supported to manage their levels of burnout so that they do not get to that stage (maybe as frequently) in their adult life.

How Do We Support Neurodivergent People to Manage Their Capacity?

I would love social skills training to be in part replaced by energy management strategies, psychoeducation and self-advocacy. I think they are such an important toolkit (neurokit) for many neurodivergent people, both adults and children. Autism and ADHD are dynamic disabilities and, as a result, our skills and needs can fluctuate on a daily, sometimes hourly basis. The supports we need will differ dependent on the environment, the demands and life circumstances. For this reason, it's very important that our clients are aware of Spoon Theory and Energy Accounting. I love to use energy levels in my practice, which involves using a visual of a battery and asking a client to identify where their energy currently lies within that scale. It's important to have check-ins throughout the day to get better at identify our energy levels. From there, we can identify patterns in our energy, for example, I notice a huge dip in energy after presentations, but a huge increase in energy after a run. I've noticed that my mind is more suited to work between 9–12 and 14–18 so I exercise in the morning and at lunchtimes to account for this. My working day is centred around my energy levels, which is a huge benefit of being self-employed as a neurodivergent person.

Self-advocacy is such a vital skill for neurodivergent people to learn because the statistics highlight just how socially vulnerable we are. Social Skills Training and ABA does not equip children with the skills to self-advocate and a lot of the time can reduce a child's ability to self-advocate. If we are taught to suppress our stims, make eye contact or communicate in ways that deviate from our natural style, we are taught to be vulnerable, because we are taught to comply. Compliance does not encourage self-advocacy and it is harmful. I was a very compliant child in school because I was eager to please everyone. I had no boundaries and constantly allowed people to be mean to me, tease me, tell lies about me and make me do things I didn't want to do. I was not liked for being myself, so I moulded myself to please others and to fit in with them. It was better, for me, to be bullied by my friends than to be sat alone at lunchtimes.

Empowering clients and providing autonomy are imperative to develop self-advocacy and prevent social vulnerability. This includes body autonomy because body autonomy violation occurs each time we ask a person to make eye contact or put up with people hugging or touching them. Until recently, I had no body boundaries and would let people hug me, kiss my cheek or put their arms around me when it physically hurt me due to tactile sensitivity. I did not know that it was okay to ask people not to do that because my body autonomy had been violated from such a young age. I love giving clients autonomy in sessions and seeing how happy they are with being given options and control of where the session goes. Unfortunately, I see many children who look surprised and confused when I say 'please let me know if there's anything in the session that you don't want to do, we can just move on'. Even with the free rein to decide whether or not they engage, clients will still say to me that they don't feel confident asking for a break or moving on in an activity, which is completely understandable. We also need to form a relationship with some people for them to feel comfortable with self-advocating, I know I certainly do.

My Experience of Monotropism

Finding the theory of monotropism was life-changing for me, and that is no exaggeration! All of my life I had had intense feelings of rage when people disrupted me from activities I was immersed in, and I could never explain or understand why. I thought I was just an irritable person to be honest. I always like to use the example of reading a book, as I've always been a huge bookworm. As a child, I would come home from school and hyperfocus in the world of books, getting lost in the characters and stories. While I sat in my safe space, blocking out the rest of the world, my parents would call me from the other room and I wouldn't process the information, though I would hear it. A few minutes later, they would enter the room and say my name a few times before my attention shifted from the book to them (the first painful attention split). They would ask me to unpack the dishwasher because tea was nearly ready and I'd say 'in a minute', immediately going back to my book because my attention had never truly left it. Five minutes later, I would still be reading the chapter, keen to get to the end because that felt complete and more comfortable, I would hear my name called with annoyance. Quickly, I'd scan the pages, knowing that any minute they'd come back in and take the book from me without having finished the chunk I was so invested in finishing. I'd panic, knowing time was running out. Eventually, they would come back in and snatch the book out of my hands in exasperation because 'tea was almost ready' and I would scream and cry and storm out the room. I would unpack the dishwasher, crashing the pots together in anger because my brain couldn't move on from the feeling of incompleteness. I couldn't move on from the emotion because it was so intense and because the issue had not been resolved. After unpacking the dishwasher, I would run back to the book and quickly finish reading it before I was called for dinner.

I cannot explain the feeling of having that book snatched out of the hand. Of not being able to finish the sentence, never mind the page or chapter. A monotropic split feels like coming out of a bubble of peace and solitude to a bombardment of sensory information, demands, verbal information, emotional and physical sessions. All those things come rushing in too quickly when I am not able to transition at my own pace and it is honestly one of the worst feelings I've ever experienced. It is physically painful. It hurts in my head and my heart and completely ruptures my sense of safeness. That might sound extreme, just because I couldn't finish a chapter, but that is reality.

Recommendation:

Here's some strategies I use to manage my monotropism and those of my clients:

- Using sand timers to transition attention more slowly, rather than alarms or sudden noises. Don't use touch to get someone's attention, it is better to place something in their visual field.
- Collaborating with the person for them to get to an agreed comfortable point before they move on (such as getting to the end of a game level or the bottom of a page of a book).
- I pick books which have midsections in a chapter or shorter chapters to read when I know I'm going to have to shift my attention more often.
- I generally try not to engage in things early in the day, where I will go into hyperfocus because I know I will struggle to do other things afterwards and I will be tired. For example, I will try to do most of my exercise or admin tasks at the start of the day and get into report writing later on.
- Not starting things when there is a short space of time with a time boundary, such as engaging in long activities before leaving the house on a morning. But making sure the person has time to engage in their interests at a better point in the day where there are not as many demands.
- Carrying around a notebook or using a phone to make notes. I will think of ideas that I want to engage in when I am out and about and can't but will make a list of them to return to later. I find it easier to move on from the idea once I know it is safely remembered in my phone notes.
- There will always be times where the person's attention has to shift suddenly to something else. I find it easier to pace myself during these times by carrying something around with me, which is attached to that focus. For example, I would have felt better being able to carry my book to the kitchen and maybe unpacking the dishwasher while I could still look at my book.
- Giving a person a time reminder can on some occasions cause anxiety but can also be helpful at other times. I find it helpful if my partner tells me we are due to leave in five minutes while I'm writing because I can decide to finish a sentence before the deadline, rather than stressing to finish after the time has passed.

Regulation

This term is at the heart of supporting 'behaviour'. I use this in inverted commas, because we all know what it means but actually behaviour as a definition is 'the way that someone behaves in a particular situation, under particular circumstances' (Cambridge Dictionary, 2024). But what we often really mean when we say 'behaviour' is actually loaded with the narrative of negative, different or unexpected ways of being within a neurotypical society and the unwritten rules we have about the 'right' ways to be. Often when used in reference to children and young people it holds a narrative of defiance or non-compliance, dare I even say naughty.

We can think about several 'types' of regulation; emotional, energy and sensory. All of these can be part of our roles as speech and language therapists, to understand, support and frame for individuals and those supporting them. Dysregulation significantly impacts communication.

> **REFLECTION**
>
> Put yourself for a moment in the last stressful situation you had, an interview, a relationship breakdown, a complaint at work. Were you functioning at your communication best?

For some neurodivergent individuals who experience high levels of stress and anxiety from being in the world, their communication skills are often likely to be impacted consistently across the day. I go back briefly here, to how useful assessments in optimal environments are, without exploring the impact of the world on the individual's communication.

Luke Beardon (2020) created the 'golden equation' for autistic individuals, but I think here we can adapt it and suggest that this is the case for all neurodivergent individuals:

$$\text{Neurodivergent person} + \text{environment} = \text{outcome}$$

So, if the outcome isn't desirable for the individual, or others in their lives, we need to look at the formula. One way to think about this is that the neurodivergent person might be lacking a skill that we need to support them to develop. Another is that the individual is just fine as they are and it is the people or the physical environment that needs to change. Perhaps it is a combination of both of those things.

There is a wonderful model used by our Occupational Therapy colleagues that I often lean in to, as an expansion I suppose of Beardon's equation, and that is the model of human occupation (Kielhofner and Burke, 1980). The model includes volition, habituation, environment and performance skills. It is a way that therapists understand and support individuals to engage in their daily activities and roles. Essentially, I would argue that is the goal of a speech and language therapist too, and we can use this to consider both the therapy we deliver, and the goals we set and recommendations we make. We have to consider the big picture, in order to develop communication skills. Below I have adapted it with more 'lay' terms for us speech and language therapists.

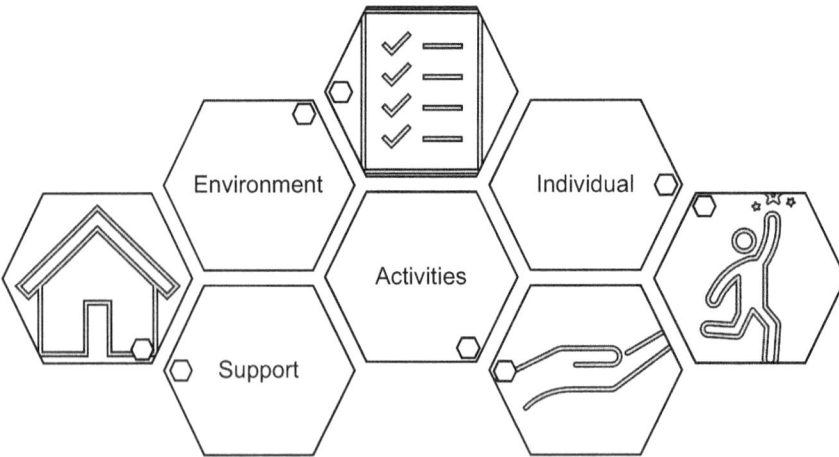

First, the individual, they are central to this. We must consider them, how they experience the world and their internal experiences too. If there is a challenge we see them experiencing, we holistically can consider what goes on around them, but equally need to be curious about their internal experiences.

If we think of the environment, when we are supporting individuals or making recommendations, the environment within which they are in will either enable or disable. So we can consider how this might be best adapted and adjusted in communication environments for that person.

I have then grouped volition and habituation here into activities: when thinking about a neurodivergent individual we can think about the activities in which they are expected to participate, what is their motivation, does this play in to their values and interests? How can we factor in preferences of activity, meeting the 'just right challenge' (Parham and Fazio, 2008) so things are stimulating but not overwhelming? If there is a mismatch between the individuals' preferences and motivation, with the tasks expected of them, we are likely to see a dysregulated response, whether this is shut down and refusal, or a more obvious physical response such as leaving the space or throwing the activity away.

Finally, the support, which links with an individual's performance capacity:

- What support do they need to engage in the activities?
- Is it the right person? Can it be any person, with the right approach?
- Do they need fluctuating support?
- What tools are supportive for the task?

If we consider this model, we can support conversations with others about which part of this might be breaking down when we observe individuals in distress or presenting with dysregulation. It can be a useful framework to promote crucial curiosity about what might be showing up for a neurodivergent individual, and I feel this is something that can be applied in the early years, through to adulthood and the workplace.

Here we must tread carefully, this is not about placing neurotypical expectations on neurodivergent people's skills, for example well they can't take turns in conversation, so we need to teach them that skill, or they can't sit still so we need to teach them too. Instead, here, we could look at teaching this person some self-advocacy about their communication style or self-awareness of their body and its need to move and ways that they can seek that movement.

So, what kind of things can we use? Well, if you are offering an affirming therapy approach basically there is not an 'off the shelf' resource which can present as a challenge if you are working particularly in a more consultative way. But we know that support strategies need to be adapted and nuanced to be meaningful, so there is a space here for good quality training and support of other individuals around the neurodivergent person so that they can work in a flexible and differentiated way to create effective outcomes.

A few good tools that can provide a 'skeleton' that you, or people you are working with who deliver the support, can then 'flesh out' are recommended:

- Autism Level Up – there are a wide range of incredible tools on their website and more recently a book that has been produced that supports energy regulation
- *Autism, Identity and Me*, by Rebecca Duffus
- *Interoception Awareness Curriculum*, by Kelly Mahler
- Energy Accounting and Spoon Management tools , such as the cutlery drawer by SENDWISE Hub.
- Social Stories and Comic Strip Conversations
- *Language for Behaviour and Emotions*, by Branagan, Cross and Parsons
- Self-Advocacy Toolkit, from the Autism Education Trust
- Sensory preferences checklists or questionnaires
- Talking Mats

In addition, we might think about adult approaches (the environment/support piece of the equation) that they can use to reduce the demands, or shift the way that they place demands on an individual:

- PACE approach, by Dan Hughes
- PANDAS model from the PDA Society
- *Declarative Language Handbook*, by Linda Murphy
- *Co-Regulation Handbook*, by Linda Murphy
- Sensory Environment Audit Tools
- Inclusive Communication Environment Tools
- Trauma-informed Practice

This is by no means exhaustive, but a place to begin some further research into things that you can use within your work. I think it is important here though to highlight that within a consultative model, if these things are being recommended to individuals to use and deliver we must ensure, in order to be affirming, that those people have got the knowledge and skills to be able to deliver these strategies in an affirming, flexible and adaptable way and that they themselves are challenging the way in which they view behaviour of neurodivergent individuals.

Connection Over Compliance

This is an important message, reframing our expectations and ways of being with neurodivergent individuals (PDA Society, 2024). We have to offer safety and security, coming from a place of curiosity and kindness. A lot of thinking stems from a behavioural approach to things, we look at the triggers and we identify strategies, reward the behaviour you want to see and ignore that behaviour you don't. Stickers, and consequences, rewards and sanctions.

I urge you seek out space to reflect and think about how and what message these kinds of behavioural strategies can create for neurodivergent individuals when they 'fail' to meet the unrealistic expectations put on them or feel shamed because of their response.

Seeking connection is at the heart of being human, we are social animals, neurodivergent or not. When we look for blind compliance, this can be met for a lot of neurodivergent individuals with experiences of trauma, questioning of the reasons for these 'rules' and what might be perceived as defiance.

When we notice behaviour with the right lens of compassion, and curiosity and kindness, we can begin to foster a sense of safety and connection. Generally, then, when individuals feel safe, connected and trust is built we find increased conversations and cooperation in those moments.

This leads us to explore any advice we might be giving to parents or professionals, or indeed the strategies we might use within therapy sessions to attempt to achieve cooperation, participation and engagement. Strategies that we might use of work first, then reward, are grounded in compliance-based approaches, Yes, it is our job to be engaging, but using compliance based approaches can be ineffective and may actually reduce potential for effective therapy outcomes.

Reward systems are often recommendations made by speech and language therapists and other professionals working in the field, however, this blanket approach again does not consider each individual and their profile and requires nuanced approaches. The faithful sticker chart, as an example, where when not thought out can create no opportunity for success, and a child then sabotages it. Or they are used in a punitive and shaming way when stickers are taken away or loud reminders made in front of others about what is needed to gain a sticker in a bid to get a child to comply through embarrassment or punishment.

> **REFLECTION**
>
> Think back to your own childhood, or perhaps even as an adult within workplaces or relationships, the impact on you when someone embarrassed you as a way of getting you to do what they asked? Or punished you for not doing as asked? Or threatened you to get you to comply? How did that feel? Is it a strong memory that you have retained? Do you want to encourage or show up for the future generation or colleagues in that way?

There are bodies of work that look into how we apply consequences, and that natural and logical consequences are generally viewed as the best way to support an understanding of the impact of one's actions. This might, for example, look like a child refusing to wear a coat to go outside for break, naturally this person is going to get cold; logically, when they say they are cold, they will have to go back inside to get their coat and must pause their play or regulation to do so. An illogical and compliance-based consequence might be that if they do not put their coat on, they cannot go outside. Here, while it might feel logical, the learning experience is then based on punishment, as opposed to a natural moment of learning. For some neurodivergent individuals their regulation of temperature is different and they genuinely might not mind being outside without a coat; for others, the demand may be too big in that moment, and we as adults need to reframe how we offer that coat; and still for others, they need that learning opportunity in a concrete way of actually getting outside, feeling the cold and then needing their coat.

As speech and language therapists we can often be a sounding board for parents and education and care staff about how to support behaviour, and these are the spaces that we need to show up for neurodivergent individuals when we are recommending and working through how they are supported. ABC charts are often used to explore behaviour of individuals, particularly within the education and care sectors. These charts look at the antecedent – what was happening before the 'behaviour', what the behaviour was, and then the consequences that the individual experienced positive or negative. While these tools can be helpful to explore perhaps regular occurrences of a particular behaviour, that the individual cannot talk about, nor can adults with curiosity unpick, they are often limiting.

For example, when we think about the 'coke bottle' or 'iceberg' models,[4] where little things that we might not see can be happening under the surface, and what we see is the behaviour, if those little things and small 'shakes' to the bottle throughout the day (before the lid flips and fizzes) an ABC chart might only catch the final 'shake' because it does not look at the big picture of that individual's experiences.

For some neurodivergent individuals, and in particular those with a PDA profile, the 'shaking' can begin from the moment they wake, with the demands of waking up and getting out of bed; for others the transition from sleep to wake can begin those 'shakes'. So, think broadly, if you are using these tools, about what you know about the individual and what might have been going on for them before the final 'shake' that caused the 'fizz'. I have struggled to find an original reference for this analogy, but I think it is a helpful way of viewing some of the behaviours we might see or hear about in neurodivergent individuals, both children and adults.

Why Can't You Just Do as You Are Told? Harriet Richardson

Gosh, I have heard this more times than I can count: 'Why can't you just …' was a common phrase that I got used to hearing. I never had the answer to the question, though since my identification, I can! I'm going to give a few examples of things that I did as a child that made absolutely no sense when seen through a neurotypical lens.

Supermarket Shopping

(Hat aged around 7)

Every week, my mum would take me food shopping and every week it would lead to a meltdown. Each time I would resist going and I would stress about it, pleading just to sit in the car. We would walk around the aisles and my mum would inspect everything to find the best quality vegetables and meats, comparing each one. We would mooch around, sometimes looking at things, which weren't on the list. I could feel the anger building and building. As we walked through the shop, my mum would try to talk to me about things and I would give grunts as responses and try to put my headphones in to listen to music. I would swing on the trolley and sometimes bump into things. I'd tip onto my tip toes and stand on the back of the trolley, seeing how far I could push it before everything fell out or I got told off. As we moved through the aisles my mum would pull the trolley along behind her, trying to help me navigate the crowds. Then all of a sudden, I rammed the trolley into the back of her heels and wouldn't say sorry.

The reason for this was quite simple, I was completely over and under stimulated at the same time. I tried to self-advocate, expressing a wish not to go but I could never explain why because I didn't understand why, and people just thought I was being difficult. The sensory environment of a supermarket is hell, people were pushing past me, getting in my way, there was music and bright lighting and I couldn't put my headphones in to block it out because my mum wanted to talk to me. Then there was the waiting, waiting for my mum to scan everything before moving on to wait somewhere else, then waiting at the check-out and waiting for her to pack. I had nothing in my hands to keep me mind occupied so I would be restless, both in body and mind. I would climb on the trolley to meet my movement needs, only to be told off. My needs weren't getting met so finally I became so dysregulated I hurt my mum.

Shower Time

I have always been well-known for taking the longest of showers. Until I moved out of my family home, this was one of my parents' biggest bugbears. I would be in the shower room for hours at times, when we needed to be somewhere or someone else needed to use warm water. I could never explain at the time why but now that I know more about autism and ADHD, this makes perfect sense and is something I still struggle with.

First, I have no concept of time whatsoever, in fact time agnosia is one of the most challenging aspects of having ADHD personally. Bathrooms don't have clocks, so I'm not able to tell how long I've been in there. Second, the amount of transitions involved in showering are extreme. Then there's the aspects of my chronic illness and sensory issues, where I cannot cope with extreme changes in temperature, such as going from warm water to cold air. This means I would procrastinate getting out of the shower because I wanted to delay that sensation. After I'd eventually got out of the shower, I would then spend hours sat in a towel doing nothing but sitting on the floor and staring at the ceiling. I couldn't cope with another transition, because I felt exhausted. I was completely in the grasp of ADHD paralysis or autistic inertia (never entirely sure which) because I had stopped and my brain couldn't get started again to tell my body to move.

It is so important that we ask the person we work with what is going on for them internally and why they are finding something difficult or acting in a particular way. Using Talking Mats really helped me to understand the perspectives and reasons for children's behaviour in SEMH settings. A lot of the time, the children had the answers for why they had done what they had done but weren't often given the chance to explain. We would often look at the child's behaviour from an external perspective and analyse it, using observations and assumptions rather than simply going to the source and problem-solving collaboratively. This is how trust and respect is formed, through being curious and trying to understand.

Homework

In primary school, my mum would sit with me to do my homework because I needed help to stay on task. She would help me practice my spelling and I would want to rush through it, dropping pencils off the table or fiddling with things rather than looking at what she was showing me. When we read books, I would jiggle the book up and down while holding it and would try to move the book away from her so I could just see it. I would write with the pen in my fist rather than between my fingers like I did in school and would not change my posture no matter how many times I was asked. This obviously led to some strain in our relationship because she was trying to help me and it looked like I was being defiant, especially when teachers never saw any of these behaviours in school.

The reason behind this was a result of ADHD. I needed someone to keep me on track because my attention span to unmotivating activities was short. Due to hyperactivity, I needed to be constantly moving and I had been sat in a chair all day at school and couldn't cope with this any longer. I dropped things off the desk so that I had excuses to move around and I fiddled to cope with having to sit in the chair. Jiggling the book up and down meant that I was getting my movement needs met, and I was able to read the book whilst I was doing this (not sure how). I would move the book away from my mum because she was sat too close to me and I wanted to move away so I wasn't experiencing tactile stimulation. My hands are hypermobile and I can only maintain a certain writing posture for so long before my hands begin to hurt, which meant I needed to use a different writing grip, which I was not allowed to use at school. My hands were exhausted from writing this way all day.

Conclusion

Ultimately this is a twofold chapter: first, how to view behaviour and take the right 'lens' to show compassion and curiosity for those behaviour differences. Second, how we can then show up in conversations to advocate for others to consider being more curious and then think about how support strategies are used.

Chapter Summary

- Your thoughts matter: how deeply you explore what you are seeing on the surface with neurodivergent individuals.
- Your curiosity matters: we have to reinforce the importance of curiosity and kindness when supporting in the moment and reflecting on the behaviours we see from neurodivergent individuals.
- Your strategies matter: and the importance of making these meaningful for each individual, with their wellbeing at the centre, considering them now and in the future.

References

Beardon, L. (2020) *Avoiding Anxiety in Autistic Children: A Guide for Autistic Wellbeing*. London: Sheldon Press.
Cambridge Dictionary (2024) 'behaviour' – definition. https://dictionary.cambridge.org/dictionary/english/behaviour (accessed on 24/8/2024).
Kielhofner, G. and J.P. Burke (1980) A model of human occupation, part 1: Conceptual framework and content. *American Journal of Occupational Therapy*, 34, 572–581.
Parham, L.D. and L.S. Fazio (eds) (2008) *Play in Occupational Therapy for Children*. St. Louis, MO: Mosby/Elsevier.
PDA Society (2024) 'Understanding behaviours'. www.pdasociety.org.uk/life-with-pda-menu/family-life-intro/understanding-behaviours/ (accessed on 25/8/2024).

10
Reflective Practice

Here We Are

Honestly, I cannot quite believe I am writing this next sentence …

But …

As we come to the end of this book (yes, it has happened, the whole thing has nearly been written!) we have to consider the next steps, the pulling together of all the learning, reflecting and exploring I hope you will have done to dive deep into your values and unconscious biases, explore social concepts and challenge, I imagine, a lot of your thinking and ways of practicing – or at least that was my experience when I began on this journey, and continue to be my experiences as I keep learning.

To centre myself for a moment: I will experience a lot of potential discomfort in feedback from the way that I have written and collated this book, and this is something I will have to sit with. That is part of learning and part of this process, being uncomfortable. This can for me be exacerbated by my rejection sensitive dysphoria, as part of ADHD. I recognise though that central to our learning is our ability to pause and reflect and, increasingly, I am becoming aware of part of that being, sitting with uncomfortable feelings. It is part of our profession; it is an expectation that we grow and develop and something that we train in and focus on throughout our careers. So we have to consider how it might feel at times to grow and develop in such a way, that is not just to find out about a new way of working, but also, that might challenge what we have been doing before.

We will meet neurodivergent individuals in all areas of our lives, in the individuals we support, the colleagues we work with, our friendships, our family, people in the supermarket, those who attend your gym. We should be looking to unapologetically champion neurodiversity-affirming practice, being the change we want to see. As Pete was quoted earlier in the book and, to adapt his words, wherever you go there will be neurodivergent people. And for them, we do this growing.

Being a Neurodivergent SLT: Harriet Richardson

From being identified as an AuDHDer, I have begun to understand what my strengths and areas of challenge are with regard to practicing as an SLT. I will never be able to specialise in speech sounds due to my auditory processing difficulties, nor would I want to. Therapy can be challenging for me due to the amount of executive function demands that are placed on me, such as prepping and planning, sending regular updates, measuring progress and so on. Schools are not the right place to me because there is too much of a social demand and keeping on top of a case load that does not tend to get discharged is very difficult for me. Instead, I have strengths in assessment and consultation, and I find that these things demand less social, executive function and communicative demand on me. I find that working in services where I conduct assessments, write a report and handover to other professionals is much easier for me to manage. I am also very good at the analytical side of speech therapy, as I notice details and connections that others might not, and I work very creatively in how I assess people. Now that I work flexibly and often remotely in self-employment, my strengths as an SLT are highlighted and I can provide great services to my clients. I am no longer surviving through a working life, which took everything out of me.

I spent a large amount of time questioning whether I could continue to be an SLT for a variety of reasons, post-identification. Not because I thought autistic people couldn't be SLTs but because I initially believed that as long as I worked in the SLT profession, I would never be healthy. Since starting to study to be an SLT, I have been in and out of burnout due to the demands it placed on me. My support needs, generally low, became much higher at certain times throughout my studying and career as a result. After my diagnosis, I wondered if I would ever be able to cope with the social and communication demands of being an SLT, needing to constantly be social and communicating with clients, their families, professionals and members of a team. I was shattered all of the time and my quality of life was very poor. I would return home from a day of work without being able to speak, needing someone to prompt me for basic self-care and in a state of constant dysregulation. Now I've moulded my working life to suit my brain, I have more capacity more generally in my life and my mental health is so much better.

When We Know Better

Hopefully we now have a better shared understanding of the perspectives of neurodivergent individuals, the nuance required to support them effectively and the ways in which we can support skill development, self-awareness, acceptance and advocacy in an affirming way. We can develop our own skills to flip the narratives that society has created and challenge the ableism within ourselves.

So, let's think about how we support ourselves further and our colleagues within the profession to create a ripple of change, because we have to change minds to make change. Part of the nuance of this is knowing how and when to approach these conversations, recognising your relationships with others and how this impacts the way in which we might speak about these topics. Be purposeful, and be strong, be an advocate, but go gentle when needed, sometimes being too strong can have a negative impact on the cause and switch people off. Remember, this is not about winning a conversation, as much as our purpose is to make changes.

Let's pause and reflect on our neurodivergent colleagues with this from Harriet:

Myth Buster: SLTs do not have to have perfect speech, language and communication to be good at their job.

So frequently, other professionals have told me that colleagues are shocked when they speak about knowing an autistic Speech and Language Therapist. They struggle to imagine how that works and how I could possibly do the job correctly. That's often because there's this narrative embedded into healthcare profession training that we must have perfect communication skills and it's ableist. As I was training to be an SLT, I overheard a clinical educator laughing with a colleague that they had had a student with a lisp before and they had failed them because 'why on earth would they be a good SLT if they can't even model the correct speech sounds?' To get onto a university course, we must prove that our communication skills are 'as expected'. Should I have known I was autistic and semi-speaking at university, I'm unsure whether I would have been allowed on the course. The HCPC's Standards of Proficiency state that we should 'be able to select, move between and use appropriate form of verbal and non-verbal communication with service users and others'. What if I am unable to speak and use AAC? Does this mean I do not meet the standards of proficiency I should as part of my role?

In a role supporting neurodivergent teenagers, an education professional used some non-literal language that I really didn't understand, and they joked that I shouldn't be an SLT because I'm supposed to be able to teach my clients this. It hit me quite hard to hear that because I'd spent a very long time being self-conscious of my language and communication differences. I felt like they were right – I wasn't up to the job. But they couldn't have been further from the truth. My own social communication differences are similar to those I see for sessions, and it has been immensely helpful for them to spend time with someone else that finds non-literal language challenging and to unpick it together. There is so much strength in vulnerability and our clients often need to see that in their therapist to feel safe to explore their own differences. I may not be able to teach them what each non-literal phrase means or how to use a certain word in a sentence, but I can show them how to self-advocate when they don't understand and not feel like they are alone in their differences. Being an autistic SLT, who is open about the challenges they face, can improve a client's self-esteem. It can create a space that is safe to make mistakes in and grow.

To say that people can only be SLTs if they have a specific vocabulary range, a specific speech sound system and neurotypical communication styles is embedded in classism, racism and ableism. Unfortunately, our profession lacks the diversity needed to cater for a range of service users and to accommodate different life experiences. This means a lot of minority groups do not receive the accommodations and tailored support they need to succeed in therapy. As a profession, we need to redefine what it means to be an SLT. There is no one way to communicate, use language and speak. To think there is makes our belief system inherently ableist, because we view our communication skills as better than others'.

Sitting with Discomfort

I imagine some of the topics may have caused you discomfort as you have read. Or perhaps you have skimmed them because they haven't felt relevant or did feel too uncomfortable.

That is ok. This journey will be at your own pace. I urge you, when you feel able to, revisit those parts of this book, seek out safe spaces to explore the content and what is showing up for you in order to grow as a professional. This can all be reflected on and written up as part of your continuing professional development records.

Some of the discomfort will come from wondering about harm you might have caused with previous support strategies you used; some might come from now seeing some of the impact that racism and supremacy have had on the lives of others, or perhaps yourself.

> 'primum non nocere'; first, do no harm
>
> (WHO, 2023)

Kate Cummings, a fabulous speech and language therapist, introduced me to this principle in conversations about gestalt language processing and trauma-informed approaches. This led me to explore the terminology a bit more. As health care professionals, we are led by the World Health Organisation, which gives us the value of doing no harm to our 'patients'. Which, in principle, is one of those 'well, of course' eye-roll kind of comments. But if we consider this on a deeper level, is it harmful as therapists not to adapt our practice?

When lived experience of neurodivergent individuals tells us about how harmful masking and compliance-based approaches can be, this information is out there, and available to us, and yet there are some who are not seeking to know more and do differently. Is this harmful?

If we are silent, when we see practice that we know is not affirming, if we sit by and let it go, are we doing harm? It is something I often reflect on and wonder about. Those conversations again are difficult to have. If we are truly seeking to do no harm, we must be highlighting and contributing to conversations that are going to shift practice in the settings where we are working, whether that is within community clinics, education provisions or elsewhere, at a systemic and political level.

This is the beginning of a process of unlearning, some of the topics will just confirm thoughts you had, perhaps validate them. However, for others this will cause challenge to beliefs and practice. The phrase I have used throughout this is don't throw the baby out with the bath water; we should not end up throwing out valuable parts of practice because of a heightened energy and enthusiasm to be more neurodiversity-affirming. It is a mindset, a lens, a set of values and our application of those, and an on-going willingness to listen, learn and grow, and it takes time.

This book has tried hard not to offer a hard and fast rule, but to note the nuance and clinical decision making that is required, the critical thinking we must apply to work better and in a more honouring and affirming way for the neurodivergent individuals that speech and language therapist's support. In that, it is a very exciting change that we as a profession can be part of, and as individuals be at the forefront of within the services we work, but there is an element of self-regulation we need to have, a pause and sit moment to process, consider and discuss how shifts in practice can be made.

Discomfort isn't easy. But it shows growth and is part of how we do better for our service users. So, find ways to manage that discomfort, seek supervision space and connection and networks that enable the conversation to continue. Please do not let it stop as you close the final page of the book.

In growth, we see change and that ultimately is what neurodiversity-affirming practice is all about, change, for the better, to enable the neurodivergent community that we serve to feel safe to be themselves, advocate for their needs and reasonable adjustments and take their place as part of the rich tapestry of society in an equitable way to their neurotypical counterparts.

Moving into Neurodiversity-Affirming Practice Is Not Supposed to Feel Comfortable. In Fact, We Might Experience a Lot of Guilt Following Our Transition: Harriet Richardson

It isn't easy to look back on your practice and evaluate the things you did previously, now viewing them as ableist and damaging to the clients we serve. As a neurodivergent SLT, this has been especially uncomfortable for me, and has caused many sleepless nights. Unknowingly, I put my clients through the same things that I was put through as a child, which caused trauma. It's hard for me to admit to myself that I have practiced unethically, using rewards for compliance, not listening to children trying to advocate and sabotaging to make them communicate. However, we often do the best we can with the knowledge we have and to be able to move on in our practice we must forgive ourselves and do better. The fear of admitting to using unethical approaches can stop many people from progressing in neuro-affirming practice. Practicing from a neuro-affirming approach is not meant to be comfortable, it is challenging in more than just a professional context. When we start to learn more about the neurodiversity paradigm, this filters into our personal lives and can impact on relationships and lifestyle. It's more than just a shift in practice, it's a shift in perspective and morals and that's a big transition to go through. Especially for lone SLTs this can be hard, as when we do these things alongside others the community aspect is beneficial. There are now lots of social media groups across the world for neuro-affirming practitioners to consult with each other, ask questions and for peer supervision, as well as a Clinical Excellence Network and working groups. Reach out to people in similar workplaces and in independent practice who are neuro-affirming for support. It is also worth looking for a supervisor who is neuro-affirming to help you to develop your practice from this lens.

What Is Your Role?

Working collaboratively with Kate Boot, we have developed the following list of suggestions for therapists to continue their development of reflective practice and take the learning from this book forward to create meaningful change in the services within which we serve.

As a therapist:

- Seek out supervision that is a safe space in order to enable you to continue your reflection and learning.

- Develop networks of other therapists and allies that you can reflect and learn and grow together with.
- Think about how you will approach these conversations with other stakeholders you talk to in the lives of neurodivergent people.
- Consider which things you will add to your toolbox for therapy strategies and how you will use these in an affirming way.

As a supervisor:

- Weave into your supervision sessions a thread of intersectionality and neurodiversity-affirming reflective points.
- Offer a 'critical friend' role to your supervisees in a way that is safe for you and them to explore their values and beliefs in relation to the concepts we have discussed.
- Find yourself a supervisor who has knowledge and learning on these areas and can continue your own growth in your supervision.
- Consider how you are supporting your neurodivergent supervisees: have you had conversations about reasonable adjustments for example?
- If you supervise therapists who are part of marginalised groups, have you considered how you make supervision a safe space for them?

As a service lead:

- Weave into your conversations with others, your policies and procedures and pathways neurodiversity and intersectionality affirming language.
- Challenge your practitioners and services you support to learn more.
- Think about how these values can show up in the way that you support other therapists who are neurodivergent, or have other intersectional identities.
- How can your learning feed into your recruitment processes and reasonable adjustments you offer during this.

For all therapists:

- Seek out further learning and consider who is producing this and specifically looking out for opportunities for learning from individuals and groups from historically and systematically oppressed groups.
- Complete the UK SLT Pride Network and RCSLT working group self and team audit tool (RCSLT, 2024).
- Plot your own position on the zones tools in relation to neurodiversity-affirming, LGBTQ+ and anti-racism in the references (EYFS, no date; RCSLT and UK SLT Pride Network, 2024; Anti-Racism Resource Guide, no date) to enable you to further identify areas of learning.
- Think concretely about things you want to change in terms of your practice I find the stop, start and keep doing model can be useful.

Things I will ...	Example
Stop Doing	Using compliance-based now/next work then reward within therapy sessions
Start Doing	Advocating for kindness and curiosity when met with conversations about the behavioural differences of neurodivergent individuals
Keep Doing	Using play within my recommendations and therapy sessions

We can think back to Chapter 1 here and Brene Brown's core values activity, and how perhaps the learning you have done might have challenged those values, or maybe created some new ones showing up for you. If you did not do that activity at the beginning of the book, here is a good space to take a moment, open up the website and get a pen and paper and begin to think deeply about yourself. You might have found this opening up throughout the book and the chapters, or now might be time with a moment to pause and reflect on the learning so far. I'd advise with a beverage of your choosing.

Supervision Tools and Ideas

In terms of how we apply and reflect on our learning and provide a structure and a format for this, you might already have ways that you do this. In which case, if they work for you and speak to your thinking style, stick with it. The main aim with supervision and reflection is offering a space to think about learning and how to take that forward with practice and give a space to decompress and re-energise. I would hope that at this point you have had some reflections throughout the chapters, and this is a space and call to document that and create some tangible actions to move forwards. So, here are a few options, alongside the stop, start and keep doing suggestions above.

Solo Supervision

Gibbs' Reflective Cycle (1988):

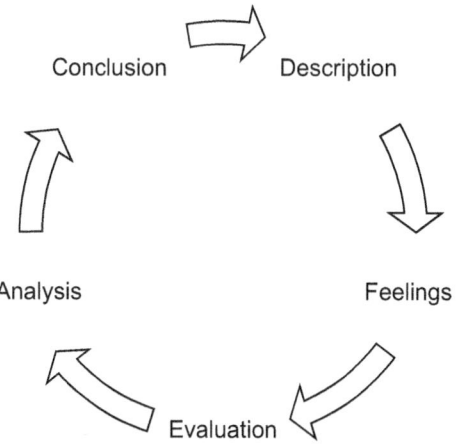

Gibbs' cycle enables a format to think about a particular piece of learning or experience in the description section and then move through the feelings, evaluation and analysis of this experience. This can be something you use for yourself to think through particular elements of learning, it may also be something you could use in supervision, or complete and take to a supervision to talk through learning or share with your team and colleagues.

> **REFLECTION**
>
> Think of a moment in the book you have had a thought that has created a space to reflect, and work through this cycle; how did that feel for you? Did it feel helpful, if not maybe try the next suggestion.

Kolb's Reflective Practice (2015)

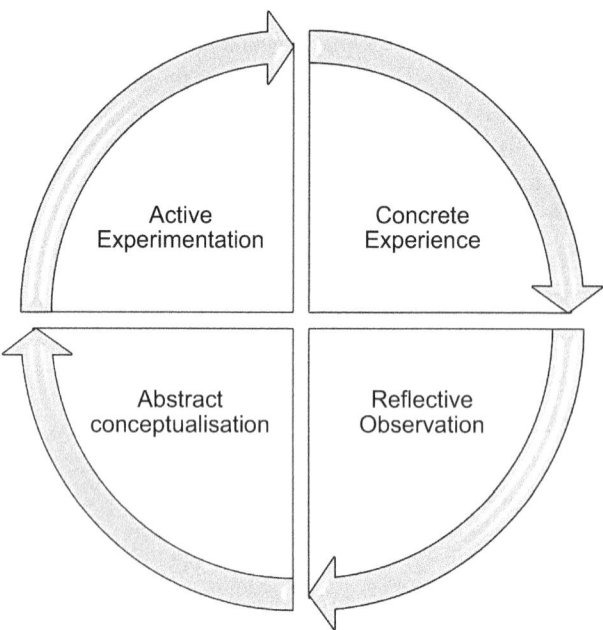

Kolb's reflective cycle has less stages than Gibb's, and begins with the concrete experience This might be something you have read, thought or observed in practice, or a conversation, any number of concrete experiences. It then follows through with your reflective observations, here you might consider things such as how you felt about it, what worked or didn't, analysing the experience or learning. Following that you can start to think about theories or concepts, this is the reflective part where you start to think about doing things differently. Finally, we then give those ideas a go and the process begins again.

> **REFLECTION**
>
> Again, give this a go for a particular thought you have had, how did this process feel for you? Did this feel better than Gibbs?

Either way, you now have two wonderful, documented pieces of CPD for your diary, so that's a win!

Group Supervision

For group supervision structures I would highly recommend the reflective case discussion model of group supervision. This format can be incredibly helpful in bringing a particular key learning opportunity to the group: this might be a tricky case you are working on within a challenging system, or a particular piece of learning you have done and want to explore its implications for practice. It encourages reflective conversations, fostering professional curiosity and takes away from a solution focussed approach, which is important when we think about neurodiversity-affirming practices in their infancy within our practice and services (Department for Education and Ruch, 2020).

As we continue as professionals, individuals and humans to learn and grow in our understanding of the world and the people in it, we will experience a plethora of thoughts and feelings, challenging us internally, and what we can do is sit with that. Equally important is to find a space to explore those externally. To make sense of the thoughts that we are experiencing, explore them and the impact on our practice. So, these cycles and processes of supervision are important and the relationship you have with your network to have these conversations. Supervision is often dictated for us, by who supervises us, which is often dictated by the systems in which we work. However, we can seek spaces to have these conversations outside of those processes if that feels safer and more secure, set up a book club to think about chapters, join a group supervision programme, find like-minded peers to read articles and reflect together, share clinical cases within peer supervision.

Applying the Learning

Below are some case studies that Fatimah and Kate worked on, that you might want to explore in a group conversation, maybe with a couple of colleagues, or your whole team. They offer a chance to practice these kinds of conversations and explore how it works on a more 'neutral' conversation, or these can be used by yourself now to apply your learning and think about how you might work within these situations.

Case Studies

This section offers a series of case studies designed to translate the concepts of intersectionality and neurodivergence into real-world contexts. These scenarios illuminate the complexities faced by individuals with intersecting identities, encouraging readers to critically examine their own practices and consider how they can better advocate for equity and inclusion.

By grounding theory in practice, these case studies provide actionable strategies and insights, bridging the gap between understanding and implementation. They are intended to inspire reflection and equip speech and language therapists with tools to challenge barriers and encourage neurodivergent-affirming, inclusive environments.

It is important to note that these case studies represent only a small selection of identities and experiences. The realities of intersectionality are vast and multifaceted, encompassing many voices, contexts and challenges that also deserve exploration. We hope these examples serve as a starting point for further consideration, dialogue, and commitment to understanding the rich diversity of lived experiences.

Case Study 1: Priya

Priya is a 46-year-old British-Tamil Hindu woman. She is autistic, dyslexic and dyspraxic, from a working-class background, and lives in a small town. Priya masks extensively in different environments, particularly in academic settings, cultural spaces and family gatherings. She experiences high anxiety around healthcare interactions, and is self-referring for concerns about her capacity to integrate socially into the environments she wants and needs to be in. She is studying for her PhD at University.

Questions for reflection:

1. How would you approach the initial assessment?
2. What would inform your choice of assessment tools?
3. What factors would you consider in therapy planning?
4. How would you approach understanding Priya's communication needs across different settings?
5. What service delivery considerations are important?

Discussion points:

The assessment and support process must consider:

- Cultural understanding of neurodivergence within Tamil communities;
- Temple attendance and religious festivals in scheduling;
- Communication expectations in extended family contexts;

- Impact of masking across university, home and community settings;
- Accessibility considering transport and financial constraints;
- Goals that recognise cultural values while supporting authentic communication.

What do you do ...

An SLT working with Priya:

- Uses only Western frameworks to understand family dynamics;
- Dismisses the importance of religious and cultural events in therapy planning;
- Recommends communication strategies that conflict with cultural expectations;
- Fails to consider financial barriers to accessing resources;
- Makes stereotypical assumptions about family views of neurodivergence;
- Sets goals without understanding cultural context.

Questions for reflection:

1. How has this SLT's cultural bias influenced their practice?
2. What systemic barriers are being overlooked?
3. What could be the immediate and long-term impact of this approach?
4. How might this affect Priya's engagement with services?
5. What changes would create more culturally safe practice?

Case Study 2: Hana

Hana is an 8-year-old refugee who is multiply neurodivergent. She lives with her mum, Dad and her twin sibling. They arrived in this country three months ago to flee conflict. Hana's parents are qualified doctors. The family is multilingual and religious. They live in temporary accommodation and are in the process of buying a house. Hana uses few words in any language, and is experiencing regular periods of frustration and distress.

Questions for reflection:

1. How would you approach your initial assessment?
2. What considerations would shape your choice of assessment tools?
3. How would you establish communication preferences and needs?
4. What factors would influence your therapy planning?
5. How would you approach parent/family collaboration?
6. What service delivery aspects need consideration?

Discussion points:

The assessment and support must consider:

- Complex interaction between trauma, neurodivergence, and language development;
- Cultural understanding of communication development and neurodivergence;
- Religious observations affecting timing and engagement;
- Housing instability impact on service access;
- Supporting authentic communication across languages;
- Building trust with healthcare systems.

What do you do …

An SLT working with Hana:

- Only assesses English language skills;
- Uses standardised assessments without cultural adaptation;
- Ignores trauma-informed practice principles;
- Sets English-only communication goals;
- Schedules sessions without considering religious observances;
- Excludes family expertise about Hana's communication.

Questions for reflection:

1. What assumptions underpin this practice?
2. How might this approach impact family engagement?
3. What barriers are being reinforced?
4. What aspects of Hana's identity are being ignored?
5. How could this harm Hana's communication development?

 Case Study 3: Rosie

Rosie is a white, 16-year-old, who is autistic, ADHD and has a diagnosed sensory processing differences. She lives with her mum and dad and goes to a mainstream Secondary school. Rosie also goes to a riding stables once a week, and a Neurodivergent Social Club. Rosie was assigned male at birth, and spent time identifying as non-binary, using pronouns they/them before becoming female and using she/her pronouns. Rosie's parents and education setting have been supportive. Rosie has an EHCP that states weekly speech and language therapy for at least 45 minutes, 1:1. She is currently presenting with semi-speaking across all settings. Following your initial assessment, Rosie identifies her main goal is to change her voice.

Questions for reflection:

1. How would you ensure Rosie's psychological safety in the therapy sessions?
2. What factors would you consider in therapy planning?
3. How would you develop a therapeutic rapport with Rosie?

Discussion points:

The assessment and support must consider:

- The intersection of gender and neurodivergence this young lady presents with;
- Systemic support of Rosie's goal and access to services to support this;
- The implications of mutism in getting her needs met across the day, and access to meaningful occupation;
- Social contexts that Rosie experiences, and how her communication needs adapt to these differing settings.

What do you do ...

An SLT working with Rosie:

- Excludes family from the discussions with Rosie around her goals;
- Identifies Rosie as too young to make decisions about her gender and works on social communication goals;
- Offers therapy sessions with a small room, that does not enable Rosie to meet her sensory processing needs;
- Uses therapy materials that speak only to cis-gender examples of social communication.

Questions for reflection:

1. What assumptions underpin this practice?
2. What barriers are being reinforced?
3. What aspects of Rosie's identity are being ignored?
4. How could this harm Rosie's communication development and well-being?

 ### Case Study 4: Malik

Malik is a 75-year-old mixed-race man, born to a Jamaican mother and a Pakistani father. He grew up in a working-class neighbourhood in Birmingham, where he experienced systemic racism and cultural tension. Malik is neurodivergent, diagnosed with ADHD in his later years. Recently, he experienced a stroke that has left him with significant swallowing and communication needs primarily around expressive language. He finds hospital settings overwhelming. Malik's family, including his daughter and son-in-law, who are also from mixed-heritage backgrounds, are involved in his care, but there are generational differences in how they perceive his neurodivergence and the challenges of his stroke recovery. His daughter is supportive, but his son-in-law tends to dismiss his neurodivergence, assuming that his needs are simply due to ageing or the stroke. Malik, who has always valued independence, resists therapy and prefers to manage on his own, feeling vulnerable in the hospital environment.

Questions for reflection:

1. How would you approach the initial assessment, considering Malik's intersectional identity, including his race, cultural background, neurodivergence, age, and recent stroke?
2. What factors would influence your choice of assessment tools, particularly considering Malik's experiences of systemic racism and cultural factors that may impact his perceptions of healthcare?
3. How can you balance Malik's desire for independence with his need for support in addressing his language and swallowing needs?
4. How would you adapt your communication and therapy plan to respect Malik's neurodivergent needs?
5. What role does Malik's family play in his therapy, and how can their cultural and generational perspectives be addressed in therapy planning?
6. What are the cultural, social and historical factors at play in Malik's care, and how can you ensure they are incorporated into the therapeutic process?
7. How do systemic inequalities (e.g., race and class) influence Malik's experience in the hospital and his interaction with healthcare services?
8. What emotional and psychological barriers might Malik face in engaging with therapy, especially given his history with systemic discrimination and potential feelings of vulnerability in the hospital?

Discussion points:

The assessment and support process should consider:

- The generational and cultural gaps in how Malik's neurodivergence and stroke recovery are understood by his family, particularly the differing views on his ADHD.
- The role of systemic racism in Malik's past experiences with healthcare and his potential mistrust of medical professionals.

- The psychological impact of growing up in a working-class, mixed-heritage household and how that may influence his self-perception and relationship with authority figures.
- How ADHD may manifest in later adulthood, and the need for adjustments in therapy to accommodate his needs.
- The intersection of race, age, and neurodivergence in healthcare settings, and how these factors may shape Malik's response to therapy.
- importance of including his family in therapy.
- The need for trauma-informed, culturally aware care that recognises the impact of past discrimination and cultural nuances in healthcare engagement.

What do you do ...

An SLT working with Malik:

- Fails to explore the impact of Malik's mixed-heritage background on his experiences of healthcare and systemic inequality.
- Uses standard assessment tools without adapting them to Malik's neurodivergence, age or cultural background.
- Does not acknowledge or address the generational differences in how Malik's family members view his neurodivergence and stroke recovery.
- Makes assumptions about Malik's ability to engage with therapy, ignoring the emotional barriers caused by his past experiences with racism and the hospital setting.
- Does not involve Malik's family adequately in understanding his needs, especially regarding their different perspectives on neurodivergence.
- Provides therapy without considering the cultural significance of race and class in Malik's identity and recovery process.

Questions for reflection:

- How has this SLT's lack of cultural awareness influenced their approach to therapy with Malik?
- What systemic and generational barriers are being overlooked in this case?
- How might Malik's intersectional identity affect his engagement with therapy and long-term recovery outcomes?
- What impact could dismissing the influence of systemic racism and cultural factors have on Malik's perception of healthcare services?
- What changes could be made to ensure a more inclusive, culturally competent approach to Malik's therapy?
- How can therapy be tailored to address Malik's unique intersectional needs while respecting his independence and acknowledging his family dynamics?

We End Where We Began

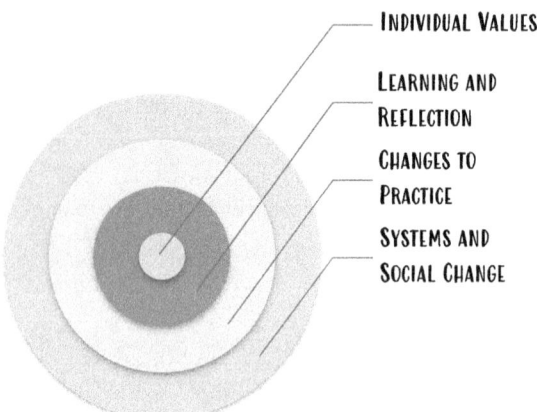

Our values are central to our being, and it is important as therapists we are aware of these and how they then radiate outwards in terms of the learning opportunities we seek, as well as the shifts we then feel able to make to our practice and in turn challenge with the systems that we work within. This is going to be different for each individual but know that whatever you are sharing with whoever you are sharing it with, you are dropping a pebble into the water, that will create little ripples, and that is hugely important.

We can also think back on the HCPC guidelines for speech and language therapists, and how with your new knowledge and learning, it with a differing lens and things that cannot be hidden once we have this awareness of them, that we must think about how we better meet those requirements to the advantage of our service users.

Conclusion

This book has aimed to open a space for you to pause, consider and reflect. To signpost you to further learning, this is not a manuscript on 'how to be neurodiversity-affirming', because I'm not certain there is 100% a definition of that. However, I hope that the aim has been achieved that you have points to reflect, places to go and seek out future learning. Where is your next place to seek out more information? I'd love to know.

Pause and think about your usual methods for reflection, how can you check in that these tools will enable you to think about intersectional and neurodiversity-affirming approaches? Think about your last supervision: is your supervisor an individual with whom you feel safe to explore this learning? If not, how you can seek a space to embed this learning?

On a very practical tangible level, we have thought about things that you might stop, keep and start doing in relation to your clinical practice. But we have to also consider how we can support further growth and shifts within the environments and systems within which we are based. How can we move the conversations forward?

A few thoughts about this:

- Who within the senior team and leaders of services in which you work can you speak to comfortably and openly?
- Which other services do you know that are doing this work well that you could seek support from or invite to speak to your service about?
- How can you have conversations within the organisations in which you work to approach conversations about for example compliance-based methods?
- What clinical excellence networks can you seek out to join to further your learning?
- Can you bring your learning to a group supervision within your service?
- Is there a space to have a team meeting with a focus on neurodiversity-affirming practice to share thoughts and reflections?
- Could you start a book club to explore chapters of this book, or other books that continue the learning you and colleagues have done?
- If you are a leader, how can you advocate for your neurodivergent staff teams as well as service users?
- How can you and your service and colleagues engage with the DE&I work within your services and support other organisations and governing bodies engaging in this work?

REFLECTION

So, are your now neurodiversity-affirming? Can one ever say honestly that you are? Or is it a process of seeking to be? Maybe there isn't an end destination. The work goes on.

A Final Note from the Author

In a conversation Fatimah suggested it might be a good idea to have a final note as we come to the end of reading. So here are a few of my reflections on this process and a call to action, to think about what tangible change and shifts you will make and hold yourself accountable to.

As we come to the end of this space of reflection and consideration together, I want to thank you for taking the time to engage in potentially challenging and uncomfortable thoughts, reflections and hopefully discussions with others.

Throughout the book there has been exploration of ways that we can reframe, rethink and reshape our practices to provide a service that is more compassionate, and inclusive across all communities. By picking up, reading and hopefully getting to the end of this book, you are showing a commitment to learning and unlearning to be more affirming. This commitment is to question traditional approaches, listen to voices that have been overlooked and work in a truly holistic way, seeing each individual as a whole, capable being, worthy of support that is honouring of their way of being.

Looking forward, our journey doesn't end here. For some, this might be the beginning, which is both overwhelming and exciting. The growth is continuous and shifts and develops with each neurodivergent individual we meet and support. The future of neurodivergent-affirming care, with better outcomes, rests on the collective willingness of our profession, and others, to challenge ourselves, to sit with discomfort and explore complex social concepts for the good of the clients we serve. Together, we can create spaces where all individuals feel safe and empowered to express themselves, seek support that honours their identity, and to thrive in environments that are genuinely inclusive.

Thank you for joining me in this effort to create a more supportive and understanding world. By bringing these values into your practice you are contributing to a future where neurodivergent-affirming care is the standard, where everyone feels seen and valued. What you do next, matters.

References

Department for Education and Ruch, G. (2020) 'The reflective case discussion model of group supervision, Practice Supervisor Development Programme'. https://practice-supervisors.rip.org.uk/wp-content/uploads/2020/06/PT_The-reflective-case-discussion-model-of-group-supervision_FINAL.pdf (accessed on 25/8/2024).

Gibbs, G. (1988) *Learning by Doing: A Guide to Teaching and Learning Methods*. London: Further Education Unit.

Kolb, D.A. (2015) *Experiential Learning: Experience as the Source of Learning and Development* (2nd ed.). London: Pearson Education.

Neurodiversity Zones of Practice. (no date) www.eyfs4me.com/neurodiversity-zones-of-practice (accessed on 25/8/2024).

Royal College of Speech and Language Therapists (2024) *Supporting LGBTQIA+ colleagues in the workplace: a guide for all*. www.rcslt.org/learning/diversity-inclusion-and-anti-racism/supporting-lgbtqia-colleagues-in-the-workplace-a-guide-for-all/#section-4 (accessed on.

RCSLT and UK SLT Pride Network. (2024) *LGBTQIA+ Zones of Practice*. Final edition. London: Royal College of Speech and Language Therapists. LGBTQIA+ Zones of Practice (rcslt.org) (accessed on 25/08/2024).

University of St Thomas libraries (no date) *Research and course guides: Anti-racism: Getting started*. https://libguides.stthomas.edu/antiracism (accessed on 25/8/2024).

World Health Organization (WHO) (2023) 'Patient safety'. www.who.int/news-room/fact-sheets/detail/patient-safety (accessed on 25/8/2024).

READING LIST

Signposts

All these books, accounts and online spaces have enabled me and my contributors to better understand neurodiversity, and how to shift the lens through which we view neurodivergent individuals by having a better understanding of their lived experience. Some of these are very personal stories, others are more specific to changing your thinking as a practitioner. Either way, they are all fantastic reads that I would recommend. This book has been in the making for 18 months plus, so note this list is definitely not exhaustive as more accounts appear and people share their knowledge and experiences.

- *We Are All Neurodiverse*, Sonny Jane Wise
- *Uniquely Human*, Barry Prizant
- *Autistic and Black: Our Experiences of Growth, Progress and Empowerment*, Kala Allen Omeiza
- *The Autistic Brain*, Temple Grandin
- *What I Want to Talk About*, Pete Wharmby
- *Natural Language Acquisition on the Autism Spectrum*, Marg Blanc
- *Unmasking Autism*, Dr Devon Price
- *Untypical*, Pete Wharmby
- *Safeguarding Autistic Girls*, Carly Jones
- *What I Wish You Knew*, HJ Richardson
- *I Will Die on This Hill*, Meghan Ashburn and Jules Edwards
- *Neurotribes*, Steve Silberman
- *Thumbsucker*, Eliza Fricker
- *The Secret Life of Rose*, by Jodie and Rose
- *PDA in the Family*, Steph Curtis
- *Unmasked*, Ellie Middleton
- *ADHD, an A-Z*, Leanne Maskell
- *Dyslexia Advocate*, Kelli Sandman-Hurley
- *Neuroqueer Heresies*, Nick Walker
- *Wired Differently*, Joe Wells
- *Caged in Chaos*, Victoria Biggs
- *Supervision in Speech and Language Therapy*, edited by Cathy Sparkes, Sam Simpson and Deborah Harding
- *Black, Brilliant and Dyslexic*, edited by Marcia Brissett-Bailey
- *PDA in the Therapy Room*, Raelene Dundon
- *A Different Way to Learn*, Naomi Fisher
- https://sltsonthesameteam.wixsite.com/rcslt-cen-slts-on-th/

- *ADHD Girls to Women*, Lotta Borg Skoglund
- *Autistic Masking*, Amy Pearson and Kieran Rose
- *Specific Learning Differences*, Diana Hudson
- *Ready, Set, Connect*, Jessi Ginsburg
- https://youtu.be/mf0HZM9p988?si=-gM3AjrIJ-2uUqAA – Dr Muna Abdi
- *A Guide to SEND in the Early Years: Supporting Children with Special Educational Needs and Disabilities*, Kerry Murphy
- *Wonderfully Wired Brains: An Introduction to the World of Neurodiversty*, Ruth Burrows and Louise Gooding
- *The Explosive Child*, Ross W Greene
- *A Vision from the Margin: Intersectional Insights on Navigating Diversity in Speech and Language Therapy*, Mariam Malik
- Selective Mutism – PDA Society – Libby Hill Q&A session www.pdasociety.org.uk/selective-mutism/
- *A Therapists Guide to Neurodiversity Affirming Practice with Children and Young People*, Raelene Dundon
- *White Women: Everything You Already Know About Your Own Racism and How to Do Better*, Regina Jackson and Saira Rao
- *Girl Unmasked: How Uncovering My Autism Saved My Life*, Emily Katy
- *All Tangled Up in Autism and Chronic Illness*, Charli Clements
- https://youtu.be/eOAEeQu9FhU?si=pmhE2-qVW2vkwo7G – Naomi Ignatius
- *The Educator's Experience of Pathological Demand Avoidance*, Laura Kerbey
- *50 Fantastic Ideas for Supporting Neurodiversity*, Kerry Murphy and Fifi Benham

Social Media Accounts

It is so important to listen to a wide range of voices within the neurodivergent community to develop practice and to ensure that you are meeting the needs of a range of different clients. Intersectionality is such a core part of the neurodiversity movement. I would love if as people read this book and explore the reading list that we can share together new accounts we find to continue to grow our community and affirming providers, people we can learn from, uplift and support.

Content creators of Colour
@itssjustliv
@natesdreamylife
@aditigangrade
@saranne_wrap
@zelue
@blackgirladhd
@autisticasfxxk
@thetruthabouttics
@autistic.qualia

@kaishawna_music
@blackautistickayla
@khadija_gbla
@flappyfroggie
@sharktizzy
@fidgets.and.fries
@autisticblackgirl
@digitalstemcell
@candy.courn

Non-speaking/minimally speaking content creators
@nonspeakers.r.us
@kaishawna_music
@fidgets.and.fries (mother to a non-speaking autistic child)
@dannywithwords

Queer content creators
@the_yorkshire_autie
@neurodivergent_advocacy
@livedexperienceeducator
@natesdreamylife
@angry_autist
@autistic_tyler
@autistiqueer
@flappyfroggie

High & medium support needs autistics
@livedexperienceeducator
@getaway_autist_mobile
@angry_autist
@autisticasfxxk
@autistic_tyler
@neuro.dinosaur
@sharktizzy
@toren.wolf

Neuro-affirming professionals
@drbeckyquicke
@autisticrealms
@kimmears16
@neurodivergent_advocacy
@fatimahbinthanif
@hat.talks.uk

@ruth_jones_slt
@amycatsslt
@theneurodivergentwomanpodcast
@communicateyourway
@carlybudd_ot
@play.learn.chat
@thespeechden
@beme_therapy
@the_adult_autism_practice
@neurodialectical
@amy_stephens_magpies
@starwalkersclinic
@yellowladybugs_autism
@audhd_therapist
@thespeechotco
@onwardsandupwardspsych
@bohospeechie
@salt_bythesea
@zeebratherapy
@lucypollardtherapies

INDEX

ABA 170
ABC charts 177
ableism 12, 17, 19, 29, 32, 61
alternative and augmentative
    communication (AAC) 97-98, 105, 107,
    111-115, 118-120, 147, 183
anti-oppressive 32
apraxia 119
assessment spaces 88, 91
attachment theory 78, 82
auditory processing 92, 99, 182
authenticity 18
autonomy 18, 77, 88, 113, 145, 151-162, 171
Ayres, Jean, Dr. 78

barriers 11, 28-29, 31-37, 86, 159-162
Bint-Hanif, Fatimah 22, 189, 197
bodily autonomy 113, 119, 155, 161
Boot, Kate 1, 4, 22, 139, 167, 185, 189
burnout 169

capacity 148-149, 159, 168-170
challenging behaviour 91
child-led 113, 116
clinical evaluation of language
    fundamentals (CELF) 87, 90-91
clinical excellence networks 40, 70, 197
code-switching 125
colourful cemantics 118
compliance 155-156, 171, 176
connection 176
consent 119, 157
continuing professional development 8,
    12-13, 59, 66, 184
Crenshaw, Kimberle 10-11, 25-26, 143
culture 10, 29, 65, 77, 113, 117, 125, 134,
    142, 154
curiosity 65, 120, 165-167, 176-177

declarative language 175
decolonialism 32
diagnosis 12-14, 33, 47-48
diagnostic labels 13, 16
disability 6, 17, 25, 30, 34, 48-49, 58-59, 63
disability justice 25, 143, 146, 151,
    153-154, 161
diversity 11, 55, 141, 150, 155, 158, 183
double empathy 50-52, 56, 96, 100, 123,
    157-158, 168
Dundon, Raelene 77, 115

emotional literacy 151, 157
emotional regulation 79, 146, 165
energy regulation 167, 175
evidence-based practice 65-66, 70-71, 73
executive functioning 46, 78, 119, 149
expressive language 80, 97, 102-105, 107,
    112, 117-118

formulation 73
functioning 45-46, 173

gender 10-11, 25, 38-39, 141-144
gender expression 38
gender identity 25, 38-39, 143, 145
gender roles 142
Gestalt Language Processing (GLP) 104-106
goals 51, 75, 93-94, 107-111, 131-134

Health Care Professions Council (HCPC) 8,
    9, 11, 31, 66, 71, 103, 183, 196
honouring 74, 84, 96-97, 116-117

identity 14, 25-27, 35-36, 48-49,
    125-126, 167
inclusive communication 23, 109, 132, 175
International Classification of Functioning
    (ICF) 58
intersectionality 22-45, 72-73, 140, 143,
    146, 151, 154, 161, 186

LEANS 131
learning disability 3, 58, 96, 148
Lewis, Talila 11, 17, 29-30, 146, 155
LGBTQIA+ 6, 25, 38-39
literacy 80, 112, 143
lived experience 4, 6-7, 45, 51, 71, 73, 89,
    140-141, 151, 154

marginalized 11, 26, 40-41
masking 26, 38, 64, 73-75, 123-125, 151, 184
Maslow 78
meaningful 4, 50-53, 108, 112-116
medical model 16-17, 29, 49, 58, 61, 67,
    119, 125
meltdown 68, 106, 123, 169
mental health 6, 15, 63-65, 83
misogynoir 153-154
monotropic 49, 54, 90, 152, 172
monotropism 54, 137, 151, 171-172
mutism 7, 49, 119-120, 168, 193

nervous system 78, 81–82, 119, 165
neurodiversity paradigm 8, 28, 31, 61–62, 70, 129
neurology 14, 16, 48, 50, 73
NICE 67, 117
nuance 70, 87, 112, 116, 129, 157–158, 182–184

oppression 17, 24–27, 29–34, 146, 151

PACE 175
pandas 175
Pathological Demand Avoidance (PDA) 81, 120, 175–177
perspective taking 146, 158
Picture Exchange Communication System (PECS) 113–116
placement 58–65, 63–65
play 54, 94, 108, 116, 133
Polyvagal Theory 78, 81
Porges, Stephen, Dr. 81
positionality 33–35
Practice-Based Evidence 67, 70, 75–76, 114
presume competence 77
presume potential 96, 115
privilege 11, 23–24, 27–28, 34–36, 113–114

reasonable adjustments 13–14, 57, 79, 88–89, 118, 120, 130, 185–186
regulation 132, 135, 167, 172–173, 175
relationships 139–161
reports 46, 86
rewards 18, 109, 115
Richardson, Harriet 5, 47, 49, 63, 67, 72–73, 79, 91–98, 105, 120–123, 126–129, 134, 168, 178, 182–185
Royal College of Speech and Language Therapists (RCSLT) 7, 11, 39, 66, 186
RSE 139–163

sanctions 176
SCERTS 128
selective mutism 120
self-advocacy 131, 140, 155, 170, 171, 175

self-awareness 150, 175
semi-speaking 120
sensory 17–18, 32, 46–47, 64–65, 92–93, 98, 156–158
sensory environment 69, 78, 89, 92, 98, 165–168, 175
sensory integration 78
sensory preferences 141, 175
sensory processing 15, 46, 78–79, 108, 110–111, 192–193
sensory seeking 166–167
sensory sensitivities 134, 160
service lead 186
sex education 139–163
shutdown 169
social communication 116, 122–138, 151–152
social model 49, 59
socioeconomic 28, 34, 37
spelling to communicate 116
standardised assessment 17, 90, 91, 192
standards 8–11, 66, 71, 155, 183
stigma 151, 160
strengths-based 49, 59, 75, 84, 88, 133, 155
student therapists 14, 59, 63, 65, 75, 183
supervision 66, 70, 148–149, 185–189, 196–197
supervisor 186
support needs 45–50
systemic oppression 29

training 58, 61–62
trauma 5–6, 15, 24, 48, 125–126, 147, 176, 185
trauma informed 12, 32–33, 141, 175, 184, 192

university 63–65, 72–73, 183

values 7–10, 181, 186–187, 196–198

World Health Organisation (WHO) 58, 184

zones of regulation 135

For Product Safety Concerns and Information please contact our EU representative GPSR@taylorandfrancis.com
Taylor & Francis Verlag GmbH, Kaufingerstraße 24, 80331 München, Germany

www.ingramcontent.com/pod-product-compliance
Lightning Source LLC
Chambersburg PA
CBHW082059230426
43670CB00017B/2898